BINGE
NO MORE
*Your Guide to Overcoming
Disordered Eating*

JOYCE D. NASH, PH.D.

New Harbinger Publications, Inc.

Distributed in the U.S.A. by Publishers Group West; in Canada by Raincoast Books; in Great Britain by Airlift Book Company, Ltd.; in South Africa by Real Books, Ltd.; in Australia by Boobook; and in New Zealand by Tandem Press.

Copyright © 1999 by Joyce D. Nash, Ph.D.
New Harbinger Publications, Inc.
5674 Shattuck Avenue
Oakland, CA 94609

Cover design © 1999 by Lightbourne Images
Image by Leo deWys/Reporters/Borze
Edited by Kayla Sussell
Text design by Tracy Marie Powell

Library of Congress Catalog Card Number: 99-74376
ISBN 1-57224-174-8 Paperback

New Harbinger Publications' Web site address: www.newharbinger.com

01   00   99

10   9   8   7   6   5   4   3   2   1

First printing

Contents

Acknowledgments   v

Preface   vii

Part 1   **Information: What You Need to Know About Disordered Eating**

Chapter 1   Eating Disorder or Disordered Eating?   3

Chapter 2   Who Binges?   29

Chapter 3   How Binge Eating Hurts   53

Chapter 4   The Causes of Disordered Eating   63

Chapter 5   Understanding Binge Eating   9

Part 2   **Intervention: How You Can Overcome Disordered Eating**

Chapter 6   Assessing Your Binge Eating Behavior   109

Chapter 7   Changing Your Eating Behavior   129

Chapter 8   Challenging Problem Thinking   149

Chapter 9   Balancing Acceptance and Change   169

Chapter 10   Improving Your Coping Skills   193

Chapter 11   Increasing Interpersonal Effectiveness   221

Chapter 12   Overcoming Backsliding   251

Resources   261

Bibliography   265

Index   279

Acknowledgments

Many people helped make this book possible. A number of people reviewed chapters and gave valuable input. Many thanks go to Judith B. Henderson, Ph.D., clinical psychologist in private practice in Minneapolis, MN, and Palo Alto, CA, who is also associated with the Eating Disorders Research Program at Stanford University and the University of Minnesota, for her thorough review of the book. Similarly, thanks go to Carol B. Peterson, Ph.D., L.P., Senior Research Scientist with the Eating Disorders Research Program, Department of Psychiatry, Medical School, University of Minnesota, and Melissa Pederson Mussell, Ph.D., L.P., Assistant Professor, Graduate Department of Professional Psychology, University of St. Thomas in Minneapolis, MN, for their critical review of the entire book. Others also deserve thanks for critically reviewing parts of the manuscript. Tony Ferrang Bloom, M.S., R.D., C.D.E., Nutrition Director for Pacific Athletic Club in Redwood City, CA, and associated with Courtside Club in Los Gatos, CA, reviewed the nutrition information, as did Elyse C. Robin, R.D., registered dietitian in private practice in San Francisco. Diane Weil, M.F.C.C., and Michael Matze, Ph.D., M.F.C.C., critically reviewed the information relating to family systems. Many thanks go to all those who took time from their busy schedules to offer their helpful comments. Additional sincere thanks go to all those who taught me so much about eating disorders: my clients, many of whose stories appear here in disguised form. Finally I want to thank my husband for his patience and forbearance during those many evenings and weekends when I was at the computer and he was left by himself.

Preface

Binge eating is not a moral failure. Contrary to popular belief, binge eating is not the result of carbohydrate craving or an addiction to sugar or food. And it does not result from yo-yo dieting (losing and then regaining weight multiple times). Binge eating is part of a disordered eating pattern that may qualify as an eating disorder.

Most often, binge eating is associated with bulimia nervosa,[1] an eating disorder characterized by binge eating followed by attempts to compensate for calories consumed. Binge eating is also the central feature in a recently recognized eating disorder—binge eating disorder or BED. Less well-known is the fact that many people who suffer from anorexia nervosa also binge periodically.

In addition, untold numbers of people have *subclinical eating disorders*—any of a number of conditions that do not meet the stringent criteria necessary to qualify for a diagnosis of anorexia or bulimia—or they are so preoccupied with food and weight that their eating behaviors are not normal.[2] Often they also struggle with some form of binge eating. Taken together, millions of Americans are in the grip of both a binge eating problem and disordered eating.

The eating binge is often the paradoxical consequence of attempts to restrict caloric intake with the intention of losing weight or maintaining weight loss. Unable to cope with hunger or deprivation, the eating disordered person succumbs to the overwhelming urge to eat. For many, stress and associated negative emotions trigger the binge. Many failures at weight management occur because bouts of excessive eating cancel out efforts at caloric restriction.

An estimated 97 million adults in the United States, or 55 percent of the population, are overweight or obese.[3] According to data from the 1980 and the 1991 surveys of the National Health and Nutrition Examination Studies, the prevalence of those who are overweight and/or obese showed a dramatic increase in the 1980s.[4]

With such rising levels of overweight and obesity, more and more people are engaging in weight management efforts. According to the NHANES III 1988-1991 survey, on average, 30 percent of males and 53 percent of females reported that they had tried to lose weight in the past twelve months.[5] The more overweight, the more likely these respondents were to be dieting, although some people who were not overweight also reported dieting.

At any given time, tens of millions of people—more than a quarter of all adult men and half of all adult women—are dieting, even if they aren't overweight. Many see themselves as binge eaters. Of those seeking treatment for obesity, an estimated 20 percent to 50 percent are binge eaters.[6] The more severely overweight a person is, the more likely it is that binge eating is a problem. Younger and younger children are also dieting, which is often a precursor to binge eating. As a result, disordered eating is reaching epidemic proportions.

Binge eating undermines success in managing weight, impairs health, diminishes the quality of life, and causes untold misery for millions. Eating disorders are accompanied by increased risk for additional psychological issues, such as depression, anxiety, substance abuse, and personality disorders. Most eating binges produce—and are influenced by—painful emotions. The end result is that the binge eater hates herself, her body, and her behavior.[7]

Binge No More helps readers to understand their own binge eating problems and to take appropriate action. Readers will identify with the experiences of other binge eaters whose stories are told in a number of vignettes, and learn how to change their own eating disordered behavior. Rather than providing a one-size-fits-all approach to finding a solution to binge eating, *Binge No More* offers a variety of cognitive-behavioral, coping, and interpersonal strategies for addressing the factors involved in maintaining an eating disorder. As such, it integrates principles and techniques from cognitive-behavioral therapy, interpersonal psychotherapy, and dialectical behavior therapy.

This book is grounded in the latest scientific literature and informed by clinical experience. It is intended for those who have a problem with binge eating or who think they do. It provides help to those suffering from binge eating disorder, bulimia, anorexia, and their subclinical variations. The book should also be a helpful adjunct to weight management programs, as well as a valuable resource to professionals working with all types of eating disorders. Parents of children with disordered eating, and family members and friends concerned about a loved one's eating disorder, will benefit from reading this book.

Binge No More consists of twelve chapters divided into two parts. Part I, Information: What You Need To Know About Disordered Eating, provides information and background understanding of eating disorders. Part II, Intervention: How You Can Overcome Disordered Eating, helps you to take action. Each chapter addresses an important aspect of binge eating as it occurs in various eating disorders.

Chapter 1, Eating Disorder or Disordered Eating?, distinguishes between eating disorders and disordered eating, and discusses the role that binge eating plays. The characteristics of binge eating disorder, bulimia nervosa, and anorexia nervosa, as well as other less recognized eating disorders, are described. The question of whether obesity is itself an eating disorder or the result of disordered eating is considered. Warning signs of disordered eating are given. The issue of recovery—what it is and whether it is possible—is addressed. This chapter concludes with a discussion of various types of help, including the use of medication that can be important in overcoming disordered eating.

The main focus of Chapter 2, Who Binges?, is on who is vulnerable to developing disordered eating. Certain groups of people seem to be more at risk for developing an eating disorder than others are. Eating disorders in men are also addressed. The prevalence of binge eating, eating disorders, and appearance concerns is also discussed. Information is provided on the variety of problems that can accompany disordered eating, including substance abuse, mood disorders, and personality problems.

Chapter 3, How Binge Eating Hurts, is unique because it discusses not only the psychological pain and physical damage that binge eating brings to the binge eater, but also how the disordered eating behavior affects the binge eater's family and friends. The fact that eating disorders and binge eating also help the person to cope, at least in the short-term, is not often acknowledged. Unless new and more adaptive ways of coping are developed, the chances of reducing binge eating are significantly reduced.

Chapter 4, The Causes of Disordered Eating, addresses the various biological, cultural, interpersonal, environmental, developmental, psychological, behavioral, and cognitive factors that can contribute to the development or maintenance of disordered eating. The role of shaming in the family, teasing or rejection by peers, life transitions (i. e., going away to college), hypersensitivity to stress, vulnerability to negative emotions, perfectionistic thinking, interpersonal conflict, self-concept and sense of identity, coping style, and self-talk, and so forth, are all considered in this chapter.

Chapter 5, Understanding Binge Eating Behavior, first addresses the varieties of binge eating. These include the hunger binge, the deprivation binge, the stress binge, the opportunity binge, the vengeful binge, the pleasure binge, and the habit binge. The various stages of a binge—tension building, tension release, recovery, and new beginning—are considered next. The chapter ends with in-depth consideration of the various antecedents or triggers that set a binge in motion, as well as the consequences that reinforce binge eating.

Chapter 6, Assessing Your Binge Eating Behavior, marks the transition from understanding disordered eating to learning what to do about it. The chapter begins with a discussion of the ABCs of a behavior pattern and how behavior consists of events linked together in chains. The foundation of change is self-monitoring, and the reader learns how to use the forms provided in this chapter to track and analyze eating behavior patterns. Next the reader is led to analyze her records systematically in order to identify the triggers that elicit binge eating and the reinforcers that maintain it. The chapter ends with a discussion of weighing and assessing body fat, and sets the stage for using the techniques and interventions set forth in subsequent chapters.

Chapter 7, Changing Your Eating Behavior, helps the reader to "normalize" eating by adopting a series of planned eating times for meals and snacks. Feared, avoided, and problem foods are identified and the reader learns how to deal with such foods in order to take them off the "forbidden foods" list. Techniques for coping with cravings are suggested, and a list of tips for preventing binge eating is provided. The reader is taught to use self-reward to shape and maintain desirable behavior patterns.

Chapter 8, Challenging Problem Thinking, begins with a discussion of how thinking influences feelings and feelings inform thinking. This is followed by a consideration of the cognitive errors that create problem thinking and some exercises focused on how to correct them. Next, self-talk and the internal "voices" of disordered eating are discussed. These voices include The Critic, The Worrier, The Caretaker, The Excuse-Maker, The Victim, The Enforcer, The Voice of Negativity, and The Voice of the Eating Disorder. The reader learns how to challenge these voices and to counteract their effects by programming positive self-talk in the voice of The Coach or The Wise Self. Characteristics of positive and negative self-talk are considered, and the reader learns how to use reminder cards to create a more favorable balance of self-talk. The chapter ends with a discussion of how to increase positive thoughts and reduce negative thinking.

Chapter 9, Balancing Acceptance and Change, addresses the important question of just how malleable is the human body. The reader is encouraged to evaluate the difference between what can be changed and at what cost, versus what can't be changed and must be accepted. The focus of this chapter is on helping the reader overcome body image dissatisfaction. Various strategies for facilitating appearance acceptance include reducing negative body talk and avoidance behaviors, changing domino thinking, making friends with the body, coping with distressing situations, using stress inoculation, and enhancing self-esteem.

Chapter 10, Improving Your Coping Skills, begins with a discussion of stress, appraisal, and coping. The use of problem-focused coping is advocated for situations that can be influenced, and adaptive emotion-focused coping for situations that are not controllable and for the emotions that accompany any stressful situation. The reader learns to use strategies such as eliciting the relaxation response, engaging in meditation, and seeking social support, rather than relying on the escape and avoidance strategies typical of those with an eating disorder. Borrowing from the work of Marsha Linehan,[8] this chapter introduces the reader to the use of mindfulness, distress tolerance, and emotion regulation skills for managing painful emotions. The chapter concludes with a discussion of a core emotion in all eating disorders—shame.

Drawing from the work of Gerald Klerman[9] and his associates, Chapter 11, Increasing Interpersonal Effectiveness, begins with the premise that all eating disorders occur in an interpersonal context and that relationship issues are often the cause of stress and negative emotions. Nonreciprocal expectations, broken promises, intolerance of others' shortcomings, threats to self-worth, misunderstandings, and inappropriate behavior often trigger interpersonal disputes. An eating disorder often functions as a way of coping with interpersonal problems. This chapter shows the reader how to improve interpersonal effectiveness by using anger productively, communicating effectively, managing conflict, and being assertive.

Chapter 12, Overcoming Backsliding, which is the final chapter, describes the relapse process. Inevitably, humans experience lapses and departures from desired behavior. The key is to prevent a lapse from turning into a full-blown relapse and a return to binge eating as a coping behavior. This chapter discusses the need to identify and cope with high-risk situations. It discusses how to recover from a first slip, adopt an alternative attitude toward the change process, and right an unbalanced lifestyle to prevent or recover from backsliding, and to continue progressing toward healthy eating behavior.

The Resources section of this book provides names, addresses, and Web sites for organizations that provide information and resources for those dealing with an eating disorder.

Throughout *Binge No More*, the personal stories of people are included. Although these vignettes stem from the experience of actual people, particulars have been changed to protect their identity and confidentiality.

Notes

1. In this book, the formal name for an eating disorder is often shortened to make reading easier. Thus, bulimia nervosa may be referred to as simply "bulimia" and anorexia nervosa as "anorexia." Similarly, someone who suffers from bulimia nervosa is termed a "bulimic," and someone who suffers from anorexia nervosa is called an "anorexic." Those with binge eating disorder may be referred to as "obese binge eaters."

2. Drewnowski, A., D. K Yee, C. L Kurth, and D. D. Krahn. 1994. Eating pathology and DSM-III-R bulimia nervosa: A continuum of behavior. *American Journal of Psychiatry*, 151, 1217–1219.

3. National Institutes of Health. 1998. Http//www.nhlbi.nih.gov/nhlbi/nhlbi.htm.

4. Kuczmarski, R. J., K. M. Flegal, S. M. Campbell, and C. L. Johnson. 1994. Increasing prevalence of overweight among U.S. adults. *Journal of the American Medical Association*, 272, 205–211.

5. Federation of American Societies for Experimental Biology, Life Sciences Research Office. 1995. *Third Report on Nutrition Monitoring in the United States: Volume 1.* Prepared for The Interagency Board for Nutrition Monitoring and Related Research. Washington, DC: U.S. GPO.

6. Bruce, B., and D. Wilfley. 1996. Binge eating among the overweight population: A serious and prevalent problem. *Journal of the American Dietetic Association, 96,* 58–61; Wing, R. R., and C. G. Greeno. 1994. Behavioural and psychosocial aspects of obesity and its treatment. *Baillieres Clinical Endocrinology & Metabolism, 8,* 689–703.

7. In this book, the female pronoun is used because the majority of those who seek help for eating disorders are female.

8. Linehan, M. M. 1993. *Cognitive-Behavioral Treatment of Borderline Personality Disorder.* NY: Guilford; Linehan, M. M. 1993. *Skills Training Manual for Treating Borderline Personality Disorder.* 125.

9. Klerman, G. L., M. M. Weissman, B. J. Rounsaville, and E. S. Chevron. 1984. *Interpersonal Psychotherapy of Depression.* New York: Basic Books.

Part 1

Information:
What You Need
to Know About
Disordered Eating

Chapter 1

Eating Disorder or Disordered Eating?

Mary Ann. Mary Ann spoke tearfully. "When it comes to eating, I lose it. I have a stressful job that keeps me running all day long. When I get home at night I'm exhausted. After I get everyone's dinner, I'm ready to collapse. That's when the eating really starts. It's not that I'm hungry. I just want to stop thinking about everything I have to do, and eating helps me do that. But I don't like how I look or feel. I don't feel like having sex anymore, and that's causing trouble in my marriage." Mary Ann is a thirty-eight-year-old, married woman who runs her own business and still has two teenagers at home. She is about fifty pounds overweight.

Peter. Peter seemed both angry and frightened as he spoke. "I started gaining weight about age thirty when I started having financial problems, and it's been going up steadily ever since. I'm now forty years old and I weigh over 300 pounds. I binge continuously all day long. I can't control myself. I've stopped seeing friends and I spend my time alone—eating. I hate how I look, but I have no control over my eating." Peter works two full-time jobs as a computer programmer.

Binge Eating Disorder

Mary Ann and Peter both suffer from an eating disorder only recently recognized, called *binge eating disorder* or BED. It involves persistent and frequent binge eating that is not accompanied by the regular use of the kinds of compensatory behaviors (for example, vomiting, abuse of laxatives) that characterize bulimia nervosa.

Unofficially termed "compulsive overeating" or "emotional eating," BED affects nearly 2.0 percent of the population.[1] (Rates are similar among both white men and women and black women.) Binge eating disorder is often accompanied by overweight. Some 8.0 percent of obese women in the community may suffer from BED, and an estimated 2.0 percent to 5.0 percent of all adults, regardless of weight, do as well.[2] Between 25.0 percent and 35.0 percent of those who seek treatment for obesity have BED.[3] The more severely overweight a person is, the more likely it is that binge eating is a problem.[4] Binge eating disorder affects slightly more women than men, exhibiting a ratio of 3:2.

Meredith. Meredith, a twenty-eight-year-old nurse, described her eating problem. "I don't eat breakfast but sometimes I'll eat a reasonable lunch—usually half a bagel, maybe with low fat cream cheese. Sometimes I allow myself fat-free potato chips as a snack and I'll eat fat-free cookies. Even so, I'm frequently hungry. There's always food to eat on the ward, but finding the time to eat a regular meal is hard. There's always a crisis or something that needs to be done immediately. Generally I try to stay away from the yummies people are always bringing in, but sometimes it gets the best of me, especially if I'm tired or cranky. Once I eat something, I figure that's it. I may as well go all the way. I know I can get rid of the calories by purging. But I feel awful afterwards. I'm so ashamed of my eating; it just proves that I can't do anything right."

Bulimia

Meredith is bulimic. The defining feature of bulimia nervosa is binge eating followed by vomiting, laxative abuse, excessive exercising, or some other way of compensating for the calories consumed. Bulimics are usually normal weight, though they may be slightly overweight or underweight. Often they were overweight at an earlier age.

Bulimia affects an estimated 1.0 percent to 3.0 percent of adolescents and young adult females, with estimates of significant but subclinical bulimic symptoms as high as 13.0 percent to 19.0 percent among female college students.[5] Nine out of ten bulimics are female.

Amy. Amy said, "I don't know why my mother and my fiancée are so upset about my weight and my eating. What's wrong with being slim?" Weighing 115 pounds at 5 feet 8 inches tall, twenty-four-year-old Amy's weight was significantly below minimum weight and she had stopped having periods. "Actually, I think I'm too fat. My stomach sticks out and I hate how I look."

On a typical day, Amy skipped breakfast and lunch but grabbed a bite of pretzel or a piece of someone else's bagel during the day. She drank eight to ten Diet Cokes a day. Her dinner consisted of steamed vegetables. But on many nights soon after dinner, Amy frequently visited the freezer. Repeatedly over the course of the evening, she ate spoonfuls of ice cream or sorbet right out of the box in the freezer, until one or more cartons were finished. Although Amy had been somewhat heavy in high school, her weight had taken a nose-dive two years earlier when her boyfriend broke up with her and she had suffered through a severe depression, resulting in substantial weight loss.

Anorexia

Amy is anorexic. *Anorexia nervosa* involves self-imposed starvation to maintain a lower than normal weight. One guideline for determining when someone meets the threshold for being anorexic is defined as weighing 85 percent or less than what is expected for that age and height, or having a body mass index (this is discussed more fully later in this chapter) of 17.5 or less. In adult women, menstrual periods stop or become irregular, and in men, sex hormone levels fall. Young girls with anorexia fail to begin menstruation at an age-appropriate time, or their menstruation may be erratic.

Anorexia affects about 1 to 3 million Americans, mostly females in late adolescence or early adulthood. This equates to 0.5 percent to 2.0 percent of the general population, though many more fall just short of meeting the full criteria for a diagnosis of anorexia.[6] An estimated 50 percent of anorexics are also binge eaters.

Carol. Carol was a thirty-eight-year-old married woman who maintained a stable, below-normal weight and engaged in running several times a day. Every day she went out for an hour run on her lunch hour, and she usually went for another run after work. If something stressful happened at work, she would leave to go for another run. She reported being in great pain and feeling exhausted during her runs, but spurred herself on with internal taunts such as, "You're nothing but a wimp; stop complaining." During the day she drank water but ate nothing. At night she often allowed herself a glass of wine, which would trigger a binge—usually involving several large bags of lettuce, but sometimes resulting in her picking through the garbage can for scraps. The next day she would exercise to atone for her indiscretion. This same behavior would often follow any incident in which she ate what she perceived to be a "normal" meal.

Exercise Anorexia

Although the primary characteristic of anorexia is self-starvation, excessive exercise can be an additional feature. Anorexia can take a less well-known form. This variation of anorexia is called *exercise anorexia,* or sometimes "activity anorexia" or "anorexia athletica." Although still primarily affecting females, more men are developing exercise anorexia. Those afflicted may be either mildly or seriously underweight.

Eating Disorders and Disordered Eating

Each of the preceding vignettes is a variation on a theme: Eating is a solution to another problem, and the sufferer may or may not be able to put into words what the problem is. An eating disorder can function to shut off feelings, provide escape from emotional pain, block out troubling thoughts, distract attention from problems, help cope with stress, or, in the case of anorexia, provide a sense of control and even a sense of identity.

Profile of a Binge

Eating disorders present many faces, and binge eating is often part of the presentation. According to the American Psychiatric Association, a *binge* is characterized by losing control and eating, within a discrete period of time—usually two hours—an amount of food that is definitely larger than most people would eat in a similar period of time and under similar circumstances.[7] However, most ordinary people define a binge as just losing control over eating.[8] Factors like the amount of food eaten, numbers of calories consumed, or eating because of negative emotions are less important than the feeling of being out of control.

Some binges involve eating large amounts of food; some just a bite of something forbidden. For many people with an eating disorder, but especially for those who are anorexic, a binge may mean eating anything at all, regardless of quantity. Eating high-fat or high-calorie food, eating in unusual places (as in the car), or eating at particular times of day, for example, at night, may cause many people to label eating as a "binge."

Some binges have a distinctive beginning and end and occur within a discrete time period; others seem to have a less discernible course and may last for days. An example of the latter is the *grazing binge*, which involves eating more or less continuously throughout the day. Feeling out of control is the hallmark of all binges. Binge eating refers to eating that results from the loosening of constraints that define a desired way of eating, leading ultimately to a perceived loss of control over eating behavior.

Binge Eating Disorder

The central characteristic of binge eating disorder is the binge. Eating binges are often triggered by negative moods such as anxiety, depression, loneliness, or boredom, and eating serves to block out thinking and feeling. Obese binge eaters are distressed about being unable to control their eating. In some cases, the obese binge eater was once anorexic or bulimic. Most obese binge eaters have a long history of repeated efforts to diet. Some continue to try dieting, whereas others have given up all efforts because of repeated failures.

Unlike the anorexic or the bulimic, the BED person does not seek to be thin—she would be happy to be average or somewhat above average weight. People with BED are often sedentary and may have obesity-related physical problems that interfere with exercising. Because of their considerable dissatisfaction and shame about their bodies, people with BED may avoid sexual relations, and some obese binge eaters are in marriages that have been asexual for many years.

Simple Overeating

Those with BED are not simply overeaters. Most people overeat from time to time, and many feel they often eat more than they should. Some people worry about breaking self-imposed eating rules, but generally they do not eat objectively excessive amounts of food and they do not experience loss of control. Some people do eat large amounts of food in a single sitting and may even do so regularly. Although they may become overweight, if they suffer little or no distress because of their eating or their weight, they do not qualify for a diagnosis of binge eating disorder. The key components in making a diagnosis of BED are that the sufferer feels she loses control over eating, is overly concerned or distressed about her body weight or shape, and experiences guilt and shame related to eating.

The BED Binge

In BED, a binge may not have a readily definable beginning or end and may last for days, rather than for an hour or two as is typical of bulimia or the bingeing anorexic. The duration of the binge can vary greatly. Binge days are more the norm than are discrete binge episodes. Some binges end with the sufferer going to sleep; others continue for days; and still others take the form of continuous snacking throughout the day with no defined meal times. In some cases, the BED binge takes the form of night eating, with excessive calories being consumed mainly between 6 P.M. and going sleep. The BED eating binge may be characterized by rapid eating, eating when not physically hungry, eating until uncomfortably full, eating alone to avoid embarrassment, and feeling disgusted with oneself, depressed, angry, or very guilty after overeating.

Origins of Binge
Eating Disorder

Binge eating can become a problem at any age, although BED is more likely than other eating disorders to develop later in life. Most people who seek help for BED are older—in their thirties, forties, and fifties. Men are more likely to develop BED than other eating disorders. Those with BED usually eat for emotional reasons: to comfort themselves, avoid upsetting situations, numb painful emotions, or distract themselves from boredom. Some are unable to report a specific trigger for a binge but may report a feeling of low-level, persistent tension and anxiety that is relieved by binge eating. At times the BED binge has a dissociative quality, resulting in the obese binge eater "numbing out" or "spacing out."

Some BED people binge because they feel good and want to make their good feelings last longer.

Co-occurring Problems

Usually BED sufferers have varying degrees of obesity. Most have a long history of repeated efforts to diet. They frequently feel desperate about their difficulty in controlling food intake. The more severe the obesity, the greater the risk of obesity-related health problems such as diabetes and sleep apnea. Obese binge eaters may report that their eating behavior interferes with their work, their ability to feel good about themselves, and their relationships with other people—including their sexual relationships. They report higher rates of self-loathing, disgust about body size, depression, anxiety, somatic concern, and interpersonal sensitivity.

Bulimia Nervosa

The defining feature of bulimia nervosa is the *binge/purge syndrome*, which involves frequent binge eating followed by the regular use of some means of compensating for the calories consumed. Most often this involves purging by vomiting, which is employed by 80 to 90 percent of bulimics. Vomiting is induced by stimulating the gag reflex; this involves putting fingers down the throat until the reflex occurs or drinking excessive amounts of fluid to make vomiting easier. Some bulimics consume syrup of ipecac to induce vomiting. Eventually, they learn to vomit at will. In some cases, vomiting becomes a goal in itself, and can be accomplished after eating only a small amount of food.

Other purging behaviors include the misuse of laxatives and diuretics. About a third of bulimics use laxatives after binge eating. Fasting for a day or more and exercising excessively are other means of compensating for calories consumed. In rare cases, bulimics misuse thyroid medication or insulin if they are diabetic, or employ the use of enemas or other means to eliminate calories or to compensate.

Those with bulimia place an excessive emphasis on body shape and weight, which almost exclusively define their self-worth. Self-esteem is a direct result of their self-evaluations of shape and weight and how they believe that others evaluate them. Bulimics depend on the approval of others to feel okay about themselves. To obtain this approval, they conform to what they think others want of them, and they hide anger, distress, or other negative feelings from themselves, as well as from others.

Bulimics frequently compare themselves to others and to internally held, frequently perfectionistic standards. Although they may appear competent and fun to be with on the surface, bulimics are often plagued by self-doubt, have low self-esteem, and feel depressed, lonely, ashamed, and empty inside. They have great difficulty talking about their feelings, which almost always include anxiety and deeply buried anger. Shame accompanies bulimia and, as a result, bulimics attempt to conceal their symptoms. The bulimic usually wants help in overcoming the eating disorder.

The Bulimic Binge

Binge eating in bulimia usually takes place in secret, and a binge may or may not be planned in advance. Unless interrupted by someone's intrusion, the binge often continues until the person is uncomfortably, or even painfully full. Many bulimics report that after the first few bites, they no longer taste the food they are consuming. They stop thinking and feeling during the binge. Food acts as an anesthetic. The purge provides relief from anxiety about the calories consumed, but leaves the bulimic feeling exhausted and uncomfortable.

Origins of Bulimia Nervosa

Bulimia usually starts in late adolescence or young adulthood, often emerging at a developmental transition point such as leaving for college, moving away from home, or going through the breakup of an important relationship. As a rule, the development of this eating disorder was preceded by a period of restrictive dieting, which continues as a feature of the disorder. Binge eating in bulimia is typically the result of two factors—stress, which generates negative emotions, and hunger, which is caused by restrictive dieting.

Co-occurring Problems

Bulimics are often impulsive. Some bulimics may engage in shoplifting, casual sexual activity, compulsive shopping, or alcohol or drug abuse. Depression, anxiety disorders, substance abuse, and difficulties in social relationships frequently coexist with bulimia.[9] Bulimics who are substance abusers are more likely to be the victims of sexual abuse than are bulimics who don't abuse substances.[10]

Anorexia Nervosa

Anorexia nervosa involves the refusal to maintain normal body weight. Excessive food restriction is the primary behavioral feature of anorexia, and sufferers typically follow current popular or faddish weight loss advice. Although rarely needing to reduce their weight, they take their restrictive eating to unhealthy extremes, producing serious nutritional disturbances that can include protein depletion and electrolyte imbalance.

Anorexics have an intense fear of gaining weight or becoming fat; and they see themselves as fat, even when others see them as too thin. As weight continues to decrease, they persist in seeing themselves as fat and become even more concerned about weight gain. They develop a distorted perception of body shape and weight that can take on the proportions of delusional thinking. Some feel generally fat. Others can admit that they are thin but they focus on and obsess about certain body parts—usually the abdomen, buttocks, and thighs—being too fat. They may weigh themselves obsessively or repeatedly check their appearance in the mirror. Weight loss is viewed as an achievement, while weight gain is felt as a personal failure.

Anorexics may employ deception to hide their eating disorder from others. When others express concern, the anorexic may make it appear that she is engaging in efforts to gain weight, only to lose it again once she thinks she has evaded—at least temporarily—pressures to change.

Exercise Anorexia

There is increasing evidence that high-level exercise can play a central role in the development of certain eating disorders, especially anorexia.[11] Excessive exercise is more frequent among those with anorexia than bulimia, and can itself become a central feature in an eating disorder. "Intense athleticism" characterizes up to 75 percent of anorexia nervosa sufferers.[12]

Those with exercise anorexia—a variation of anorexia nervosa—repeatedly exercise beyond the requirements for good health; often steal time to exercise from work, school, and relationships; and focus on the challenge of the activity rather than the fun. Self-worth is defined in terms of performance, but victory is not savored. They push on to the next challenge immediately. Like those with other eating disorders, those who exercise excessively are preoccupied with food and weight, and define many foods as forbidden. They, too, may binge as a result of restricting the food they eat. For them, however, the real issues are less about weight or performance excellence than they are about power, control, and self-respect.

Others use excessive exercise as a means of purging calories and maintaining a low weight. Even in the face of injuries, they pursue a harsh regimen of exercise through sheer willpower. In addition to compulsive exercising, these people are usually fanatic about weight and diet—often severely restricting their caloric intake. In many cases, they are already anorexic or qualify for a diagnosis of subclinical anorexia, and exercise is a means of controlling appetite as well as weight.

Exercise anorexia is more likely to begin in the teens or by early adulthood than later in life. A study of 250 adolescents, aged twelve to seventeen, who were *obligatory exercisers*—those for whom exercise is the central focus of their lives, regardless of its physical or social consequences—found they share many characteristics with those who have anorexia and bulimia.[13] Those who engage in obligatory exercise have often participated in sports or physical activities since childhood, although some were never previously athletic.

Sometimes exercise anorexia develops subsequent to another illness that produced significant weight loss, and excessive exercising is used to maintain weight at a low level. Exercise anorexia also can become a means of defining self-worth in terms of athletic performance. Being able to run longer or faster; swim under challenging conditions, for example, in the ocean; or bicycle long distances may become the only part of her life where the excessive exerciser feels at least minimally competent and effective. Unfortunately, she is rarely satisfied with her athletic achievements and pushes on quickly to the next challenge. Exercise becomes the drug that temporarily blots out painful self-awareness.

The Anorexic Binge

About half of all anorexics periodically lose control and binge.[14] A binge for an anorexic may or may not consist of many calories and may involve unusual binge foods, e.g., frozen fish sticks, unheated cans of corn, salt sandwiches, large bags of lettuce. Anorexics are often self-punishing and hold themselves to unrealistically high standards. Giving in to a binge is usually followed by severe self-punishment, such as fasting, more restrictive eating, or engaging in hours of grueling exercise.

Origins of Anorexia Nervosa

Anorexia rarely begins before puberty or after age forty.[15] Most often it emerges in early adolescence, between the ages of thirteen and eighteen. In many cases, there has been a prior history of overweight. In some cases, the onset of anorexia is associated with a stressful life event, such as leaving home for college.

Typically, anorexia takes hold with younger adolescents who are often health conscious. People who become anorexic are often the good children, the "model" children—conscientious, hard working, rarely complaining, helpful, compliant, and good students. They may be "people pleasers" who seek approval and avoid conflict. Often they are others' caretakers and, typically, they put others' needs ahead of their own. This means squelching their own feelings or acting in ways that don't feel comfortable.

Anorexics are frequently perfectionists, holding themselves to unrealistically high standards. Underneath, however, they feel defective and inadequate, and must relentlessly attempt to do better. They want to be special and stand out from the crowd, but they don't know how to feel competent, worthy, and effective. They keep their feelings to themselves, misleading others that all is well. The young anorexic is often asexual, and as she grows older has difficulty participating in sexual relations.

Those who suffer from anorexia typically refuse emotional nourishment while actively depriving themselves of pleasure and satisfaction in love and work.[16] Often they seem to feel that their emotional needs are unacceptable, punishable, or deadly, to themselves or others.[17] They may find comfort and pride in their denial and suffering, which they experience as a triumphant achievement.

Those with anorexia achieve thinness mainly through self-starvation. Initially, they may begin the journey to full-blown anorexia by excluding only what they perceive to be high-calorie foods from their diet, but most eventually end up with a very restricted diet consisting of very few foods. Anorexics may also use purging, even without binge eating, or excessive exercise as additional methods of weight loss. Some also lose control and binge, although the foods they binge on may be unusual.

Co-occurring Problems

Anorexics can literally starve themselves to death. Long-term mortality is estimated at over 10 percent, with most deaths resulting from starvation, suicide, or electrolyte imbalance and cardiac arrest. Anxiety and affective disorders are the most prevalent comorbid psychiatric disorders that coexist with anorexia.[18] In addition, anorexics frequently display obsessive-compulsive traits and symptoms, and are predisposed to developing an obsessive-compulsive personality style.[19] That is, they are frequently perfectionistic, rigid, preoccupied with details, rules, lists, order, and organization, and have difficulty enjoying themselves.

Disordered Eating and Subclinical Eating Disorders

Some people who exhibit disordered eating behaviors do not fully meet the criteria needed for a diagnosis of one of the recognized eating disorders, yet they may suffer greatly from a subclinical eating disorder. A woman who maintains a below-normal weight by restricting her food intake, but who has not lost her menses, is categorized as a subclinical anorexic. Similarly, a person whose binges do not involve a large number of calories or whose binges occur less than two times a week on average is said to have subclinical bulimia. Infrequent binge eating or recently initiated binge eating without compensation (without vomiting or otherwise trying to eliminate the calories consumed during the binge) but accompanied by distress would be examples of subclinical BED. A person who purges after eating small amounts of food, or someone who chews and spits out food without swallowing exhibits a disordered eating pattern, but does not fall into one of the three recognized eating disorders—anorexia, bulimia, or binge eating disorder.

Disordered Eating Syndromes

In other cases, a disordered eating pattern has a name but has not yet been officially recognized as an eating disorder. *Night-eating syndrome* or NES affects people with varying degrees of obesity, some of whom are seriously obese. Night-eaters typically skip breakfast and perhaps lunch, but begin eating in the latter part of the day. More than a quarter of their daily food is consumed after the dinner hour, and night-eaters eat continuously throughout the evening hours and sometimes into the early hours of the morning.[20] They may awaken frequently during the night and have difficulty falling asleep again unless they eat. Night-eaters are fully aware of their eating behavior and often feel tense, anxious, upset, or guilty about their eating. Sometimes, their sleep disturbance is associated with sleep apnea, which is a condition of impeded airflow and respiratory pauses during sleep. Often the night-eater also experiences daytime sleepiness.

Nocturnal sleep-related eating disorder may be a sleep-related disorder, rather than an eating disorder. Like sleepwalkers, nocturnal eaters may not be aware of arising in the middle of the night to binge. This is one woman's description of that experience: "When I woke up this morning, there were candy bar wrappers all over the kitchen, and I had a stomachache. I had chocolate on my face and hands. My husband says I was up eating last night, but I have no memories of doing so."

Nocturnal eaters may have no memories of their eating binges or only fragmentary memories. When confronted with the evidence of their binges, they are embarrassed, ashamed, and afraid they may be losing their minds. Some deny they did it, arguing that they could not possibly have suffered such a dramatic loss of control. They may suspect someone is trying to trick them. Those who are aware of their behavior are very upset by it. An estimated 10 percent to 15 percent of people with eating disorders are affected by nocturnal eating. About a third have complete amnesia for their eating and about a quarter eat strange food, e.g., cat food, salt sandwiches. Some are injured or burned during their nocturnal eating episodes.

Is Obesity an Eating Disorder?

Traditionally, *obesity* has been defined as weighing 20 percent or more than the expected weight for age, height, and body build, as given in standard height and weight tables. For example, if a 5'6" woman is expected to weight no more than 145 pounds, obesity for her would begin at 174. However, body weight measured on the scale is not a good indicator of body fat, the important variable in obesity.

Measuring the *body mass index*, or BMI, provides another way of defining overweight and obesity. BMI adjusts for height and applies equally to men and women. BMI is a reasonable substitute for assessing the percentage body fat because it correlates reasonably well with body fat percentage.[21] Additionally, BMI is easy to determine and is a useful indicator of health.[22]

BMI classification boundaries, the so-called "cut-points," are somewhat arbitrary. Most recently, a BMI between 19 and 25 has been declared as a healthy range. Overweight is defined by having a BMI greater than 25 but less than 30. Obesity is defined as having a BMI greater than 30. Similarly, a BMI of less than 19 is underweight, and a BMI of 17.5 or less marks the range that meets one of the criteria for anorexia nervosa. To calculate your exact BMI, multiply your weight in pounds by 700. Then divide your answer by your height in inches. Once more divide that answer by your height in inches. The resulting figure is your BMI. (Table 1.1 provides an easier way to determine BMI without having to use a complicated formula.)

Most health professionals think of obesity as a medical problem because of the attendant health risks. Eating habits that lead to obesity can contribute to increased cholesterol and triglycerides in the blood, and to high blood pressure. Obese people are at greater risk for heart disease, cancer, diabetes, endocrine problems, gall bladder disease, lung and breathing problems, and arthritis. The fatter the person, the higher the risk.

However, obesity also has psychological aspects that make it more difficult to categorize as just a medical condition. Not only are the obese at risk for BED, self-hatred and body dissatisfaction are pervasive among the obese, and they suffer much scorn and discrimination because of their size. Not surprisingly, obese binge eaters are more likely to suffer from depression, anxiety, and other psychological problems.

The hallmarks of all eating disorders are extreme body dissatisfaction and significant psychological distress associated with eating. Using these two criteria, obesity can be the result of or concomitant with an eating disorder, if not itself an eating disorder. When someone is obsessed about food, eating, and weight, suffers guilt or shame about eating, detests her appearance or is terrified of becoming fat, and uses eating (or not eating) as a means of coping, the diagnosis of an eating disorder is appropriate.

Types of Treatment

The best treatment for an eating disorder is one that is custom-tailored to each person's unique circumstances. This may involve only one or a combination of the following treatments:

- Nutrition counseling

- Psychotherapy
- Medication
- Medical management, or education about weight management.

Ideally, treatment of an eating disorder includes the attention of a physician and/or a psychiatrist, a therapist trained to work with eating disorders, and a dietitian or nutrition counselor. Experts generally agree that, if possible, intervention should begin at the least invasive level, and more components added as necessary and appropriate. Self-help is often the first level of treatment tried.

Self-Help

Some people with eating disorders respond well to simple information provided in an easy-to-understand format.[23] For certain people with BED, self-help manuals and books have been shown to be helpful. *Binge No More* is such a book. Based on proven techniques and principles drawn from cognitive-behavioral therapy, interpersonal therapy, and dialectical behavior therapy, it promotes coping skills, improved interpersonal functioning, and size acceptance grounded in research showing the importance of these components to overcoming disordered eating. Some people, however, need additional assistance in implementing these techniques.

Table 1.1: Determine Your Body Mass Index (BMI)

BMI	17	18	19	20	21	22	23	24	25	26	27	28	29	30	35	40
4' 10"	81	86	91	96	100	105	110	115	119	124	129	134	138	143	167	191
4' 11"	84	89	94	99	104	109	114	119	124	128	133	138	143	158	173	198
5'	87	92	97	102	107	112	118	123	128	133	138	143	148	153	179	204
5' 1"	90	95	100	106	111	116	122	127	132	137	143	148	153	159	185	211
5' 2"	93	98	104	109	115	120	126	131	136	142	147	153	158	164	191	218
5' 3"	96	102	107	113	118	124	130	135	141	146	152	158	163	169	197	225
5' 4"	99	105	110	116	122	128	134	140	145	151	157	163	169	174	204	232
5' 5"	102	108	114	120	126	132	138	144	150	156	162	168	174	180	210	240
5' 6"	105	112	118	124	130	136	142	148	155	161	167	173	179	188	216	247
5' 7"	109	115	121	127	134	140	146	153	159	166	172	178	185	191	223	255
5' 8"	112	118	125	131	138	144	151	158	164	171	177	184	190	197	230	262
5' 9"	115	122	128	135	142	149	155	162	169	176	182	189	196	203	236	270
5' 10"	119	26	132	139	146	153	160	167	174	181	188	195	202	207	243	278
5' 11"	122	129	136	143	150	157	165	182	179	186	193	200	208	215	250	286
6'	125	133	140	147	154	162	169	177	184	191	199	206	213	221	258	294
6' 1"	129	137	144	151	159	166	174	182	189	197	204	212	219	227	265	302
6' 2"	132	14	148	155	163	171	179	186	194	202	210	218	225	233	272	311
6' 3"	136	144	152	160	168	176	184	192	200	208	216	224	232	240	279	319
6' 4"	140	148	156	164	172	180	189	197	205	213	221	230	238	246	287	328

Table 1.1 Instructions: Find your height in the left-hand column. Trace across the row until you find the cell that is closest to your present weight. Once you find it, move up the column to the row labeled "BMI" to find your body mass index. BMIs in italics indicate unhealthy ranges. A BMI below 19 puts you at risk for anorexia; a BMI between 25 and 29 puts you at risk for being overweight. Obesity is defined as any BMI 30 or above.

Self-Help Groups

Sometimes support can be found in self-help groups led by lay people. One such group is Overeaters Anonymous (OA). Based on the Twelve-Step model of Alcoholics Anonymous, OA promotes finding a spiritual (although not necessarily religious) solution to overeating by "working the steps" under the guidance of a sponsor. OA and other types of support groups provide a means of reducing isolation and alienation, and finding a community in which there is understanding and acceptance of shared experience and pain. Support groups by themselves, however, are often not sufficient treatment to correct an eating disorder. To be most effective, they should be integrated into a comprehensive treatment plan.

Psychotherapy

Another means of obtaining support for overcoming disordered eating is to seek the services of a trained therapist experienced and skilled in working with eating disorders. Such therapists may provide either individual or group therapy. Mental health professionals who may hold one of several degrees provide psychotherapy.

Psychologists

Psychologists hold either a Ph.D. or a Psy.D. and have extensive training in human behavior and emotions, as well as in assessment and testing for emotional or educational functioning. Some psychologists obtain special training in the treatment of eating disorders. Several national organizations maintain a referral list and can provide sufferers of eating disorders with referrals to qualified therapists. (See the Resources section at the back of the book for information on contacting them.)

Psychiatrists

Some people confuse psychologists with psychiatrists. Psychiatrists are medical doctors and have an M.D. degree. They are especially trained in the understanding and management of medications, and only an M.D. can prescribe medication. Although many psychiatrists also provide psychotherapy, their unique competency is in the prescription of medications. A psychiatrist is usually a vital member of the treatment team, especially for anorexia and bulimia. Medication, as an adjunctive treatment, can help reduce binge eating and purging, as well as relieve the depression and anxiety that frequently accompany an eating disorder.

Licensed Therapists

Other types of licensed therapists include licensed clinical social workers (LCSWs) and marriage, family, and child counselors (MFCCs). Some nurses receive special training to provide psychotherapy. These therapists usually hold a master's degree, have fewer years of formal education in human behavior compared to psychologists, and do not write a dissertation to obtain their degree.

Both psychologists and other licensed therapists may have special training in working with families. Eating disorders frequently afflict young people who are still living at home with their families, and family interactions may contribute to or exacerbate an eating disorder. Including the family in therapy is especially important in the treatment of anorexia. Family counseling can help to change old patterns of communication and create healthier new ones.

Nutritional Counseling

Nutritional counseling helps to debunk food myths and promote healthier food choices. Nutritional rehabilitation is critical to treatment, especially in the case of anorexia, and a nutritionist is an important part of the treatment team. Although people with eating disorders may know a great deal about nutrition, often their knowledge is distorted in ways that support the eating disorder. For example, the fact that bananas are more dense in calories than other fruits may translate to "Bananas are fattening," which becomes "If I eat a banana I'll get fat," which places bananas on the forbidden foods list. In addition, the nutritionist can help with issues such as portion control. Lack of understanding of correctly sized portions can contribute excess calories and make weight management more difficult. The help of a dietitian or nutritionist can be valuable for anyone suffering from disordered eating.

Medication

Medication can also play an important part in helping to alleviate an eating disorder.[24] Medication alone is rarely helpful but can be useful in combination with psychotherapy. The combination of antidepressant treatment and cognitive-behavior therapy has been shown to be effective for both bulimia nervosa and binge eating disorder.[25]

Medication for Bulimia Nervosa

Research suggests that antidepressant medication can be helpful in the treatment of bulimia and possibly BED.[26] The most frequently prescribed antidepressants for eating disorders are the selective serotonin reuptake inhibitors (SSRIs), especially Prozac (fluoxetine). Tricyclic antidepressants such as Norpramin (desipramine) and Tofranil (imipramine) also have been used in the treatment of bulimia.

Although all antidepressants have roughly equal efficiency and perform better than placebos, the "average" decrease in binge frequency is only about 55 percent, and not everyone is helped by these medications. Some people stop using medication because of side effects, which can include anxiety, nervousness, headache, drowsiness, dry mouth, upset stomach, nausea, and a variety of other reactions. In those for whom the medication works, if the medication is discontinued, relapse occurs in more than 60 percent. Those with the most severe bulimic symptoms obtain the best results with a combination of medication and psychotherapy.

Medication for Binge Eating Disorder

Research on the usefulness of medication with BED is in its infancy, but initial work suggests that antidepressants can be helpful for this eating disorder, especially if an underlying depression coexists with the eating disorder.[27] Medication in combination with cognitive-behavioral treatment shows some promise.[28] Use of a single antidepressant agent results in the recovery of about 25 percent of patients entering treatment for BED, but some of these patients relapse once the medication is discontinued.[29]

Redux (dexfenfluramine) and "fen-phen," which consisted of fenfluramine (Pondimin) and phentermine (Ionamine)—a combination of drugs that was never tested or approved to be used together—were popular weight loss drugs until recently. Redux and Pondimin, the fenfluramine half of the fen-phen combination, were found to cause serious deterioration in heart valves and were banned from the market by the FDA in mid-1997.

The phentermine half of fen-phen is still available and is sometimes combined with the popular antidepressant Prozac to create "phen-pro," a drug combination without proven effectiveness.

A new prescription obesity drug, Meridia (sibutramine), which was originally developed as an antidepressant drug, was brought to market in 1998. Much like the now-banned diet drugs Redux and Pondimin (fenfluramine), Meridia boosts brain levels of serotonin and norepinephrine—neurotransmitters that are thought to help control appetite. Meridia works differently from the banned drugs, and it is believed to be safer. One study found that 65 percent of patients receiving 15 mg of Meridia daily lost more than 5 percent of their body and 39 percent lost more than 10 percent of their body weight.[30] However, in some people, Meridia can trigger an increase in blood pressure and heart rate and its efficacy in helping to alleviate overeating or obesity in the long-term is not yet established.

Xenical (orlistat) is another new drug. Unlike typical diet drugs, which suppress appetite, Xenical is a pancreatic lipase inhibitor—it blocks the absorption of up to 30 percent of fat consumed, thus reducing a portion of calories consumed.

With Xenical it is necessary to follow a low-fat diet. Failure to do so produces unpleasant results. The blocked fat has to go somewhere, and the end result can be diarrhea, bloating, and gas. Fat-soluble nutrients are swept away as well, and vitamin supplementation is necessary. A study found that 55 percent of patients receiving Xenical lost more than 5 percent of their body weight, and 25 percent lost more than 10 percent of their body weight.[31] In addition, Xenical slowed the rate of weight regain.

All of these must be used in combination with a low-fat, low-calorie diet and regular exercise to produce clinically significant results, and none are a quick and easy answer for losing weight.

Ineffective Medications

In their attempts to cope with binge eating, some people use over-the-counter medications advertised as helpful for reducing appetite and for weight loss. Most of these contain caffeine, phenylpropanolamine, benzocaine, or fiber. Caffeine, a stimulant and diuretic, and phenylpropanolamine are popular ingredients because they suppress appetite and enhance weight loss when they are used as part of a low-calorie diet.[32] Benzocaine numbs the tongue briefly, reducing taste sensations, which in turn lowers caloric intake in the short run. Also on the market are weight-loss pills containing fiber that supposedly fill the stomach and provide a feeling of fullness, which is presumed to reduce eating. Some of these pills are moderately effective for short-term weight loss, but the weight reduction involves loss of fluid, not fat,[33] and they can lead to dehydration and abuse. All of these pills are accompanied by the admonition to follow a low-calorie diet. In the long run none help overcome binge eating.

Medication for Anorexia Nervosa

In contrast to the research results in bulimia nervosa, controlled trials have not provided consistent evidence for the usefulness of antidepressant drugs in the treatment of anorexia nervosa.[34] Alternative medications are being investigated for use with this eating disorder, and the results are not yet known.[35] Some preliminary evidence suggests that Prozac may be helpful in preventing relapse in weight-restored anorexics. In addition, medication can be helpful in managing concurrent problems that occur with anorexia, such as depression or obsessive-compulsive disorder, but none have been shown to assist weight gain reliably or to alter other core features of the disorder.[36]

Medication in the Treatment of All Eating Disorders

In all types of eating disorders, one of the biggest obstacles to successful treatment with medication is compliance. Purging eliminates the medication from the system, and erratic compliance with taking medication (or outright refusal, usually by the anorexic) results in failure to reach and maintain adequate blood levels of the medication. When medication is taken as prescribed, binge eating is usually reduced by 50 percent to 90 percent, and approximately one-third or fewer achieve elimination of binge eating.

Weight Reduction Efforts

Controversy exists about the role of weight reduction and control efforts in the treatment of obesity.[37] Because obesity is often associated with binge eating disorder, this question arises: Should binge eating and obesity be treated separately or concurrently?[38] Some people question whether anything but severe obesity should be treated at all because of the high level of treatment failures that engender false hope and continued psychological distress.[39]

Restrictive dieting is strongly implicated as a precursor to binge eating for normal-weight bulimics, as well as for some obese binge eaters. This fact, together with the observation that binge eaters do less well in weight control programs, led to the initial assumption that binge eating must be treated before successful weight control can take place.[40] Subsequent research suggested that weight loss treatment that also addresses binge eating as a problem can be helpful, especially for those with severe binge eating problems.[41] Moderate binge eaters and the non-bingeing obese were helped by a standard behavioral weight loss treatment that taught healthy eating habits (not restrictive dieting) and advocated adequate exercise.

Not all obese binge eaters engage in restrictive dieting that leads to binge eating. One study found that less than 9 percent of obese binge eaters entering a weight-control program reported having been on a strict diet at the point when binge eating began, and 64 percent said that binge eating had preceded their obesity.[42]

Other research found that 49 percent of obese binge eaters confirmed that binge eating had preceded any attempts to lose weight by dieting.[43] In fact, many obese binge eaters are helped by a weight loss approach that takes a cognitive-behavioral focus.[44] Such a program also advocates following a balanced diet that is low in fat and high in carbohydrates, as well as regular exercise. Rather than striving to achieve a specific goal weight, however, newer thinking in the treatment of obesity is redefining what the goal of a weight management intervention should be.

Exercise

Adequate exercise that increases or maintains cardiovascular functioning, muscle strength, and flexibility is essential for good health. Regular exercise has been shown to be critical to maintaining normal weight. Obese binge eaters rarely get adequate exercise, whereas excessive exercise that impairs health is more likely to characterize those with anorexia or bulimia. In the latter two eating disorders, exercise may be used to compensate for calories consumed or used to provide a sense of power and accomplishment which serves to create or maintain a fragile identity. For some, being an athlete or avid exerciser provides a rationale to eat indiscriminately, even if it leads to gaining excess weight.

How much is too much exercise? Cardiovascular health requires that 2000 to 3500 calories be burned off each week in aerobic exercise such as running, jogging, dancing, bicycling, or brisk walking. The recommendation is to exercise three to five days a week for no less than thirty minutes per session and as much as sixty minutes. Beyond that, health benefits decrease and the risk of injury increases.

Regular, adequate exercise helps with stress management and provides a sense of well-being that can be helpful in curbing binge eating. On the other hand, excessive exercise points to a potential eating disorder that may need professional intervention.

Notes

1. Bruce, B., and W. S. Agras. 1992. Binge eating in females: A population-based investigation. *International Journal of Eating Disorders, 12,* 365–373; Smith, D. E., M. D. Marcus, C. Lewis, M. Fitzgibbon, and P. Schreiner. 1998. Prevalence of binge eating disorder, obesity, and depression in a biracial cohort of young adults. *Annals of Behavioral Medicine, 20,* 227–232; Spitzer, R. L., M. Devlin, B. T. Walsch, D. Hasin, R. Wing, M. Marcus, et al. 1992. Binge eating disorder: A multisite field trial of the diagnostic criteria. *International Journal of Eating Disorders, 11,* 191–203.

2. Bruce, B., and W. S. Agras. 1992. Binge eating in females: A population-based investigation. *International Journal of Eating Disorders, 12,* 365–373.

3. Marcus, M. D., R. R Wing, and D. M. Lamparski. 1985. Binge eating and dietary restraint in obese patients. *Addictive Behaviors, 10,* 163–168; Spitzer, R. L., M. Devlin, B. T. Walsch, D. Hasin, R. Wing, M. Marcus, et al. 1992. Binge eating disorder: A multisite field trial of the diagnostic criteria. *International Journal of Eating Disorders, 11,* 191–203; Spitzer, R. L., M. J. Devlin, B. T. Walsh, D. Hasin, R. Wing, M. Marcus, et al. 1992. Binge eating disorder: Its further validation in a multisite study. *International Journal of Eating Disorders, 13,* 137–153; Telch, C. F., W. S. Agras, and E. M. Rossiter. 1988. Binge eating

increases with increasing adiposity. *International Journal of Eating Disorders, 7,* 115–119.

4. Telch, C. F., W. S. Agras, and E. M. Rossiter. 1988. Binge eating increases with increasing adiposity. *International Journal of Eating Disorders, 7,* 115–119.

5. American Psychiatric Association. 1994. *Diagnostic and Statistical Manual of Mental Disorders. 4th ed.* Washington, DC; Craighead, L. W. 1995. Conceptual models and clinical interventions for treatment of bulimia and binge eating. In L. VandeCreek (Ed.), *Innovations in Clinical Practice: A sourcebook: Vol. 14* Sarasota, FL: Professional Resource Exchange. 67–87.

6. American Psychiatric Association. 1994. *Diagnostic and Statistical Manual of Mental Disorders. 4th ed.*

7. Ibid.

8. Pratt, E. M., S. H. Niego, and W. S. Agras. 1998. Does the size of a binge matter? *International Journal of Eating Disorders, 24,* 307–312; Telch, C. F., E. M. Pratt, and S. H. Niego. 1998. Obese women with binge eating disorder define the term binge. *International Journal of Eating Disorders, 24,* 313–317.

9. Brewerton, T. D., R. B. Lydiard, D. B. Herzog, A. W. Brotman, P. M. O'Neil, and J. C. Ballenger. 1995. Comorbidity of Axis I psychiatric disorders in bulimia nervosa. *Journal of Clinical Psychiatry, 56,* 77–80.

10. Deep, A. L., L. R. Lilenfeld, K. H. Plotnicov, C. Pollice, and W. H. Kaye. 1999. Sexual abuse in eating disorders subtypes and control women: The role of comorbid substance dependence in bulimia nervosa. *International Journal of Eating Disorders, 25,* 1–10.

11. Davis, C., S. Kaptein, A. Kaplan, M. P. Olmsted, and D. B. Woodside. 1998. Obsessionality in anorexia nervosa: The moderating influence of exercise. *Psychosomatic Medicine, 60,* 192–197; Davis, C., D. K. Katzman, S. Kaptein, C. Kirsh, H. Brewer, K. Kalmbach, et al. 1997. The prevalence of high-level exercise in the eating disorders: Etiological implications. *Comprehensive Psychiatry, 38,* 321–326.

12. King, A. 1963. Primary and secondary anorexia nervosa syndromes. *British Journal of Psychiatry, 109,* 470–479.

13. Brehm, B. J., and J. J. Steffen. 1998. The relation between obligatory exercise and eating disorders. *American Journal of Health Behavior, 22,* 108–119.

14. Casper, R. C., E. D. Eckert, K. A. Halmi, S. C. Goldberg, and J. M. Davis. 1980. Bulimia: Its incidence and clinical importance in patients with anorexia nervosa. *Archives of General Psychiatry, 37,* 1030–1034; Garfinkel, P. E., H. Moldofsky, and D. M. Garner. 1980. The heterogeneity of anorexia nervosa. *Archives of General Psychiatry, 37,* 1036–1040; Hsu, L. K. G., A. H. Crisp, and B. Harding. 1979. Outcome in anorexia nervosa. *Lancet, i,* 61–65.

15. American Psychiatric Association. 1994. *Diagnostic and Statistical Manual of Mental Disorders. 4th ed.*

16. Bion, W. R. 1959. Attacks on linking. *International Journal of Psychoanalysis, 40,* 308–315.

17. Foxe, G. 1998. Observations on the anorectic personality. *AABA Newsletter,* Summer, 7–8.

18. Herpertz-Dahlmann, B. M., C. Wewetzer, E. Schulz, and H. Remschmidt. 1996. Course and outcome in adolescent anorexia nervosa. *International Journal of Eating Disorders, 19,* 335–345.

19. Jarry, J. L., and F. J. Vaccarino. 1996. Eating disorder and obsessive-compulsive disorder: Neurochemical and phenomenological commonalities. *Journal of Psychiatry and Neuroscience, 21,* 36–48; Wonderlich, S. A., W. J. Swift, H. B. Slotnick, and S. Goodman. 1990. DSM-III-R personality disorders in eating-disorder subtypes. *International Journal of Eating Disorders, 9,* 607–616.

20. Stunkard, A. J., W. J. Grace, and H. G. Wolff. 1955. The night-eating syndrome: A pattern of food intake among certain obese patients. *American Journal of Medicine, 19,* 78–86.

21. Smalley, K. J., A. N. Kneer, Z. V. Kendrick, J. A. Colliver, and O. E. Owen. 1990. Reassessment of body mass indices. *American Journal of Clinical Nutrition, 52,* 405–408.

22. Kushner, R. F. 1993. Body weight and mortality. *Nutrition Review, 51,* 127–136.

23. Carter, J. C., and C. G. Fairburn. 1998. Cognitive-behavioral self-help for binge eating disorder: A controlled effectiveness study. *Journal of Consulting and Clinical Psychology, 66,* 616–623.

24. Jimerson, D. C., B. E. Wolfe, A. W. Brotman, and E. D. Metzger. 1996. Medications in the treatment of eating disorders. *The Psychiatric Clinics of North America,* 19(4), 739–754.

25. Agras, W. S. 1997. Pharmacotherapy of bulimia nervosa and binge eating disorder: Long-term outcomes. *Psychopharmacology Bulletin, 33,* 433–436; Goldbloom, D. S., M. Olmsted, R. Davis, J. Clewes, M. Heinmaa, W. Rockert, et al. 1997. A randomized controlled trial of fluoxetine and cognitive behavioral therapy for bulimia nervosa: Short-term outcome. *Behavior Research & Therapy, 35,* 803–811.

26. Agras, W. S. 1997. Pharmacotherapy of bulimia nervosa and binge eating disorder: Long-term outcomes. *Psychopharmacology Bulletin, 33,* 433–436; Walsh, T. B., and M. J. Devlin. 1998. Eating disorders: Progress and problems. *Science, 280,* May 1387–1390.

27. Grilo, C. M. 1998. The assessment and treatment of binge eating disorder. *Journal of Practical Psychiatry and Behavioral Health, 4,* 191–201.

28. Wilfley, D. E., and L. R. Cohen. 1997. Psychological treatment of bulimia nervosa and binge eating disorder. *Psychopharmacology Bulletin, 33,* 437–454.

29. Agras, W. S. 1997. Pharmacotherapy of bulimia nervosa and binge eating disorder: Long-term outcomes. *Psychopharmacology Bulletin, 33,* 433–436.

30. Aronne, L. J. 1998. Modern medical management of obesity: The role of pharmaceutical intervention. *Journal of the American Dietetic Association, 98* (Supplement 2), S23–S26.

31. Ibid.

32. Schteingart, D. C. 1995. Phenylpropanolamine in the management of moderate obesity. In T. B. Van Itallie, and A. P. Simopoulos, eds., *Obesity: New Directions in Assessment and Management.* Philadelphia: The Charles Press. 220–226.

33. Weintraub, M., and G. A. Bray. 1989. Drug treatment of obesity. *Medical Clinics of North America, 73,* 237–250.

34. Devlin, M. J., and B. T. Walsh. 1995. Medication treatment for eating disorders. *Journal of Mental Health UK, 4,* 459–468; Ferguson, C. P., M. C. La Via, P. J. Crossan, and W. H. Kay. 1999. Are serotonin selective reuptake inhibitors effective in underweight anorexia nervosa? *International Journal of Eating Disorders, 25,* 11–17; Leach, A. 1995. The psychopharmacotherapy of eating disorders. *Psychiatric Annals, 25,* 623–633; Walsh, T. B., and M. J. Devlin. 1995. Pharmacotherapy of bulimic nervosa and binge eating disorders. *Addictive Behaviors, 20,* 757–764.

35. Jimerson, D. C., B. E. Wolfe, A. W. Brotman, and E. D. Metzger. 1996. Medications in the treatment of eating disorders. *The Psychiatric Clinics of North America,* 19(4), 739–754.

36. Johnson, W. G., J. Y. Tsoh, and P. J. Varnado. 1996. Eating disorders: Efficacy of pharmacological and psychological interventions. *Clinical Psychology Review, 16,* 457–478; Leach, A. 1995. The psychopharmacotherapy of eating disorders. *Psychiatric Annals, 25,* 623–633.

37. Kirschenbaum, D. S., and M. L. Fitzgibbon. 1995. Controversy about the treatment of obesity: Criticisms or challenges? *Behavior Therapy, 26,* 43–68.

38. Porzelius, L. K., C. Houston, M. Smith, C. Arfken, and E. Fisher. 1995. Comparison of a standard behavioral weight loss treatment and a binge eating weight loss treatment. *Behavior Therapy, 26,* 119–134.

39. Garner, D. M., and S. C. Wooley 1991. Confronting the failure of behavioral and dietary treatments for obesity. *Clinical Psychology Review, 11,* 729–780.

40. Telch, C. F., W. S. Agras, and E. M. Rossiter. 1988. Binge eating increases with increasing adiposity. *International Journal of Eating Disorders, 7,* 115–119.

41. Porzelius, L. K., C. Houston, M. Smith, C. Arfken, and E. Fisher. 1995. Comparison of a standard behavioral weight loss treatment and a binge eating weight loss treatment. *Behavior Therapy, 26,* 119–134.

42. Wilson, G. T., C. A. Nonas, and G. D. Rosenblum. 1993. Assessment of binge-eating in obese persons. *International Journal of Eating Disorders, 13,* 23–33.

43. Spitzer, R. L., M. Devlin, B. T. Walsch, D. Hasin, R. Wing, M. Marcus, et al. 1992. Binge eating disorder: A multisite field trial of the diagnostic criteria. *International Journal of Eating Disorders, 11,* 191–203.

44. Aronoff, N. J. 1997. Obesity-related eating patterns. In S. Dalton, ed., *Overweight and Weight Management: The Health Professional's Guide to Understanding and Practice.* Gaithersburg, MD: Aspen Publishers. 107–141.

Chapter 2

Who Binges?

Eating disorders and disordered eating are on the rise and becoming a major public health concern.[1] Increasing numbers of people are developing disordered eating and are at risk for a full-blown eating disorder. Particular groups of people have been found to be at greater risk of developing an eating disorder, including athletes, models, dancers, and those in the entertainment industry. Although these groups are at higher risk, most people who develop an eating disorder do not come from one of these groups.[2] Those at risk for developing an eating disorder can be grouped in various ways—by gender, age, physical characteristics, occupation, and activities. Many factors contribute to the development of an eating disorder,[3] and these are discussed further in chapter 4.

Who Is at Risk?

Being female, especially in Western societies that idealize thinness, puts women and girls at risk for developing eating disorders.[4] Today, more and more children and adolescents are dieting and developing eating disorders. Increasingly, males are also developing eating disorders. Athletes and people in high profile occupations or those that have standards for body weight are also at risk. Those who are overweight are at risk for developing binge eating disorder (BED).

Children, Adolescents, and Young Adults

Initially, those who fall prey to an eating disorder are often bright, attractive young women between twelve and twenty-five years of age. The focus on thinness and dieting, however, is moving downward from adolescence to prepubescence—a time when young girls are still growing and developing. Younger and younger children are becoming worried about being or becoming fat, and as adolescence nears, this fear becomes wide-reaching.[5]

Concerns about weight and shape were investigated in a study of 368 females aged eleven to sixteen years. It found that 14.5 percent of eleven- to twelve-year-olds, 14.9 percent of thirteen- to fourteen-year-olds, and 18.9 percent of the fifteen- to sixteen-year-olds exhibited significant weight and/or shape concerns.[6] A study of 239 children, aged eight- to ten-years old, also showed that socially defined standards for thinness, discontent with body shape, and preoccupation with body weight and dieting are both internalized and expressed at a very early age.[7] Such concerns can precipitate dieting and disordered eating and set the stage for later eating disorders.[8]

Dieting is often a precursor to the development of an eating disorder,[9] putting more and more young people at risk. In a study of middle-class white girls, 40 percent of fourth graders reported that they sometimes diet and 33 percent stated that they "very often" worried about being fat.[10] Yet another study of lower-middle class girls, three-fourths white and one-fourth black, found that 28 percent of second-graders, 33 percent of fourth-graders, and 35 percent of sixth-grade girls confirmed that they had dieted to lose weight.[11] In a study of eight- to thirteen-year-olds, 45 percent indicated a desire to be thinner and 37 percent reported that they had tried to lose weight.[12]

Two out of five preadolescent girls have engaged in weight-loss efforts, and one study found that 13 percent of adolescent girls, though not yet diagnosed with a full-blown eating disorder, engaged in obvious anorexic or bulimic behaviors.[13] A 1997 study of teenagers ranging in age from 12 to 17 found that 38 percent of girls and 12 percent of boys were dieting. Most of the girls were within a normal weight range.[14] One study of 1,373 high school students identified bulimia in 9.6 percent of females and a little over 1 percent of males.[15] About one out of every one-hundred young women between the ages of ten and twenty are starving themselves, sometimes to the point of death.[16] Every year, three of every one hundred adolescent and young adult women are diagnosed with bulimia nervosa,[17] and four out of one hundred college-aged women have bulimia.

In a study of first-year college women, 10 percent were classified as "dieters at risk" and another 31 percent as "intensive dieters."[18] Dieters at risk were those who binged and purged but did so less than two times a week as required for the official diagnosis of bulimia or binge eating disorder. There were intensive dieters who binged and engaged in restrictive dieting but they did not purge in any way or meet the other criteria for BED. By the following semester, many of these subclinical cases had developed a full-blown eating disorder. Altogether, 44 percent of college women studied reported significantly disturbed eating behavior.

Overweight and Obese People

Over half of all adult Americans, both male and female, are overweight and a third are *obese*—more than 20 percent above normal, healthy weight. An estimated 20 percent to 50 percent of these are binge eaters.[19] In one population study, obesity was associated with a substantially higher prevalence of binge eating disorders, which affected mainly Caucasian men and women but also black women.[20] In adolescents and young people, being overweight is strongly associated with dieting—a risk factor for developing an eating disorder.[21] Those who were overweight or obese at younger ages are more likely to become binge eaters and to be less competent at managing their weight, more likely to eat in response to negative emotions or in positive social settings, and less likely to resist temptation.[22] Higher degrees of obesity combined with a history of *weight cycling*—frequently losing and regaining weight—are more often associated with the development of binge eating disorder.[23]

Males

Even though an eating disorder is commonly seen as a "female issue," more and more men are developing eating disorders. An estimated 5 to 10 percent of those diagnosed with anorexia nervosa and about 10 to 15 percent of bulimics are male. Community-based studies of these eating disorders have established a ratio of one male for every ten females with either anorexia or bulimia.[24] In binge eating disorder, every two out of five people with BED are males. A study of 135 males being treated in a hospital for eating disorders found that sixty-two or 46 percent were bulimic, thirty or 22 percent were anorexic, and forty-three or 32 percent met criteria for eating disorder not otherwise specified.[25] Generally, males develop an eating disorder later than females, although more and more young males are becoming weight-sensitive.

Beginning in grade school, boys are less likely than girls to consider themselves overweight or in need of dieting. Typically, young boys are more concerned about becoming taller and more muscular than they are about being too big, and some degree of overweight is more acceptable in males of all ages. By early adulthood, the number of males who want to increase their weight about equals the number of males who want to lose weight, whereas females almost always want to lose weight. By adulthood, males tend to see themselves as overweight at higher weights, while females describe themselves as overweight when they are actually closer to an ideal body weight. Adult women feel thin only when they are below 90 percent of ideal body weight, whereas men rate themselves as thin until they are as high as 105 percent of an ideal body weight.[26]

Males who develop an eating disorder are more likely than females to have been overweight at some point before developing the disorder. Many boys begin dieting to avoid being teased for childhood obesity, to improve athletic appearance, or to avoid developing Dad's obesity-related medical condition.

Chuck. At age thirty-eight, Chuck arrived at a therapist's office and described the events that had contributed to his developing an eating disorder. Chuck and his brother, Bob, lost their mother when Chuck was seven. Divorced from Chuck's father for several years, she had been ill for some time before she died, and Chuck remembers being scared and lonely when she was sick. Chuck and Bob were sent to live with their father and his new wife after their mother's death. Chuck's father was highly critical of Chuck's weight, calling him "Fatso" and often sending him to bed without dinner saying, "You're too fat to eat." Chuck's stepmother frequently joined in the criticism and taunts. Chuck would retreat to his room in tears. Although persistently overweight as a child, by adulthood, Chuck's weight had ballooned to nearly 300 pounds, even though he tried diet after diet. Despite threats from his employer to put him on restriction if he didn't shape up, Chuck could not curb his obsessive eating.

Homosexual Males

Some, but by no means all, males with eating disorders are members of the gay community, where men are judged on their physical appearance much in the same way that women are judged in the heterosexual community.[27] It is estimated that approximately 21 percent of males with an eating disorder are gay.[28] In a study of 135 males with eating disorders being treated at a hospital, 42 percent of those treated for bulimia identified themselves as either homosexual or bisexual, and 58 percent of those who were anorexic identified themselves as asexual.[29] Adolescent boys who develop anorexia frequently have gender-identity questions, and the increased probability of a gay-orientation in males with eating disorders has been confirmed by research.[30] The desire to lose weight is more common in males with a homosexual orientation, but the desire is still less prevalent among males than among heterosexual females.

Heterosexual Males

Although heterosexual males are not exposed to the same intense pressure to be thinner as women and gay men are, men are becoming more concerned about appearance and more interested in being attractive and fit. Since the mid-1970s, increasing numbers of men—34 percent of those surveyed in 1985, up from 15 percent in 1972—are generally dissatisfied with their looks. Weight was cited as the most disliked aspect of appearance, and more specifically, the size of their stomachs. In today's competitive workplace, achieving and maintaining an attractive appearance is seen as an advantage.

Athletes

Participating in a sport or activity that demands thinness increases the risk of developing disordered eating. Runners, jockeys, figure skaters, and gymnasts are generally at higher risk than most football players are, although there are exceptions. For example, two 1995 articles appeared in the *San Jose Mercury News*[31] reporting that Dennis Brown, a twenty-seven-year-old Super Bowl defensive end, revealed that he was bulimic as the result of trying to keep his weight down and avoid criticism from his coaches and other team officials.

Wrestlers may try to shed pounds quickly before a match so they can compete in a lower weight category, and body builders may seek to achieve high definition by depleting body fat and fluid reserves. Depending on the sport, male athletes are at risk for developing disordered eating.

Certain pressures and responsibilities may increase the risk of an athlete's developing an eating disorder.[32] When a lucrative contract, scholarship, or approval from peers or parents is on the line, the athlete may try to reduce weight in order to shave fractions of a second off his or her performance. Coaches may pressure athletes to lose weight and may use severe training to punish those who fail to comply.

Stress from participating in high profile activities and from excessive training, performance anxiety, and increasingly demanding competition may set the stage for binge eating followed by attempts to compensate if weight gain is an issue. Pressure to succeed academically contributes to stress as well. Injury can trigger depression and compulsive behaviors, including binge eating.

The Military

Military men and women are required to maintain certain weight and fitness standards, which can put them at risk for eating disorders. The prevalence of anorexia nervosa, bulimia nervosa, and other eating disorders was investigated in a sample of 1,425 active-duty Navy males aged eighteen to fifty-five years-old.[33] Results indicated that 2.5 percent suffered from anorexia nervosa, 6.8 percent from bulimia nervosa, and 40.8 percent from other eating disorders. Anorexia and bulimia existed throughout all ranks and ages. Eating disorders represented attempts to meet standards for body weight and to pass fitness requirements, although fasting, vomiting, and the use of diet pills and laxatives were employed year-round as well as during fitness training periods.

High Profile Occupations

Those in high profile jobs in which appearance plays an important role in interpersonal relationships may be at a higher risk than those with more relaxed appearance standards, such as warehouse workers, construction workers, or computer programmers. Some examples of high profile jobs include sales and marketing, retail sales, fashion merchandizing, design, and so forth. Similarly, dancers, ballet students, models, and entertainers are also at higher risk because of their concerns about appearance or body weight.[34]

Complicating Factors

Eating disorders seldom occur alone, and other conditions or disorders can complicate the picture. These may include substance abuse, depression, anxiety disorders, and personality disorders.

Substance Abuse and Eating Disorders

Those with an eating disorder may also exhibit other addictive behaviors.[35] About 25 percent of all eating disorder patients indicate a current or prior history of substance abuse.[36] Bulimics are more likely to be substance users than are anorexics, and anorexics who binge and purge abuse substances more than restricting anorexics.[37]

In one study, 73 percent of bulimics admitted to using alcohol and 35 percent used it at least weekly, while only 30 percent of anorexics indicated they used alcohol at all and 12 percent used it weekly.[38] In another study, 25 percent of bulimics admitted to drinking more than 36 drinks per week and 10 percent drank more than 50 drinks per week.[39] Marijuana was used by 25 percent of bulimics but only 5 percent of anorexics.[40] Eighteen percent of bulimics but only 3 percent of anorexics used amphetamines. Other substances used by bulimics included tranquilizers (14 percent), cocaine (13 percent), barbiturates (10 percent), and hallucinogens (8 percent). A third of bulimics but only a little more than one-fifth of anorexics smoked cigarettes.

Research on the use of substances by those with binge eating disorder has produced mixed results. Some studies have found that binge eaters have lower rates of substance use than normal-weight bulimics and about the same rate of use as non–binge eaters.[41]

Other studies have found that bulimics and obese binge eaters abuse alcohol about equally.[42] Those who have a dual diagnosis of both an eating disorder and substance abuse or dependence have higher rates of hospitalization, attempted suicide, and failure to take medication than those with a single diagnosis, and treatment must take into account both diagnoses.

Depression and Eating Disorders

Binge eaters, bulimics, and anorexics suffer more psychiatric difficulties, especially depression, than those without an eating disorder. One study reported that the lifetime prevalence rates for major depression in women seeking treatment for bulimia or binge eating disorder were 74 percent and 48 percent respectively.[43] Another study found that clinical samples of obese binge eaters had prevalence rates of 65 percent for major depression or dysthymia (chronic, low level depression that lasts for years) and 70 percent for anxiety disorders. One study compared obese binge eaters in the community and obese people who did not binge and who were not seeking treatment. The obese binge eaters were found to have a significantly higher lifetime prevalence rate of major depression—49 percent compared to 28 percent for the obese who did not binge—but similar rates of other psychiatric disorders.[44]

Some experts have suggested that depression is the *result* of an eating disorder, rather than a cause; and if the eating disorder can be alleviated, the depression will disappear.[45] Others argue that for anorexics depression is secondary and relates to their physical exhaustion and underlying feelings of awareness of wretchedness and hopelessness.[46] After restoring nutritional balance, this depression must be accessed and resolved for recovery to take place. However, research indicates that negative moods frequently precede an eating binge, and these moods are at least temporarily relieved by the binge episode. For these reasons, antidepressant medication is often helpful in the treatment of an eating disorder.

Symptoms of Depression

Depression can range from relatively mild to quite severe, with serious implications for mental health. Symptoms may include feeling down most of the time, crying a lot, having difficulties sleeping, either overeating or having little appetite, showing little interest in activities that used to give pleasure, having difficulty concentrating, and experiencing fatigue or agitation. The depressed person usually lacks self-confidence, engages in self-blame, isolates himself or herself from others, has a pessimistic outlook for the future, and dwells on unhappy past events. Feelings of inferiority and guilt may also be present.

Furthermore, depression can be expressed as physical symptoms such as headaches, backaches, gastrointestinal disturbance, irritability, and so forth. Not all of these symptoms need be present for a diagnosis of depression. When depression is severe, the sufferer may even wish to die. Suicidal ideation is an important indicator of Major Depression and the person experiencing it should be seen by a mental health professional as soon as possible.

Anxiety Disorders

Anxiety disorders come in several varieties and are believed to "set the stage" for the development of some eating disorders. In one study, 60 percent of anorexics and 57 percent of bulimics reported having an anxiety disorder concurrently with their eating disorder, while 90 percent of anorexics and 94 percent of bulimics reported that the anxiety disorder preceded the onset of their eating disorder.[47] Generalized anxiety disorder in adults, or overanxious disorder in children, involves the tendency to worry about many things. In obsessive-compulsive disorder, intrusive thoughts and obsessions create anxiety that is sometimes managed by engaging in compulsive behaviors such as hand washing, counting, and checking. Social phobia is an anxiety disorder in which there is excessive worry about being in social situations in which the person thinks she might be judged.

Anorexics are particularly likely to suffer from obsessive-compulsive disorder, whereas bulimics are often phobic in social situations. Both tend to suffer from overanxious disorder. Post-traumatic stress disorder, or PTSD, results when a person suffers a traumatic event such as a rape, sexual abuse, witnessing a murder, or is involved in a natural catastrophe such as an earthquake. In one study of bulimics, 36.9 percent had a history of PTSD.[48]

Obsessive-Compulsive Disorder

For some people, binge eating and subsequent purging helps alleviate the psychological pressure created by obsessional thinking. The obsessive and compulsive aspect of eating disorders may in some instances link them to another formidable psychiatric problem, obsessive-compulsive disorder or OCD.[49] OCD is an anxiety disorder defined by the presence of obsessive thoughts, images, or impulses that are experienced as intrusive, inappropriate, and distressing. Compulsions are repetitive behaviors or mental acts (such as repeating a phrase) that a person feels driven to perform. Typically, obsessions increase anxiety and compulsions are used to reduce tension.

Obsessive-compulsive disorder is thought to have important cultural components that define the specific content of the obsessions. It is quite possible that the influence of the current culturally defined thin-body ideal causes some women with OCD to develop eating disordered symptoms because this is the form their obsessions and compulsions take. Extensive exercising is a common feature of anorexia nervosa (sometimes labeled exercise anorexia) and it, too, may be linked to OCD.[50]

Two studies found that 37 percent of their sample who met the diagnostic criteria for either anorexia or bulimia also met the criteria for OCD.[51] Additional research supports these findings.[52] An eating disorder accompanied by OCD needs to be treated with interventions appropriate to OCD.

Personality and Eating Disorders

Personality traits are enduring patterns of perceiving, feeling, relating or reacting to, interacting with, and thinking about the environment, other people, and oneself. These patterns are exhibited in a wide range of social and personal contexts.[53]

The foundation of personality is established early in childhood and influenced by both hereditary and environmental factors. Personality traits evolve as a consequence of the temperament a person is born with and the treatment he or she receives in the family and later from peers. As a result, the person develops a distinctive way of viewing the world, the self, and others, which influences how he or she relates to others. Habits, attitudes, beliefs, and emotional responses become enduring patterns that are brought to bear in many situations.

When personality traits are inflexible or they cause problems in relationships or in functioning adaptively in life, this is called a personality disorder. Over the past two decades, clinicians and researchers have become increasingly aware that personality disorders occur in a significant minority of people with an eating disorder. Because of their personality organization, they often have greater difficulty recovering from an eating disorder. Dennis and Sansone[54] provide a useful overview of the interaction of various personality organizations and eating disorders.

Borderline Personality Organization

One personality disorder that affects some people with eating disorders is called borderline personality organization (BPO). Those with a borderline personality organization have unstable, intense, or chaotic relationships in which they vacillate between idealizing and devaluing the other person.[55] When things don't go their way, people with BPO may become critical, irritable, and hostile, often complaining of mistreatment and blaming others for their problems. They tend to be extremely sensitive to perceived slights, which can trigger angry reactions. Ruth is an example of a person with a borderline personality organization.

Ruth. When Ruth sought help from the psychologist at the community college where she was studying to be a dental technician, she appeared to be about sixty pounds overweight. She complained that she was having difficulty making and keeping friends, and she wasn't getting along with any of her teachers. At age twenty-eight, Ruth had already changed career directions twice. Ruth expected her widowed mother who lived on social security to underwrite her living expenses, and when her mother objected, Ruth complained bitterly about her mother's present and past failures as a parent. Following these rages, Ruth often became distraught, seeing herself as unlovable. At such times, she would binge on food or get drunk.

The person with BPO may exhibit a wide array of symptoms, the most common of which is unpredictable mood swings marked by anxiety, depression, or frequent and inappropriate displays of anger. Sometimes these "rage reactions" result in verbal abuse of others or even physical fights. Borderline individuals may be uncertain about their careers, long-term goals, values, sense of self, or sexual orientation. They have markedly low self-esteem and may believe unequivocally that they are "bad." They are often impulsive and may engage in substance abuse, overspending, frequent and unrestricted sexual relations, shoplifting, reckless driving, and so forth. Some people with BPO engage in self-mutilating behavior—cutting or burning themselves. Recurrent suicidal behavior, gestures, or threats are also common.

An eating disorder—usually bulimia or binge eating—is a common part of a borderline presentation. Eating disorder behaviors serve a variety of functions for those with BPO. The pursuit of thinness may help them enhance their normally low self-esteem. Because they have a limited ability to self-soothe in the face of stress, binge eating can serve as a coping behavior, and purging may help them regain a sense of self-control. Self-starvation, excessive exercising, laxative abuse, and vomiting may be used for self-punishment or as an expression of their deep-seated anger. The combination of binge eating and purging allows borderlines to numb themselves to intolerable emotional pain.[56]

Eating disordered patients who have BPO are less likely to benefit from time-limited and conventional treatment and are more likely to require an intensive and lengthy course of therapy. Effective treatment may take years instead of months. In addition to the usual interventions needed for dealing with eating disorders—normalization of eating patterns, challenging and changing distorted thinking, and developing effective coping skills, treatment should incorporate strategies for managing self-destructive behaviors, stabilizing mood, improving interpersonal functioning, reworking negative self-concept, and enhancing self-esteem.

One study of women with eating disorders who also had borderline symptoms found that these women had a more difficult time recovering from their eating disorder, and that they demonstrated greater emotional maladjustment and distress. These included less satisfaction with life, fewer perceived positive changes in eating disorder symptoms, and the need for continued mental health treatment.[57]

Histrionic Personality Organization

Those with a histrionic personality disorder have a persistent need for attention, acceptance, and approval by others. They like being in the spotlight and tend to be dramatic, exhibitionistic, and even seductive. Histrionic individuals are extremely sensitive to the moods and thoughts of others. They are alert to potential criticism or rejection, and they may manipulate others to avoid disapproval or to gain validation. To this end, they may feign helplessness, exaggerate or fabricate stories, throw tantrums, become sick with vague illnesses, or act provocatively. Although histrionic people usually make friends easily, these relationships are often superficial and lacking in warmth, genuineness, integrity, and loyalty. Histrionic individuals become easily bored, frustrated, or disappointed, and are prone to mood swings. Generally, they are not deep thinkers, but they may be talented in the dramatic arts or other creative endeavors.[58]

Claire. At age twenty-six, Claire had traveled a lot in her job as an events coordinator. She came to therapy because she was upset that her fiancée had abruptly ended their engagement. Now she was seeing an old boyfriend again, but they were having the same kinds of difficulties she and her fiancée had had. Claire admitted that she frequently tried to get her boyfriend (and previously, her fiancée) to tell her he loved or missed her, and when he did not comply, she would cry hysterically and threaten to end the relationship. At other times, she would take offense at some apparent insensitivity or oversight on his part and angrily confront him. Either of these situations left Claire emotionally distraught. Eating binges helped distract her from these feelings, and the subsequent purges removed the threat of gaining weight.

Histrionic individuals' extreme preoccupation with being socially acceptable and desirable can easily extend to overconcern about weight, shape, and appearance, leading them to engage in chronic dieting. Dieting in turn sets the stage for binge eating. The binge/purge cycle helps them deal with negative feelings and alleviates feelings of boredom or emptiness. Bulimia or anorexia with binge eating are the most likely eating disorders for histrionics.

The person with a histrionic personality organization needs to decrease her dependence on others for approval and work toward self-reliance. She needs to learn how to develop healthier and deeper relationships, as well as greater self-awareness. The usual treatment interventions aimed at normalizing eating patterns, breaking the binge/purge cycle, and restoring weight if necessary are often threatening to histrionics because they are convinced that appearance is their main asset. Finding other ways to define self-worth is an essential component of lasting recovery.

Avoidant Personality Organization

Anorexia is a common eating disorder for those with an avoidant personality organization. These are shy individuals who want to have relationships, but their fear of disapproval, ridicule, and rejection by others keeps them from reaching out. Consequently, they are often isolated and unhappy, with low self-esteem and significant self-doubt about their ability to relate to others. They often feel like misfits, and their fear of social embarrassment, judgment, and feeling awkward causes them to avoid opportunities to be with people.[59] Consider Jillian's history:

Jillian. At age thirty-two Jillian was tall, slender, and strikingly attractive. At the therapist's office, she tearfully explained that she had had only one brief relationship in her life, and that he had "dumped" her because she was "so fat and ugly." Subsequently, she began dieting and exercising, but she was convinced no one could ever find her attractive. Although Jillian had obtained an MBA at a good school, she now worked as an executive assistant in a small manufacturing firm. Trembling with emotion, she explained that she had become so distraught in her first job as a sales representative that she had had a "nervous breakdown" and quit.

When she was growing up, Jillian had always been the tallest child in the class. She was called "bean pole" by the other kids and not included in their activities. In high school she focused all of her energies on studying and making good grades. As a result, she had no friends and never dated. Continuing this pattern in college and graduate school, Jillian consoled herself that someday she would "make it big" and prove her worth. When her first job turned out badly, she fell into a deep depression. Eventually she discovered running and began to train to run a marathon, all the while counting calories and restricting her eating to certain foods. Sometimes she was so overcome by hunger that she binged. When this happened, she increased the length of her exercise routines for a few days. Running gave her a sense of accomplishment and control and helped to distract her from her fear of being alone forever. She was also convinced that if she could lose more weight, someone might find her acceptable for a love relationship.

Anorexia, especially the restricting type, is common among avoidant individuals, as is excessive exercising. For them, losing weight or maintaining a low weight may be synonymous with disappearing and helps them to feel less vulnerable to judgment and criticism. In other cases, the eating disorder substitutes for interpersonal relationships. It serves as a focus of attention that fills time and creates a sense of purpose, achievement, and power. In some cases, the fantasized result of the disordered eating behavior—a thin body—offers some hope of social connectedness.

Avoidant eating-disordered individuals are reluctant to seek help because they fear they will be criticized or that their inadequacies will be exposed. When they do seek help, it is usually at the insistence of a family member or concerned other, or because of a crisis in their life. Therapy is often a lengthy and difficult process. The person with an avoidant personality needs to build a sense of self-worth by discovering the strengths, abilities, and talents she may have overlooked or devalued. Eventually she needs to explore the painful memories that led to her serious mistrust and fear of ridicule and rejection by others. Gradually and with the support of the therapist, the avoidant person must attempt to establish relationships with others. Group therapy is often frightening for the avoidant person, and some find it difficult to undertake this therapeutic approach.

Dependent Personality Organization

Fearful of abandonment, those with a dependent personality organization have a pervasive sense of inferiority and helplessness. At times they are hesitant to make decisions and allow someone else, usually a spouse or parent, to provide them with structure, guidance, and direction. Dependent people sacrifice themselves to their relationships, subordinate or deny their own needs, assume personal responsibility for all of the problems in their relationships, and provide care and support to others— usually at the expense of their own needs. Their desire to be taken care of causes them to be submissive in relationships, allowing others to take the initiative and assume responsibility for major areas of their lives, such as where they should live, who their friends are, and what kind of job to pursue. Because they fear losing the relationship, they often have difficulty expressing disagreement and are unable to become appropriately angry. Their passivity may even lead them to accept verbal, sexual, or physical abuse.[60]

Donna. At her husband's insistence, Donna made an appointment with a therapist. He felt she needed to do something about the extra thirty-five pounds she had gained since the birth of their two children. Her excess weight was a turn-off to him sexually. In the first session, Donna tearfully admitted that she was a binge eater. Eating helped her feel better when Earl was off playing golf, going to the gym, or working, leaving her to parent the kids alone. In fact, the entire family's schedule revolved around Earl's activities. When they did socialize, it was always with Earl's friends. Donna also detailed her husband's efforts to get her to lose weight. Several years previously, he had enrolled her in Weight Watchers. Then he set her up with a personal trainer. When the nutritionist she saw at his insistence mentioned that Earl was too involved in making decisions for her, Donna did not go back to that nutritionist, saying that she didn't want to cause trouble with her husband.

Dependent personality organization is fairly common among those with eating disorders, especially anorexia nervosa.[61] In particular, restricting anorexics may have a dependent personality organization,[62] although conceivably some who have BED also have a dependent personality.

Binge eating allows dependent persons to nurture themselves without having to seek support or emotional connection from others or take much time away from their caretaking duties. In addition, binge eating helps distract them temporarily from the depression, isolation, and anxiety they frequently feel. Anorexia that results in very low weight and the possible concomitant physical debilitation prevents caregivers from separating from their care recipients and eliminates the possibility of independent functioning.

The person with a dependent personality needs to develop self-confidence and increase her self-esteem. She must learn to be more independent in her thinking and functioning, and to develop greater self-awareness through verbalizing her feelings, desires, and needs. The dependent personality needs to resolve fears about functioning independently and autonomously, and to develop greater tolerance for the anxiety that is associated with self-reliance. Both social skills training and assertiveness training can be very helpful.

Obsessive-Compulsive Personality Organization

An obsessive-compulsive personality organization (OCPO) differs from obsessive-compulsive disorder, or OCD. The latter is characterized by intrusive and unwanted thoughts or images, which produce anxiety. Compulsive behaviors such as counting, checking, and hand washing are employed to control anxiety. The person with OCPO is overly concerned with orderliness and logic.

Steve. Steve's wife Sharon insisted that he come to therapy with her. She was a binge eater, and some of Steve's habits were part of the problem. Steve was the chief financial officer of a small computer software firm. He arose regularly at 5 A.M. to go to the gym and work out before going to the office. After eating his regulation breakfast which consisted of a bowl of cereal with skim milk and one cup of coffee, he ate nothing else during the day. He worked long hours, often not arriving home until 8 or 9 in the evening. By that time, Sharon had already eaten and gotten the kids to bed. Steve expected the house to be orderly and spotless, even though Sharon also worked full-time outside the house. When he arrived home, he expected Sharon to have cooked his evening meal, which was to be prepared from a heart-healthy cookbook, and to join him at dinner. If his wife failed to prepare the meal to his exacting standards, he lectured her on the evils of saturated fat and red meat. Steve took pride in his runner's body, which he maintained by regular exercise and attending carefully to his diet.

The hallmarks of obsessive-compulsive personality disorder include perfectionism, rigid adherence to rules and regulations, inflexible thinking, stubbornness, and excessive devotion to work—usually at the expense of having fun. Obsessive-compulsive individuals are often preoccupied with being industrious, self-disciplined, productive, and responsible, although they can be distracted by details and get bogged down by procrastination or inefficient time management. They are often perceived as moralistic, self-righteous, inflexible, stingy, punitive, overly rational, and lacking in warmth and empathy.

Those with an obsessive-compulsive personality organization are likely to be restricting anorexics or anorexics who engage in excessive exercise.[63] For them, the eating disorder provides a means of achievement, which is expressed by weight loss. For some, counting calories, measuring pounds lost, employing routines and rituals to control hunger, and focusing on self-imposed, strict rules for eating allows them to retreat from the relationship and achievement demands of adolescence and early adulthood. Obsessive-compulsive people are not comfortable experiencing or expressing emotion—which feels to them like being out of control. Exhibiting high levels of perfectionistic thinking, they prefer to intellectualize and rationalize rather than feel. For others, the eating disorder provides a sense of power and can be an expression of opposition to authority figures.

Obsessive-compulsive people generally resist therapy, which they fear threatens their way of staying in control. Indeed, an important goal in therapy is for them to learn to identify, label, and express feelings. As they become better at tolerating emotional experiencing, the arena of interpersonal relationships can be addressed. Obsessive-compulsives need to learn how to tolerate feelings of vulnerability and frustration when all is not perfect, and to be more emotionally expressive with others.

Notes

1. Goldman, E. L. 1996. Eating disorders on the rise in preteens and adolescents. *Psychiatry News, 24*, 10; Hoek, H. W., A. I. Bartelds, M. A. Bosveld, et al. 1995. Impact of urbanization on detection rates of eating disorders. *American Journal of Psychiatry, 152*, 1272–1278; Hsu, L. K. G. 1996. Epidemiology of the eating disorders. *Psychiatric Clinics of North America, 19*, 681–700.

2. Franko, D. L., and P. Orosan-Weine. 1998. The prevention of eating disorders: Empirical, methodological, and conceptual considerations. *Clinical Psychology: Science and Practice, 5*, 459–477.

3. Stice, E., C. Ziemba, J. Margolis, and P. Flick. 1996. The dual pathway model differentiates bulimics, subclinical bulimics, and controls: Testing the continuity hypothesis. *Behavior Therapy, 27*, 531–549.

4. Vaz, F. J. 1998. Outcome of bulimia nervosa: Prognostic indicators. *Journal of Psychosomatic Research, 45*, 391–400.

5. Phelps, L. and E. Bajorek. 1991. Eating disorders of the adolescent: Current issues in etiology, assessment, and treatment. *School Psychology Review, 20*, 9–22.

6. Cooper, P. J., and I. Goodyear. 1997. Prevalence and significance of weight and shape concerns in girls aged 11-16 years. *British Journal of Psychiatry, 171*, 542–544.

7. Shapiro, S., M. Newcomb, and T. B. Loeb. 1997. Fear of fat, disregulated-restrained eating, and body esteem: Prevalence and gender differences among eight- to ten-year-old children. *Journal of Clinical Child Psychology, 26*, 358–365.

8. Calam, R., and G. Waller. 1998. Are eating and psychosocial characteristics in early teenage years useful predictors of eating characteristics in early adulthood? A 7-year longitudinal study. *International Journal of Eating Disorders, 24*, 351–362.

9. Kendler, K. S., C. MacLean, M. Neale, R. Kessler, A. Heathy, and L. Eaves. 1991. The genetic epidemiology of bulimia nervosa. *American Journal of Psychiatry, 148*, 1627–1637; Patton, G. C., E. Johnson-Sabine, K. Wood, A. H. Mann, and A. Wakeling. 1990. Abnormal eating attitudes in London schoolgirls—A prospective epidemiological study: Outcome at twelve month follow-up. *Psychological Medicine, 20*, 383–394.

10. Gustafson-Larson, A. M., and R. D. Terry. 1992. Weight-related behaviors and concerns of fourth-grade children. *Journal of the American Dietetic Association, 92*, 818–822.

11. Thelen, M. H., A. L. Powell, C. Lawrence, and M. E. Kuhnert. 1992. Eating and body image concerns among children. *Journal of Clinical Child Psychology, 21*, 41–46.

12. Maloney, M. J., J. B. McGuire, S. R. Daniels, and B. Specker. 1989. Dieting behaviors and eating attitudes in children. *Pediatrics, 84*, 482–489.

13. Killen, J. D., C. B. Taylor, M. J. Telch, K. E. Saylor, D. J. Maron, and T. N. Robinson. 1986. Self-induced vomiting and laxative and diuretic use among teenagers: Precursors of the binge-purge syndrome? *Journal of the American Medical Association, 255,* 1447–1449.

14. Patton, G. C., J. B. Carlin, Q. Shao, M. E. Hibbert, et al. 1997. Adolescent dieting: Healthy weight control or borderline eating disorder? *Journal of Child Psychology and Psychiatry and Allied Disciplines, 38,* 299–306.

15. Gross, J., and J. C. Rosen. 1988. Bulimia in adolescents: Prevalence and psychosocial correlates. *International Journal of Eating Disorders, 7,* 51–61.

16. Lucas, A. R., M. Beard, W. M. O'Fallon, and L. T. Kurland. 1991. 50-year trends in the incidence of anorexia nervosa in Rochester, Minn.: A population-based study. *American Journal of Psychiatry, 148,* 917–922.

17. Fairburn, C. G., and S. J. Beglin. 1990. Studies of the epidemiology of bulimia nervosa. *American Journal of Psychiatry, 147,* 401–408

18. Drewnowski, A., D. K. Yee, C. L. Kurth, and D. D. Krahn. 1994. Eating pathology and DSM-III-R bulimia nervosa: A continuum of behavior. *American Journal of Psychiatry, 151,* 1217–1219.

19. Bruce, B., and D. Wilfley. 1996. Binge eating among the overweight population: A serious and prevalent problem. *Journal of the American Dietetic Association, 96,* 58–61; Spitzer, R. L., M. Devlin, B. T. Walsch, D. Hasin, R. Wing, M. Marcus, et al. 1992. Binge eating disorder: A multisite field trial of the diagnostic criteria. *International Journal of Eating Disorders, 11,* 191–203; Spitzer, R. L., M. J. Devlin, B. T. Walsh, D. Hasin, R. Wing, M. Marcus, et al. 1992. Binge eating disorder: Its further validation in a multisite study. *International Journal of Eating Disorders, 13,* 137–153.; Wing, R., and C. G. Greeno. 1994. Behavioural and psychosocial aspects of obesity and its treatment. *Baillieres Clinical Endocrinology & Metabolism, 8,* 689–703.

20. Smith, D. E., M. D. Marcus, C. Lewis, M. Fitzgibbon, and P. Schreiner. 1998. Prevalence of binge eating disorder, obesity, and depression in a biracial cohort of young adults. *Annals of Behavioral Medicine, 20,* 227–232.

21. Canals, J., G. Carbajo, J. Fernandez, C. Marti-Henneberg, and E. Domenech. 1996. Biopsychopathologic risk profile of adolescents with eating disorder symptoms. *Adolescence, 31,* 443–450; Patton, G. C., J. B. Carlin, Q. Shao, M. E. Hibbert, et al. 1997. Adolescent dieting: Healthy weight control or borderline eating disorder? *Journal of Child Psychology and Psychiatry and Allied Disciplines, 38,* 299–306.

22. Grissett, N. I., and M. L. Fitzgibbon. 1996. The clinical significance of binge eating in an obese population: Support for BED and questions regarding its criteria. *Addictive Behaviors, 21,* 57–66.

23. Adami, G. F., P. Gandolfo, B. Bauer, and N. Scopinaro. 1995. Binge eating in massively obese patients undergoing bariatric surgery. *International Journal of Eating Disorders, 17,* 45–50.

24. Fairburn, C. G., and S. J. Beglin. 1990. Studies of the epidemiology of bulimia nervosa. *American Journal of Psychiatry, 147,* 401–408.

25. Carlat, D. J., C. A. Camargo, and D. B. Herzog. 1997. Eating disorders in males: A report on 135 patients. *American Journal of Psychiatry, 154,* 1127–1132.

26. Anderson, A. E. 1995. Eating disorders in males. In K. D. Brownell and C. G. Fairburn, eds., *Eating Disorders and Obesity.* New York: Guilford. 177–182.

27. Beren, S. E., H. A. Hayden, D. E. Wilfley, and C. M. Grilo. 1996. The influence of sexual orientation on body dissatisfaction in adult men and women. *International Journal of Eating Disorders, 20,* 135–141; Siever, M. D. 1994. Sexual orientation and gender as factors in socioculturally acquired vulnerability to body dissatisfaction and eating disorders. *Journal of Consulting and Clinical Psychology, 62,* 252–260.

28. Anderson, A. E. 1995. Eating disorders in males. In K. D. Brownell and C. G. Fairburn, eds., *Eating Disorders and Obesity.* New York: Guilford. 177–182.

29. Carlat, D. J., C. A. Camargo, and D. B. Herzog. 1997. Eating disorders in males: A report on 135 patients. *American Journal of Psychiatry, 154,* 1127–1132.

30. Anderson, A. E. 1995. Eating disorders in males. In K. D. Brownell and C. G. Fairburn, eds., *Eating Disorders and Obesity.* New York: Guilford. 177–182.

31. *San Jose Mercury News,* 26 January 1995, section F. "49ers Say Brown Hid Weight-Loss Regimen; *San Jose Mercury News,* 27 January 1995, section E.

32. Lapiano, D. A., and C. Zotos. 1992. Modern athletics: The pressure to perform. In K. D. Brownell, J. Rodin, and J. H. Wilmore, eds., *Eating, Body Weight, and Performance in Athletes: Disorders of Modern Society.* Philadelphia: Lea and Febiger. 275–292.

33. McNulty, P. A. F. 1997. Prevalence and contributing factors of eating disorder behaviors in active duty Navy men. *Military Medicine, 162,* 753–758.

34. Abraham, S. 1996. Characteristics of eating disorders among young ballet dancers. *Psychopathology, 29,* 223–229; Clark, N. 1994. Counseling the athlete with an eating disorder: A case study. *Journal of the American Dietetic Association, 94,* 656–658; Olson, M. S., H. N. Williford, L. A. Richards, J. A. Brown, and S. Pugh. 1996. Self-reports on the Eating Disorder Inventory by female aerobic instructors. *Perceptual Motor Skills, 82,* 1051–1058.

35. Mitchell, J. E., S. Specker, and K. Edmonson. 1997. Management of substance abuse and dependence. In D. M. Garner and P. E. Garfinkel, eds., *Handbook of Treatment for Eating Disorders. 2nd ed.* New York: Guilford Press. 415–423; Newman, M. M., and M. S. Gold. 1992. Preliminary findings of patterns of substance abuse in eating disorder patients. *American Journal of Drug and Alcohol Abuse, 18,* 207–211.

36. Katz, J. L. 1990. Eating disorders: A primer for the substance abuse specialist: I. Clinical features. *Journal of Substance Abuse Treatment, 7,* 143–149.

37. Casper, R. C., E. D. Eckert, K. A. Halmi, S. C. Goldberg, and J. M. Davis. 1980. Bulimia: Its incidence and clinical importance in patients with anorexia nervosa. *Archives of General Psychiatry, 37,* 1030–1034; Garfinkel, P. E., H.

Moldofsky, and D. M. Garner. 1980. The heterogeneity of anorexia nervosa. *Archives of General Psychiatry, 37,* 1036–1040.

38. Jones, D. A., N. Cheshire, and H. Moorhouse. 1985. Anorexia nervosa, bulimia and alcoholism: Association of eating disorder and alcohol. *Journal of Psychiatric Research, 19,* 377–380.

39. Brisman, J., and M. Siegel. 1986. Bulimia and alcoholism—Two sides of the same coin? *Journal of Substance Abuse and Treatment, 1,* 113–118.

40. Bulik, C. M. 1987. Drug and alcohol abuse by bulimic women and their families. *American Journal of Psychiatry, 144,* 1604–1606.

41. Hudson, J. I., H. G. Pope, J. Wurtman, D. Yurgelun-Todd, S. Mark, and N. E. Rosenthal. 1988. Bulimia in obese individuals: Relationship to normal-weight bulimia. *Journal of Nervous and Mental Disease, 176,* 144–152; Marcus, M. D., R. R. Wing, L. Ewing, E. Kern, W. Gooding, and M. McDerott. 1990. Psychiatric disorders among obese binge eaters. *International Journal of Eating Disorders, 9,* 69–77; Wilson, G. T., C. A. Nonas, and G. D. Rosenblum. 1993. Assessment of binge-eating in obese persons. *International Journal of Eating Disorders, 13,* 23–33.

42. Mitchell, J. E., R. Pyle, E. D. Eckert, D. Hatsukami, and E. Soll. 1990. The influence of prior alcohol and drug abuse problems on bulimia nervosa treatment outcome. *Addictive Behaviors, 15,* 169–173; Schwalberg, M. D., D. H. Barlow, S. A. Alger, and L. J. Howard. 1992. A comparison of bulimics, obese binge eaters, social phobics, and individuals with panic disorders or comorbidity across DSM-III-R anxiety disorders. *Journal of Abnormal Psychology, 101,* 675–681.

43. McCann, U. D., E. M. Rossiter, R. J. King, and W. S. Agras. 1991. Nonpurging bulimia: A distinct subtype of bulimia nervosa. *International Journal of Eating Disorders, 10,* 679–687.

44. Telch, C. F., and E. Stice. 1998. Psychiatric comorbidity in women with binge eating disorder: Prevalence rates from a non-treatment-seeking sample. *Journal of Consulting and Clinical Psychology, 66,* 768–776.

45. Cooper, P. J., and C. G. Fairburn. 1986. The depressive symptoms of bulimia nervosa. *British Journal of Psychiatry, 148,* 268–274.

46. Crisp, A. H. 1997. Anorexia nervosa as a flight from growth: Assessment and treatment based on the model. In D. M. Garner and P. E. Garfinkel, eds., *Handbook of Treatment for Eating Disorders. 2nd ed.,* New York: Guilford Press. 248–277.

47. Bulik, C. M., P. F. Sullivan, J. L. Fear, and P. R. Joyce. 1997. Eating disorders and antecedent anxiety disorders: A controlled study. *Acta Psychiatrica Scandinavica, 96,* 101–107.

48. Dansky, B. S., T. D. Brewerton, D. G. Kilpatrick, and P. M. O'Neil. 1997. The National Women's Study: Relationship of victimization and posttraumatic stress disorder to bulimia nervosa. *International Journal of Eating Disorders, 21,* 213–228.

49. Wall, D. 1998. Obsessive compulsive disorder and eating disorders. *AABA Newsletter,* Summer. New York: American Anorexia Bulimia Association. 4–5.

50. Davis, C., S. Kaptein, A. S. Kaplan, M. P. Olmsted, and D. B. Woodside. 1998. Obsessionality in anorexia nervosa: The moderating influence of exercise. *Psychosomatic Medicine, 60,* 192–197.

51. Thiel, A., A. Broocks, M. Ohlmeier, G. E. Jacoby, and G. Schufler. 1995. Obsessive-compulsive disorder among patients with anorexia nervosa and bulimia nervosa. *American Journal of Psychiatry, 152,* 72–75; Thiel, A., M. Zuger, G. Jacoby, and G. Schussler. 1998. Thirty-month outcome in patients with anorexia or bulimia nervosa and concomitant obsessive-compulsive disorder. *American Journal of Psychiatry, 155,* 244–249.

52. Kaye, W. H., T. Welzin, and L. K. Hsu. 1996. Anorexia nervosa. In E. Hollander, ed., *Obsessive Compulsive Related Disorders.* Washington, DC: American Psychiatric Press.

53. American Psychiatric Association. 1994. *Diagnostic and Statistical Manual of Mental Disorders. 4th ed.* Washington, DC.

54. Dennis, A. B., and R. A. Sansone. 1997. Treatment of patients with personality disorders. In D. M. Garner and P. E. Garfinkel, eds., *Handbook of Treatment for Eating Disorders. 2nd ed.* New York: Guilford Press. 437–449.

55. Ibid.

56. Ibid.

57. Sansone, R. A., and M. A. Fine. 1992. Borderline personality as a predictor of outcome in women with eating disorders. *Journal of Personality Disorders, 6,* 176–186.

58. Dennis, A. B., and R. A. Sansone. 1997. Treatment of patients with personality disorders. In D. M. Garner and P. E. Garfinkel, eds., *Handbook of Treatment for Eating Disorders. 2nd ed.* New York: Guilford Press. 437–449.

59. Ibid.

60. Ibid.

61. Gartner, A. F., R. N. Marcus, K. Halmi, and A. Loranger. 1989. DSM-III-R personality disorders in patients with eating disorders. *American Journal of Psychiatry, 146,* 1585–1591; Kennedy, S. H., G. McVey, and R. Katz. 1990. Personality disorders in anorexia nervosa and bulimia nervosa. *Journal of Psychiatric Research, 24,* 259–269; Norman, D., M. Blais, and D. Herzog. 1993. Personality characteristics of eating disordered patients as identified by the Millon Clinical Multiaxial Inventory. *Journal of Personality Disorders, 7,* 1–9; Wonderlich, S. A., W. J. Swift, H. B. Slotnick, and S. Goodman. 1990. DSM-III-R personality disorders in eating-disorder subtypes. *International Journal of Eating Disorders, 9,* 607–616.

62. Piran, N., P. Lerner, P. E. Garfinkel, S. H. Kennedy, and C. Brouillette. 1988. Personality disorders in anorexic patients. *International Journal of Eating Disorders, 7,* 589–599; Steiger, H., K. Liquornik, J. Chapman, and N. Hussain. 1991. Personality and family disturbances in eating disorder patients:

Comparison of "restricters" and "bingers" to normal controls. *International Journal of Eating Disorders, 10,* 501–512.

63. Davis, C., S. Kaptein, A. S. Kaplan, M. P. Olmsted, and D. B. Woodside. 1998. Obsessionality in anorexia nervosa: The moderating influence of exercise. *Psychosomatic Medicine, 60,* 192–197; Lilenfield, L. R., W. H. Kaye, C. G. Greeno, K. R. Merikangas., K. Plotnicove, C. Pollice, et al. 1998. A controlled family study of anorexia nervosa and bulimia nervosa: Psychiatric disorders in first-degree relatives and effects of proband comorbidity. *Archives of General Psychiatry, 55,* 603–610.

Chapter 3

How Binge Eating Hurts

In the long run, binge eating hurts. It has physical, psychological, and social consequences that far outweigh the short-term benefits of avoiding unpleasant emotions or providing a quick means of nurturing oneself. The restrictive dieting and purging that often accompany binge eating are important contributors to the medical and psychological complications that are incurred with an eating disorder.

Medical Complications of Eating Disorders

Starving, stuffing, and purging can lead to physical damage and sometimes death. Eating disorders detrimentally affect cells, tissues, organs, and systems in the body. The most lethal effects occur among anorexics, with 6 percent to 20 percent eventually dying from the disorder—usually as the result of the complications of starvation, electrolyte imbalances, or from suicide. Although all eating disorders incur some physical damage, very serious medical complications are common in anorexia nervosa. While anorexics frequently minimize the physical consequences of their situation, bulimics report a number of complaints and may seek medical help. Often these are nonspecific complaints such as "heartburn," "constipation," or "feeling bloated." Obese binge eaters usually seek medical help, often requesting medication for a runaway appetite, or for help with other problems such as joint damage and pain that can accompany severe obesity. The obese are also at risk for developing Type II diabetes.

Gastrointestinal Disturbances

The binge/purge cycle frequently disrupts the functioning of the gastrointestinal system, resulting in complaints of stomach bloating, constipation, and abdominal pain. Delayed gastric emptying is commonly encountered in those with anorexia nervosa and in some people with bulimia. Because of restrictive dieting, food stays in the stomach longer and does not pass through the intestines as rapidly as would be expected.

This contributes to the feeling of fullness and "bloating" that is so upsetting to anorexics and bulimics and tends to trigger a purge and possibly deter further eating. Paradoxically, improvement in the gastric emptying rate can take place only by eating food on a regular basis and learning to tolerate the temporary anxiety associated with feelings of fullness. Likewise, normalizing the eating pattern, eating frequent small meals, and increasing fiber and fluid intake is the best way to treat constipation.

In rare cases, rapid overeating can cause acute dilation of the stomach, perforation, or bleeding, all of which trigger severe abdominal pain. Uncontrolled vomiting, which can be triggered by the use of syrup of ipecac or by acute pancreatitis, also can result in gastrointestinal bleeding.[1]

Some obese binge eaters complain of irritable bowel syndrome (IBS). This is characterized by bouts of constipation or diarrhea accompanied by abdominal discomfort, gas, and bloating. IBS is thought to be triggered by stress, but it may also be aggravated by consumption of high-fat foods and certain other foods, such as cruciferous vegetables like cabbage, broccoli, and cauliflower. Binge eaters with IBS should keep their meals low in fat and high in fiber by emphasizing whole grains, fruits, and vegetables. In addition, they should avoid caffeine and alcohol. Engaging in regular exercise will help them cope better with stress and improve their gastrointestinal functioning.

Fluids and Electrolytes

Electrolytes are minerals such as sodium and potassium that are dissolved in the blood and other body fluids. These minerals are needed for the proper functioning of nerves and muscles, including heart muscle. When the electrolyte balance is upset—usually by vomiting, abusing laxatives and enemas, or engaging in abrupt and excessive overeating after prolonged caloric restriction—the result can be muscle cramps, tremors, spasms, and in some cases, cardiac arrest.

Electrolyte abnormalities are relatively common in those with eating disorders, especially those who binge/purge. Some deaths have been linked to these problems, and electrolyte abnormalities are also associated with cardiac arrhythmia and other heart problems. *Edema,* which involves the accumulation of excess fluid in cells, tissues, and various cavities, can be a reaction to dehydration caused by vomiting, or abusing laxatives or diuretics. This fluid retention can be interpreted as weight gain by some, causing renewed dieting and attempts to lose weight. Severe caloric restriction may also upset electrolyte balances.

Cardiovascular System

Various cardiac abnormalities, including irregular heartbeat and cardiac arrest, have been described in eating disordered patients. Some cardiac dysfunction is associated with electrolyte abnormalities. Slowed heart rate and low blood pressure frequently accompany starvation incurred in anorexia nervosa. Ipecac, when used repeatedly for purging purposes, is stored in muscle tissue, including the heart, which can result in muscle weakness. Obese binge eaters have both increased risk of high cholesterol and high blood pressure, both risk factors for cardiovascular disease.

Bones and Metabolism

The low estrogen levels associated with anorexia and bulimia are important contributors to loss of bone mass and osteoporosis, resulting in increased risk of fractures, especially later in life. Various other abnormalities related to mineral absorption have also been observed. Hypoglycemia, or low blood sugar, can develop either after fasting or in response to binge eating and vomiting episodes. Dieting results in loss of muscle mass with a subsequent decrease in metabolism. Anemia and malnutrition are likely among anorexics. Joint problems are frequent among obese binge eaters, who may also exhibit a slowed metabolism.

Skin and Hair

Many persons with anorexia nervosa develop lanugo— downy, soft body hair—occurring on the face, the forearms and other surfaces of the body. It can be accompanied by loss of scalp hair. The skin becomes dry and blotchy with an unhealthy gray or yellow cast, and nails may turn brittle. In bulimics, calluses, abrasions, or scars may appear on the back of the hand from inducing the gag reflex necessary for vomiting. Small hemorrhages in the eye are also caused by the increased intraocular pressure associated with vomiting. Those who are severely overweight may develop skin rashes where skin rubs together or where moisture is trapped.

Teeth

Recurrent vomiting is associated with significant and permanent loss of dental enamel, as well as with chipped teeth and an increased frequency of dental cavities. Brushing the teeth after vomiting only accelerates this process and should be avoided. Periodontal disease has also been reported as the result of purging.

Menstrual/Reproductive Complications

Amenorrhea or the failure to ovulate and menstruate is a hallmark of anorexia. Because of lowered levels of sex hormones, anorexics are usually not interested in having sexual relations, and even when they are, infertility is common because the hormone deficiencies and low body fat inhibit ovulation. If pregnancy does occur, anorexics have a higher than normal frequency of spontaneous abortions and low-birth-weight babies.

Between 75 percent and 85 percent of women with bulimia nervosa also lose their periods for more than three months, and 50 percent to 70 percent are amenorrheic for twelve months or more. During the course of bulimia, twice as many bulimic women complain of infertility as women in the general population. Although bulimia can inhibit sexual desire or arousal, bulimics are frequently sexually active. Bulimics who do become pregnant are at greater risk for miscarriage and for postnatal depression.[2]

Significant obesity is often associated with binge eating disorder. With higher levels of obesity, ovulation becomes less frequent and menstrual irregularities (especially spotting or minimal menstruation) is more frequent. Less frequent ovulation reduces the chances of pregnancy, and high weight is frequently associated with pregnancy complications. Although no research data delineate the effect of obesity or binge eating disorder on sexual desire or performance, clinical experience with obese binge eaters suggests that the higher rates of self-loathing, disgust about body size, self-consciousness, and body dissatisfaction can all negatively affect sexual functioning.

Other Problems

Eating disorders have been associated with kidney damage, liver damage, and a weakened immune system. Icy hands and feet and general intolerance to cold are common experiences for anorexics. Fainting spells and mental fuzziness, as well as bad dreams and sleep disruption, can be a by-product of starvation. Swollen glands in the neck produce the characteristic "chipmunk cheeks" of bulimia. Those who suffer from obesity and binge eating disorder have a higher risk of gallbladder disease, cancer, and diabetes. Their ability to move around easily may be decreased, limiting their physical activity and their ability to burn calories.

Psychological Complications of Eating Disorders

It is a sad paradox that the person who undertakes restrictive dieting and weight loss to improve self-esteem and bolster self-confidence often ends up with more problems than she started with. For example, the anorexic often begins self-starvation as a means to feel more in control of herself and/or her life. Instead, the anorexia comes to control her.

Anorexia

The anorexic lives by rigid rules for eating and exercise, and breaching a rule results in hostility directed at herself. As self-starvation progresses, she experiences obsessive thoughts about food and engages in elaborate rituals to keep hunger and eating in check. Eventually anorexia becomes the central focus in her life and can even become a substitute for a sense of self.

Chapter 1 began the story of Carol, who used excessive exercise and restrictive dieting to control her weight. She worried obsessively about gaining weight, and when her anxiety became too great, she relieved it by running. Plagued by anxiety and self-doubt, Carol often took time off from work in the middle of the day to run, which, naturally, caused problems on the job. On occasions when she succumbed to a binge, she was filled with terror that she might gain weight. Sometimes she used syrup of ipecac to purge. She admitted that she could not imagine her life or herself without anorexia. Although married, Carol's identity was not self-defined as a wife or mother; her identity was as an anorexic. "Without anorexia," Carol would say, "I am nothing."

Anorexics have difficulty understanding that their low weight or their anorexic behaviors pose a serious health problem. In the early stages of anorexia, before their weight falls into the danger zone, they may take pride in their appearance and find it hard to comprehend why others think they are too thin. They resist attempts to get them to seek treatment, regarding this as interference in their right to self-determination. In the later stages of anorexia, when their weight is so low it threatens life, the ability to think clearly becomes seriously impaired. Depression sets in at some point, often accompanied by thoughts of suicide. In the last stages of anorexia, one core thought dominates—"I am bad and I don't deserve to live."

Bulimia

Bulimics also engage in extensive self-criticism and self-blame, which contribute to feelings of guilt, shame, anxiety, and self-doubt. Repeated failed attempts to stop the binge/purge cycle result in feeling helpless and hopeless that recovery is even possible. Depression is often a fellow traveler with bulimia.

Meredith's story was also described in Chapter 1. In the grip of bulimia, Meredith felt ashamed of her binge/purge behavior. Her repeated attempts to restrict eating resulted in losing control and bingeing, leaving her feeling hopeless and depressed. During her binges, she was often terrified of being discovered. To maintain secrecy, she hid food so she could eat it without being observed. Much of the time, Meredith felt as if she didn't belong to the same world that everyone else inhabited.

Binge Eating Disorder

Those with binge eating disorder (BED) share many of the same psychological complications characteristic of bulimia. In addition, obese binge eaters often encounter social rejection, ostracism, and discrimination because of their weight. Their self-esteem suffers and they lose confidence in ever being able to manage their weight.

Like Mary Ann, whose story was introduced in chapter 1, people with BED feel ashamed and disgusted with their weight and body shape, and they often avoid situations where they feel exposed. They may attempt to conceal their weight by wearing bulky or dark clothing and avoid calling attention to themselves in social gatherings. Unable to control their overeating, binge eaters feel helpless to change their behavior. As noted previously, depression is a common accompaniment to BED.

How an Eating Disorder Hurts Others

Disordered eating hurts family and friends, as well as the person with the eating disorder. Others observe problematic behaviors, such as the refusal to eat or obviously poor eating or exercise habits, and develop concerns about what these behaviors mean. They may notice that food is missing, that more and more money is being spent on food, or that their loved one's health is obviously being affected. These behaviors and their consequences lead the concerned family member, partner, or friend to react in various ways. They may feel confused, helpless, worried, guilty, angry, or even disgusted. Family members and friends often want to help but don't know what to do, or they become frustrated when their efforts to help fail.

Renee. Twenty-four-year old Renee trained so excessively for a triathlon that her professional trainer became alarmed. The trainer warned Renee that she was pushing herself beyond what was considered good training. Despite being afraid of water and swimming, Renee arose daily at 5:30A.M. to swim for thirty minutes in San Francisco Bay, followed by a long, punishing run that included the steepest hills she could find—all before going to work. Renee's workouts often were so vigorous that she would become nauseated and throw up. She refused to eat in front of anyone, which caused problems in her relationship with her boyfriend Carl. If she went to dinner alone with him, Renee would not order or eat anything. He liked going out with friends and socializing over dinner. When Renee was pressured to go out to dinner with friends, which she tried to avoid, she would order only if she felt forced to do so, and then she would not eat or would pick at the food. Carl's friends sometimes tried to get Renee to eat, which made her retreat into angry silence. Carl would then become angry with Renee, accusing her of embarrassing him in front of his friends. Carl's patience with Renee's eating habits was wearing thin, and by the time they arrived in a therapist's office, he was threatening to end their relationship.

Here are more examples of the impact an eating disorder can have on others. Daniel brought his girlfriend home to visit during spring break at the university they both attended. Sherri declined to eat dinner with the family, which upset Daniel's mother, especially when she observed that Sherri would often eat a whole half-gallon of ice cream later in the evening, only to disappear into the bathroom shortly afterwards. Daniel's mother told Daniel in no uncertain terms that Sherri was not welcome back. Shortly afterward, Daniel and Sherri broke up.

Ken invited his friend Marla to have dinner at his home. He spent considerable time planning and preparing the menu and staging a nice evening. Everything seemed to go well enough until the end of the dinner, when Marla excused herself to go to the bathroom. About fifteen minutes later, she reappeared. Ken was shocked and confused when he detected the smell of vomit.

Mary Ann was introduced in chapter 1. She is the thirty-eight-year-old married woman who runs her own business, still has two teenagers at home, and is about fifty pounds overweight. After a long, hectic day at the office, she often arrived home exhausted and stressed. Despite eating a reasonable dinner, she couldn't stop eating. Her husband frequently made negative comments such as, "Do you really need that?" or "Haven't you had enough?" Her teenage daughter didn't say anything to her mother, but she was increasingly restricting her own eating. Occasionally, Mary Ann wondered why her daughter never invited friends over.

Mary Ann's daughter was apparently on her own route to disordered eating, spurred by the shame that her mother's overeating caused and the fear that she too might become obese. Mary Ann's binge eating also was pinching the family budget. The families of both bulimics and binge eaters bear an extra financial burden because of the excess food eaten and, in the case of bulimics, purged. Similarly, those who chew and spit out food without swallowing may run up the cost of food for the family without receiving any nutritional benefits.

The avoidance behaviors and the compulsive exercising engaged in by anorexics, the purging of bulimics, and the overeating habits of those with binge eating disorder create consternation among the friends and family members of the person exhibiting the disordered eating behavior. In addition to the conduct itself, the consequences of such behaviors cause problems for significant others. These can include the following:

- The development of fat phobia in family members

- The added cost of wasted food

- The loss of the eating disordered person's companionship

- The need for family members to care for the eating disordered person

- The cost for treatment of an eating disorder

- Shock and concern from seeing the emaciated body of someone with anorexia can cause the observer to feel considerable alarm and distress.

An eating disorder can impact a relationship in several significant ways. Here are some:

- The extreme body dissatisfaction that is typical in all eating disorders may interfere with a couple's healthy sexual relationship.

- To the extent that the eating disorder elicits avoidance behaviors, the social activities of a couple or a family may be curtailed.

- If the eating disorder creates health problems, the partner or another family member may of necessity become a caretaker.

Robert. Ann, Robert's wife, was disgusted with his appearance and fearful for his health. They had been married thirty years, and five-foot, eight-inch–tall Robert had always been overweight. Over the past ten years, however, he had gained steadily; he was up to an all-time high of 387 pounds. Because of his sleep apnea (a condition, often found among the obese, in which the sleeper temporarily stops breathing), he could no longer sleep in their bed, and had to sleep sitting up in an easy chair. Robert had to sit on the toilet to urinate, rather than stand, because he could not see his penis in order to direct his urine stream. At one point, he got a rash on his scrotum, which he was not able to reach to apply salve. Ann had to do it for him. Robert tried to hide his overeating from Ann by restricting his binges to restaurants and other places outside their home. Ann suspected what he was doing, which increased her frustration and resentment.

Family and friends can become angry and wonder, "How can he/she do this to me?" In some cases, family members may feel guilty, wondering what role they may have played in the eating disorder. This is especially true when the eating disordered person is a child or young person still living in the home. Naturally, parents experience alarm and concern when a child of any age develops an eating disorder. At first, parents may deny that a problem exists, but their denial usually gives way to efforts to help. Often a parent is the first to call a mental health professional to ask what can be done. If the child is living at home, the parent may seek treatment for her or him. If it is an adult child, the parent may express their concerns and offer to help. At other times, friends or partners may be the first to notice a problem. It is often difficult to know how to help.

Notes

1. Mitchell, J. E., C. Pomeroy, and D. E. Adson. 1997. Managing medical complications. In D. M. Garner and P. E. Garfinkel, eds., *Handbook of Treatment for Eating Disorders. 2nd ed.* New York: Guilford Press. 383–393.

2. Abraham, S. 1998. Sexuality and reproduction in bulimia nervosa patients over 10 years. *Journal of Psychosomatic Research, 44*, 491–502.

Chapter 4

The Causes of Disordered Eating

Many factors contribute to vulnerability for the development and maintenance of modern-day eating disorders. These include external events and the abilities and resources the person has for coping with such events. Cultural messages as well as the influence of family, friends, and peers, mold attitudes toward the self and others and can set up a vulnerability to developing an eating disorder. Certain turning points in life, such as beginning to date, leaving home for college, or the breakup of an important relationship often trigger the onset of an eating disorder. How a person reacts to and copes with such events depends in part on her temperament, way of thinking, coping style, and interpersonal skills. In addition, the contribution of heredity to the development of an eating disorder is only beginning to be known.

The influences from the past that triggered the onset of an eating disorder may not be what keeps the disorder in place in the present. A difficult family situation and teasing about weight or shape by peers in grade school may have created a sensitivity to weight issues, and a chance remark by a coach about the need to lose weight may be what initiated the disordered eating, but other factors maintain the eating disorder today. Most often these include restrictive dieting and how one copes with stress and negative emotions. Even so, it helps to understand how an eating disorder got started.

Cultural Factors

Since the 1960s and the advent of the Barbie doll and the super-model Twiggy, at five feet, seven inches and 98 pounds, the culturally defined standard of beauty promoted in the media has become increasing thinner and unrealistic. TV, movies, and magazines flood people with messages about the rewards of being thin. The message is that popularity, friends, success, power, and romantic relationships come to those who are thin and beautiful. Those who do not match up to cultural ideals are portrayed as failures, bad, morally lax, weak, out of control, stupid, laughable, lonely, disapproved of, and rejected.

Between 1959 and 1988, the number of diet and exercise articles in women's magazines escalated significantly.[1] In the 1990s, the emphasis of magazine articles shifted somewhat from weight loss to exercise and fitness, although the focus on thinner is better persisted. At least half and likely more of all young girls and women read such magazines, making them vulnerable to the "thin-is-best" propaganda. Nearly all watch television, where advertisements of women with unrealistically thin bodies are seen frequently. Despite the fact that the images of models in magazines are frequently computer-enhanced, these pictures are viewed as realistic representations of what women should—and can—look like. Repeated exposure to such magazine and television images encourages the internalization of attitudes about slenderness and an unrealistic body image ideal. Those girls and women who adopt and endorse the thin ideal, who participate in their own sexual objectification, and who are dissatisfied with some aspect of their appearance, are the most vulnerable to developing eating pathology.[2]

Over the last several decades, the health industry and the government, as represented by the Surgeon General and the National Institutes of Health, have launched massive media campaigns to persuade Americans to change their diet, reduce fat intake, lose weight, and exercise more. Spurred by this health consciousness, the sought-after body ideal for both males and females now promoted in the media is taut, lean, muscled, and physically fit.

Joining the trend, some physicians issue dire warnings to overweight patients and often unknowingly compliment patients with a nonobvious eating disorder on their fine weight management. (These same physicians may overlook an eating disorder in a male because of the cultural stereotype that denotes eating disorders as typically a female issue.) Body weight and shape have become a focus of concern in everyday life, most especially for women, and the media provide constant reminders.

It seems clear that media messages play a role in the development of negative body image and body dissatisfaction. Unfortunately, these messages often get translated into actual discrimination and ostracism of the overweight and the less physically attractive. Children in grade school and adolescents in high school taunt and torment others based on body weight and appearance, even when such criticism is not warranted on any objective basis. Such teasing and rejection provides the impetus for dieting at younger and younger ages, setting the stage for the development of an eating disorder. Culturally defined standards for thinness and appearance that are accepted and internalized create dissatisfaction with the body and a disturbed body image, producing shame and devaluing self-worth.

Still, not everyone who is exposed to idealized images in the media develops an eating disorder. Other risk factors are to be found in the particular constellation of family, personality, and behavioral factors that characterizes any given person.

The Interpersonal Context

The development and maintenance of an eating disorder takes place in an interpersonal context that includes the influences of family, peers, friends, and important others. Interactions between family members teach children about themselves and what to expect of others. Often, adverse experiences within the family, especially those that impinge on self-esteem and self-confidence, contribute to the onset of extreme dieting, binge eating, and purging, and some of these experiences may also serve to perpetuate the illness.[3] The family is a crucial influence, along with certain personality factors that provide either immunity or vulnerability to an eating disorder.[4]

Profiles of Eating-Disordered Families

Although the characteristics of families of eating-disordered patients can vary considerably,[5] a common profile of the bulimic family describes the parents as controlling and affectively negative, with the child reacting in a resentful, yet appeasing, way.[6] Bulimics often perceive their families as conflicted, disorganized, detached, disengaged, or nonnurturing.[7] Observation of interactions between family members confirms that they can indeed be less than supportive and sometimes even hostile.[8] An investigation of 105 patients with bulimia found that patients viewed their families as having low cohesiveness, a lack of emphasis on independent and assertive behavior, and a high level of conflict coupled with a low emphasis on open expression of feelings.[9] Another study found that bulimics experienced their mothers as more withdrawn and less friendly than did non–eating-disordered individuals, and saw their fathers as behaving toward them with significantly less friendliness.[10]

Not as much is known about the family context of binge eating disorder. One study found that women with BED described their parents' parenting style as "affectionless control."[11] Compared to the families of obese women who did not binge eat, the families of obese binge eaters were less cohesive, less emotionally supportive, expressed more conflict, and tended not to support individual independence.

Bulimics and those with BED are similar in many ways, and it seems reasonable to assume that they have similar family backgrounds. Often these families are chaotic and conflictual with hostile and rather neglectful parents. Both bulimics and obese binge eaters are likely to have a family history of substance abuse, but the BED sufferers are less likely than those with bulimia to have suffered sexual abuse.[12]

Families of anorexics are frequently described as controlling, overprotective, enmeshed, rigid, and conflict-avoidant.[13] Often the parents convey expectations for high achievement to the children.[14] Children in such families develop a poor sense of identity and effectiveness, which manifests as a sense of lack of power, autonomy, control,[15] and personal ineffectiveness.[16] They are usually compliant and dependent in childhood and misuse eating in an attempt to assert their independence and gain control of their lives in adolescence.[17]

Anorexics perceive their families as generally stable, nonconflictual, cohesive, and with no lack of nurturance. Compared with "normal" families, anorexic families show more rigidity in their family organization, have less clear interpersonal boundaries, and tend to avoid open discussions of disagreements between parents and children.[18] In such families the unspoken rule is that it is not okay to express negative feelings. Communication within the family leaves little room for the expression of feelings, including those of anger, fear, anxiety, or shame,[19] and discourages individuation.[20]

Trauma and Eating Disorders

Children of chaotic families are at greater risk for serious traumatic experience—especially sexual and physical abuse—and this begs the question whether such trauma predisposes such children to developing an eating disorder. Depending on the population studied, the occurrence of sexual trauma in eating disorder patients can be quite high.[21] Most often, these were bulimic patients. However, a review of a number of studies found that sexual abuse does not occur any more frequently among those with eating disorders than in the general population.[22] Nevertheless, sexual abuse and, to a lesser extent, physical abuse, can be a contributing factor to the development of some types of eating disorders,[23] especially bulimia.[24] Childhood sexual abuse is associated with various forms of psychopathology and may contribute to greater levels of comorbidity in eating-disordered individuals.

Abuse of all kinds, including psychological abuse, represents a form of boundary violation in which the separateness and integrity of the child's physical and/or psychological self are treated with gross disregard.[25] Psychological abuse includes frequent yelling, insults, criticism, guilt-inspiring statements, ridicule, embarrassment in front of others, and attempts to make the child feel like a bad person.[26] Abusive experiences constitute major stressors and predispose the child to the development of all manner of psychopathologies, including eating disorders.

When a parent is unable to provide a safe and predictable environment for a child, or when the parent is not willing or able to be emotionally supportive, the child is vulnerable to developing persistent anxiety and other negative emotions. The message children in such families get is that there is something wrong with them; that they are inadequate or somehow not good enough for those who supposedly love and care for them. This results in shame—the experience of oneself as an unattractive and an undesirable person; a person one does not wish to be, accompanied by an awareness of having low status or of being devalued.[27] Shame is a central emotion for many people with an eating disorder. (See chapter 10 for an in-depth discussion of shame.) Restrictive diet-ing or excessive exercise resulting in weight loss can be an attempt to undo shaming experienced in the family. Failed attempts to lose weight or change body shape incur more shame, a core affect in binge eating.

Criticism and Teasing

Perceived pressure to be thin from family, peers, friends, and dating partners is another factor contributing to disordered eating. Criticism regarding weight or shape makes the person criticized even more vulnerable to media messages about the ideal body, which leads to body dissatisfaction and vulnerability to develop-ing eating pathology.[28]

Both males and females are at greater risk for an eating dis-order if they were fat or overweight as children, especially if they were teased or criticized because of it. Frequently those with BED were put on diets at an early age by overly concerned or weight-obsessed parents. In an attempt to control the child's eating and weight, these parents may have instituted rules about eating. Often these rules were applied only to the heavier weight child or to the girls but not the boys in the family.

Judy. As a twenty-year-old college student, Judy had a good relationship with her mother and she adored her maternal grand-mother. Unfortunately, Judy's relationship with her father, who had been divorced from Judy's mother for some fifteen years, was much less supportive.

At five feet, ten inches and 195 pounds, Judy was a college varsity basketball player who enjoyed her status as a skilled ath-lete. Although her mother was caring and encouraging, Judy was aware of her mother's concern about Judy's weight as well as for her own. Mom was an attractive, well-dressed woman with a pro-fessional career who garnered compliments and approving looks wherever she went. Likewise, grandma at seventy-two was a petite fashion plate. Mom and grandma liked shopping for clothes and frequently exchanged fashion and health tips.

Judy never told her mom how uncomfortable she felt on their shopping forays. Neither did she mention her discomfort when she came home from school on visits and her mother either commented that Judy looked as if she had lost some weight, or said nothing at all about Judy's appearance—signaling to Judy that her mother thought she'd gained weight. Judy was self-conscious about her size and she frequently felt overly large and clumsy around the women in her family, despite their apparent love and support.

Her father was another story. Although Dad himself was overweight, he freely criticized Judy for her lack of self-discipline. When Judy visited him, he restricted what she was allowed to eat. At one point he told her point-blank how embarrassed he was to introduce her to his friends because of her size. It never occurred to Judy to reject these criticisms or defend herself. In her heart, she believed he was right. She was ashamed of her size and generally tried to avoid noticing her own eating behavior. She frequently overindulged in sweets, rationalizing that as an athlete she could afford the calories. Besides, eating helped distract her from painful self-awareness of her weight, her sadness at not matching up to her mother's unspoken expectations for her, and her painful experiences in her relationship with her father.

Beth. At the age of fourteen, Beth was beginning to change from a chubby child into a beautiful adolescent. However, she was convinced she was fat and ugly. She was especially ashamed of her hips and thighs. At school the kids had taunted her, calling "Hippo, Drippo. Better not eat no mo'." Even her father seemed to join in, suggesting she shouldn't wear jeans because they accentuated her hips. Beth's grandmother addressed her as "Miss Piggy," and her brother once drew pictures of Beth depicting her as grossly fat. But the worst hurts came from interactions with her mother.

Her mother worked at a stressful job and didn't have much patience for a fourteen-year-old's needs. When Beth complained about her friends or family calling her names and taunting her, Mom's response was that Beth ought to go to the gym more often and watch what she ate. When Mom got angry, she made cutting remarks such as, "When I was pregnant I was thinner than you are now." Mom usually had several glasses of wine during the evening, and on a few occasions when she drank too much, she said that she wished Beth had never been born.

Naturally, Beth became very distressed about her weight and body shape, and pleaded with her parents for help. To appease Beth, they usually agreed to her requests. Beth succeeded in getting them to pay for a course of hypnotherapy, buy certain diet foods, take her to a dietitian, and purchase over-the-counter appetite suppressants and a variety of other weight-loss products and services. When none of these worked, Beth resorted to temper tantrums, binge eating, and taking to her bed for days at a time. Despite antidepressant medication, Beth's condition worsened, and at several points she threatened suicide. Her exasperated, overwhelmed, and angry parents feigned unconcern, saying they hoped she wouldn't create a mess in the house when she killed herself.

Clearly, Beth was playing the role of the Problem Child. Beth's "problem" was her unhappiness, which was expressed in various ways—binge eating, fighting with her parents, demanding she be given whatever she wanted, and even threatening suicide. Of course, Beth's unhappiness was also partly created by the roles her parents played. Beth's mother was the "Unavailable One" and her father the "Ineffective One." Beth's acting out—including her eating disorder—was an attempt to get her parents to respond to her needs, but they mostly reacted with criticism, rejection and invalidation, thus causing Beth to act out even more. The family's situation was chaotic, openly conflicted, and hostile.

Parental Influences

When someone develops an eating disorder, it can be a sign that there is something wrong in the family. Families with a member who has an eating disorder vary tremendously. Some look okay on the surface; others have obvious problems such as alcoholism, drug or gambling addictions, financial problems, interpersonal conflict, abuse, or family violence. A number of less obvious factors in the family also can contribute to the development of an eating disorder in a vulnerable offspring. Some of these include poor boundaries, inconsistent parenting, high levels of criticism, overconcern about appearance, and unrealistic expectations for high achievement.

Her father aside, Judy's family situation seemed okay. Her mother was supportive and caring, and Judy was a good student and a good athlete. The problem in Judy's family was overconcern about appearance and weight. Looking good was synonymous with being worthwhile, and this belief had been passed on from grandma to Mom and now to Judy. Implicit and explicit messages were constantly being given to Judy about what to eat and not to eat, and her need for greater self-control.

The Mother/Daughter Relationship

A good deal of research has demonstrated how the mother/daughter relationship relates to eating problems. Food-related interactions between mother and child, and maternal attitudes toward weight can influence the development of an eating disorder. A mother's investment in her own thinness increases her preadolescent daughter's vulnerability to dieting,[29] and mothers who practice disordered eating are more likely to have daughters who develop pathological eating.[30] Such mothers also had longer dieting histories, thought their daughters should lose more weight, and saw their daughters as less attractive than they could be if they were slimmer.

Daughters of mothers with disordered eating often adopt that parent's attitudes toward weight and shape, as well as copy the mother's eating habits. This is especially true when a daughter is indeed heavier and she sees dieting as a way of increasing self-worth.[31] In some cases, mothers actually pressure their daughters to be thin, even enrolling them in weight-reduction programs at an early age. With the onset of normal adolescent weight gain, girls whose mothers are overweight or weight-preoccupied frequently become quite fearful of gaining weight and may begin dieting.[32] These girls may engage in extreme weight control efforts like rigorous dieting and/or excessive exercise to avoid becoming obese as well.

The Father/Daughter Relationship

Fathers can also play a role in making their daughters vulnerable to eating disorders. Weight-concerned fathers make it known to both their spouses and their daughters that their being overweight is not okay. One father went so far as to snatch food out of his daughter's hands whenever he thought she was eating too much. Such men may or may not extend this dictum to themselves. The fact that Judy's father did not attend to his own excess weight did not stop him from criticizing her. In other cases, men who are conscious and concerned about their own weight may pressure the women in the family to watch what they eat and exercise more.

Sometimes it is not the father's attitude and concern about his daughter's or his wife's weight that is the problem; it is his own obesity and the attendant shame this brings to his daughter that instigates her own dieting behavior. In other cases, a parent's alcohol or drug abuse produces an unpredictable and chaotic environment, and the eating disorder provides the illusion of control in an uncontrollable and frightening situation. Laura's story, which follows, is an example of someone who started dieting and eventually developed anorexia because of her revulsion with her father's obesity as well as with his alcoholism.

Laura. Sixteen-year-old Laura fretted. "I don't know why everyone is saying I'm too thin. Compared to the other girls in my ballet class, I'm fat. I'm the biggest one there. My dad is really fat, and I don't ever want to look like he does. He cooks for the family because Mom works and he doesn't. I won't eat anything he cooks because it is always fatty and greasy. He drinks, too. When he picks me up at school I can smell alcohol on his breath. I'm scared to be in the car with him. While he's cooking, he's got a glass of wine in his hand, and by the time dinner is over, he's polished off two bottles of wine. When I won't eat what he cooks, he gets mad and yells at me about what an ungrateful child I am."

The Family

Families differ in their degree of being either well functioning or dysfunctional. Highly *functional* families encourage a positive and confident self-concept in children, and parents teach children to understand the language of emotions. Well-functioning families encourage all members to express their feelings, thoughts, desires and fantasies while respecting the rights and boundaries of others. Communication between family members is clear, direct, honest, supportive, and respectful. Each family member takes responsibility for acknowledging and helping to resolve problems. Differences are worked out through negotiation, and compromises are reached. Rules are flexible and fair. The atmosphere is open and spontaneous. Mistakes are forgiven and viewed as learning tools. All members of the family are encouraged to explore and express their uniqueness and pursue their path in life. Anxiety is low. Trust is high.

What makes a family dysfunctional? Two dimensions help define *dysfunction* in the family—the enmeshment/disengagement, or boundary, dimension and the hostile/conflict-avoidant, or emotional, dimension. Dysfunction within a family can be understood as a combination of these two dimensions.

The Enmeshment/Disengagement Dimension

The *enmeshment/ disengagement dimension* relates to the ego boundaries—each person's experience of self—in the family. Good ego boundaries allow each person to know his or her limits, rights, and roles in the family. With good ego boundaries, each person has the experience of integrity, independence, and autonomy, while still feeling he or she is an integral, valued, and loved member of the family.

Enmeshment is a term that refers to the violation or fusion of boundaries. In an enmeshed family, members intrude upon one another either physically or psychologically. The spouse who opens and reads the other spouse's mail without permission, or the parent who reads a child's diary, has breached the other person's boundary—because everyone has the right to privacy. The parent who tells a child what to think or feel, or who contradicts the child's assertions of how she thinks or feels, breaches a psychological ego boundary. The parent's ego intrudes on the child's ego or sense of self. Fused boundaries between parent and child make the psychological processes of separation and individuation—necessary for becoming a fully functioning adult—difficult if not impossible. Poor or fused boundaries within a family can lead to physical or sexual abuse.

Disengagement is characterized by "walled" boundaries.[33] The person with walled boundaries is emotionally and sometimes physically unavailable to other members of the family. For example, the workaholic father who is rarely home or who is unable or unwilling to participate much in family activities has rigid boundaries that keep him from becoming engaged, emotionally or physically, with other family members. The mother who escapes nightly into alcohol or whose social activities have a higher priority than her family's needs is similarly disengaged.

One common pattern in many families is for one parent—often the father—to be disengaged and the other parent—usually the mother—to be enmeshed with one or more of the children. The children become the mother's emotional support, which is not forthcoming from her spouse. Taken to an extreme, a child may act as a stand-in spouse substitute for the needy parent, taking on roles and responsibilities not appropriate for a child of any age.

The Hostile/Conflict-Avoidant Dimension

Another useful dimension for understanding the dysfunctional family is called the *hostile/conflict-avoidant dimension*. This emotional dimension refers to whether anger is expressed openly or is internalized by some or all members of the family. Often in families, one parent is the "anger-out" person—the one who is permitted to openly and frequently express anger, while the other parent is the "anger-in" person—the one who rarely or never expresses anger. Sometimes the anger-in person loses it and engages in open fighting, but more often his or her anger is expressed in more subtle ways—"forgetting" something important to the other spouse, spending more money than the family budget allows, getting drunk, or getting fat.

In some families, both parents are openly hostile and angry, which creates a chaotic and unpredictable environment for all family members. Loud, angry fighting is a regular occurrence. Domestic violence in the form of hitting, shoving, pushing, throwing things, blocking the other person's way, or worse, are possibilities. Often this open hostility and rage is fueled by alcohol or drug use by one or both parents. Inevitably, some of the children learn to be anger-out people, while another child often tries to bring peace to the family. Sometimes a child in this type of family develops problems that have the effect of detouring the parents' negative energy from each other onto the child.

In other families, conflict is avoided whenever possible. Raised voices or angry words are not heard. The only emotions allowed to be expressed in conflict-avoidant families are positive and happy ones. In such families staying in control is the name of the game. Because they never observe conflict, children never learn how to negotiate differences and arrive at compromises. Needs must be suppressed or denied, and children don't learn to recognize or deal with negative emotions except with denial. Negative energy is often channeled and transformed into being productive and high achieving. Children in such families may develop a pattern of trying to please others, often at the expense of neglecting their own needs.

The Emerging Self-Concept

The family is the cradle of self-concept and the child's emerging self-image. Within the family the child learns what to expect of others. Experiences with caregivers become "internal working models" of the self and others and profoundly influence the child's expectations of relationships with others.[34]

Interactions with family members create a particular way of thinking and feeling that can play an important role in the development and maintenance of an eating disorder.[35] Many individuals who develop an eating disorder have a poorly developed sense of self, coupled with beliefs of ineffectiveness in dealing with others.[36] Such individuals typically come from hostile and emotionally-enmeshed family systems in which the child's personal thoughts and emotions are unacknowledged or denied.[37] Instead, the parent or other family member tells her that she doesn't feel the way she thinks she feels, or that she is wrong to feel that way, or that, in fact, she feels something other than what she thinks she is feeling.

When Beth would express her distress about her shape and weight, her mother would often respond by chiding her that she was being selfish to worry so much about herself. When there is invalidation of feelings and experience, the child is unable to organize a sense of self or to define her personal boundaries and self-worth. When a child and parent are emotionally enmeshed, the child is likely to have difficulty separating and becoming independent. The end result can be that the child adopts an interpersonal style characterized by a strong need to please others and seek others' approval, coupled with a lack of awareness of her own needs and wants. For example, Judy was unable to confront her father about his hurtful remarks because she sought to please him and protect him from her own anger, which was so deeply buried that she was unaware of it.

The Worthless Self

Families of bulimics are often hostile, unfriendly, and rejecting. Similarly, families of obese binge eaters tend to be high in conflict and less supportive of each other. These dysfunctional family interactions contribute to the development of a self-concept that is highly self-critical and rejecting, as well as less self-accepting, self-nurturing, and self-protecting.[38]

Food and eating are used to cope with negative feelings associated with the "worthless self." In addition, bulimics are less likely to nurture themselves in ways unrelated to food.[39] At their best, bulimics are less self-nurturing; at their worst they are self-attacking and exhibit hostile and neglectful self-concepts.

The People Pleaser

Eating-disordered individuals, especially bulimics, try to please others as a means of preserving a positive image of personal well-being.[40] Their sense of self-worth depends on the approval of others. This results in a strong sense of dependency and the tendency to idealize the other in interpersonal relationships. The bulimic individual tends to disclose more to others, be less able to function independently of others, and feel less in control in friendships.[41]

The High Achiever

Another type of family system that can have a heavy impact on a child's self-concept and provide fertile ground for an eating disorder is the overconcerned, overly protective parent or enmeshed family, especially if it is also a high-achieving family. In such family systems, the child is encouraged to take on more and more challenges and to succeed at everything. The child feels rewarded by pleasing the parent, and works hard to do so, sometimes pushing herself beyond her limits. Fun and playtime may be sacrificed for school work, and activities that should be fun, such as soccer or dance, become opportunities to compete and achieve. Many times, these children do not feel they have choices in their lives, and must work hard or risk losing their parents' love. These children become perfectionists who set high standards for themselves and berate themselves if they fall even a little short. Such children are at particular risk for developing anorexia. Research has found that many anorexics exhibit a poor sense of self, problems with trust, an absolute need to be in control, and difficulty in identifying and differentiating emotions.[42] Youngsters most likely to be at risk for disordered eating are those with low levels of self-esteem and high levels of anxiety.[43]

Influences from the Environment

Not all dysfunctional families produce a child with an eating disorder, and not all eating disordered individuals come from dysfunctional families. Even when a person has the advantage of growing up in a relatively well functioning family system, other factors can contribute to the development or maintenance of an eating disorder. These include the nature and influence of the child's environment—including the school, the community, and peers.

The School

Attending junior high school, high school, and college coincide with times of particular vulnerability for developing an eating disorder. The teenage years are a time when a young person is developing a sense of self and preparing for the responsibilities of adulthood. A school environment that is hostile and stressful can facilitate disordered eating. Likewise, growing up in an affluent community where appearance is valued and is used as a means of discriminating, increases the risk. Often those who develop an eating disorder had difficult school years. They may not have been accepted by their peers and may have felt like outsiders. In some cases, they actually felt threatened.

Pat. Although Pat's family was generally warm and supportive, because of political reasons Pat was bussed across town to a junior high school known for its violence and gang conflict. Students regularly brought knives and weapons to school, and fights were a frequent occurrence. Outnumbered and without any means for controlling the situation, teachers looked the other way when violence broke out. Although Pat was terrified, her parents were unable to get her school changed. Eventually Pat moved on to a high school that had similar problems. Pat's eating disorder began soon after she entered junior high and continued well into her thirties.

Peers

Peer influence is an important factor in eating and body image concerns.[44] Today, even very young children are expressing concern about body weight, and the onset of dieting is occurring at increasingly younger ages. Evidence suggests that children, especially girls, learn not only from the mass media and their families, but also from their peers that appearance, including body shape and weight, is very important.[45]

Being teased about one's weight or shape can greatly increase distress about food and eating.[46] Peers teased Beth about her hips and thighs, which made her feel rejected and angry. She began a cycle of restrictive dieting, followed by binge eating and increasing despair. Similarly, peers teased Jillian because of her height (see chapter 2), resulting in her having lifelong interpersonal problems. Excessive exercise became her substitute for relationships and disordered eating her way of coping with overwhelming anxiety.

Research demonstrates that teasing not only may lead to dieting and eventually to an eating disorder, but also such teasing can have lasting effects on self-concept and a person's satisfaction with her body.[47] The more frequent the teasing and the more upsetting it is to the person who is the target, the more likely it will negatively affect eating and body image.[48]

Peers also model behaviors and attitudes that can influence eating and body image. Adolescents and young people frequently discuss weight and dieting, sharing weight-management techniques, including the use of compensatory behaviors such as vomiting.[49] *Contagion*—female students learning bulimic behaviors from other students, or from the Internet—is an increasingly common phenomenon on college campuses.

One study showed that the most important influence of peers comes from the belief that being thin will make a person more popular.[50] The effect of this belief was stronger for girls, probably because it is an extension of the media images that associate femininity, success, and desirability with being slender and having the "ideal thin and fit body."

Developmental Factors

The vulnerability to developing an eating disorder involves a confluence of factors that includes both normative developmental tasks and individual differences.[51] Three transition points of early adolescence pose particular risk: One is the weight and fat gain that comes with menstruation and the other physical changes associated with puberty. Another is the onset of dating, and the third involves the intensification of academic demands that occurs about the same time. In one study, girls who were experiencing two or more of these developmental changes simultaneously had the highest levels of disturbed eating behaviors. When additional risk factors such as an internalized slender body ideal, perfectionistic thinking, high reactivity to stress or criticism, or difficulty differentiating emotions from physical sensations are added to those three stressors, the stage is set for the emergence of an eating disorder. Not surprisingly, eating disorders are also triggered frequently by the break up of an important relationship, going off to college, or parental divorce.

Psychological Factors

Certain psychological factors are relevant to the development of an eating disorder, while other factors sustain the current expression and maintenance of an eating disorder. The vulnerability of particular types of personality organizations to developing eating disorders was discussed in chapter 2. Additional psychological factors include comparison processes that lead to body dissatisfaction and negative emotions.

Comparison Processes

The internalization of a thin-body ideal results from culturally based, media-promoted messages, together with social pressure to be thin from family, friends, partners, and peers. This internalized image becomes the standard of comparison for actual body weight and shape, often resulting in high levels of body dissatisfaction, especially when body weight is higher than normal. This dissatisfaction results in the two most relevant factors involved in causing an eating disorder to be expressed in the here and now—dietary restraint and negative affect.[52]

Dietary Restraint

Restricting your calories and the type of food eaten is an attempt to reduce weight in the hope of attaining a weight and shape closer to the internalized ideal. Sever dieting induces a state of physical starvation with attendant fatigue, hunger, and irritability, which sets the stage for a subsequent eating binge. Any breach of self-imposed rules for eating is an occasion for self-blame and self-criticism, resulting in negative emotions including anxiety, anger, shame, fear, sadness, guilt, and depression.

Negative Emotions and Stress

Low self-esteem and a negative self-concept, coupled with high sensitivity to stress, increases the person's vulnerability to negative emotions. The emotions most likely to be associated with an eating disorder are anger, anxiety, depression, shame, and boredom. Stress comes from a variety of sources. Some are physical stresses—becoming overly hungry, fatigued, or hung over from alcohol or drugs. Feeling lonely, experiencing interpersonal conflict, or being in an unsatisfying relationship constitute relationship stresses. Not having control over one's life or choices, feeling coerced or manipulated, and not being able to relax or have fun are still other sources of stress.

When stress is overwhelming, avoidance behaviors such as binge eating may be used to cope. The binge or the binge/purge serves to shut down thinking, suppress emotions, and distract from problems that feel unsolvable. Binge eating is used to regulate mood and to create an altered state of consciousness, and purging is an attempt to undo the effects of the calories consumed. Similarly, the rituals employed to maintain restrictive eating require an intense focus that crowds out day-to-day concerns that would increase anxiety, fear, shame, anger, and depression. The eating disorder becomes a very imperfect solution to another problem.

Escape from Self-Awareness

The desire to escape from painful emotions that result from comparing oneself against high standards or ideals has also been implicated as a source of binge eating.[53] Those with an eating disorder are extremely attentive to how they appear to others and how they compare with cultural and personal standards. These standards may extend beyond the body shape and weight domains to other, non-eating-related domains such as performance at school or at work. When eating disordered individuals perceive that they fail to measure up, they experience an aversive awareness of their failures and shortcomings, which in turn generates negative affect. To escape these painful feelings, these individuals tend to use avoidant coping strategies rather than problem-solving or other coping approaches. The use of eating as an escape from discomfort is one form of avoidance coping. Likewise, food and eating are used for self-nurturance and distraction from painful affects. The binge functions to narrow the focus of attention and distract the person's attention from threats to self-esteem.

Biological Factors

Certain biological factors may influence the development or maintenance of an eating disorder. These include the contribution of physiological determinants, genes and heredity, hunger and starvation, and addiction. Physiological explanations of binge eating have centered on notions of metabolism and neurochemical imbalances.

Physiological Determinants

Science is learning more and more about the various determinants of eating behavior, energy balance, and body weight. It is now known that the brain receives signals from various parts of the body, and these signals are integrated in a complex manner to regulate metabolism and other body functions.[54] Some of these signals include hormones, neurotransmitters, and nutrients in the blood, such as glucose, amino acids, and fatty acids. For example, as the result of an increase in certain hormones, fat stores are increased beginning in puberty so that reproduction can take place. Likewise, changing levels of hormones associated with a female's menstrual cycle influence the experience of hunger. Similarly, after eating a meal, substances called peptides are released by the gastrointestinal tract that tell the brain satiety has been achieved. Depletion of glycogen stores in the body results in signals to the brain that promote eating more carbohydrate.

Disturbances in these biological signals can contribute to the development or maintenance of abnormal patterns of eating and body weight gain. Some recent studies have found that disturbances in the neurochemical systems and the neuroendocrine processes may contribute to the development of abnormal patterns of eating and body weight gain in humans.[55] Such disturbances may be at the root of problems such as food cravings, seasonal appetite disturbances, and stress-related eating. Future research may identify ways of correcting these disturbances that would be used to augment nutritional and behavioral strategies for treating eating disorders.

Carbohydrate Craving

Carbohydrate craving has been offered as one explanation for binge eating.[56] This explanation has received much attention in the media subsequent to the publication of a popular book by the researchers who did the original work on this concept.[57] Based on research with rats, early studies suggested that eating carbohydrates increases the brain's serotonin levels. Serotonin is a neurotransmitter that induces calmness, among other functions.

According to the theory, when carbohydrate cravers consume carbohydrates such as chocolate, they experience improved mood and less fatigue, whereas non-cravers report feeling more depressed and more fatigued after eating carbohydrates.[58] Presumably chocolate has a particularly potent anxiety-reducing effect for some people, and bulimics and obese binge eaters "self-medicate" with carbohydrates to modulate their emotions.

However, a number of problems with this theory became apparent soon after its introduction. For one thing, research supporting this theory involves animals, not humans. Another problem is that the introduction of even a small amount of protein abolishes the calming effect of brain serotonin.[59]

Furthermore, to the extent that binge eaters have deficits in serotonin, it is not clear whether these disturbances are the cause of binge eating or are due to the side effects of dieting.[60] Although the notion of carbohydrate craving still has appeal, especially among lay people, the research evidence supporting it remains incomplete and unconvincing.[61]

Genes and Heredity

It is not clear whether genetic factors contribute to a predisposition to developing an eating disorder per se.[62] One study that investigated the relative contribution of genetic versus environmental risk factors prompting an obsessive desire to be thin found that environment was more important.[63] However, recent advances in human genetics and molecular biology suggest that body weight and body mass are at least partly regulated by heredity.[64]

Although the contribution of heredity to body weight varies depending on which relatives are studied, the variation attributable to genes ranges between 25 percent to 40 percent.[65] Some evidence points to a single major gene as the source of higher than normal body weight, but other evidence suggests the involvement of multiple genes.[66]

The contribution of heredity can be seen in family weight patterns. Families in which one or both parents are seriously obese have two to three times the risk of having an obese child when compared to families in which neither parent is seriously obese. The likelihood of obesity in children is highest if both parents are obese and somewhat lower if only one is obese. Still, about a third of obese individuals have two normal weight parents. Furthermore, obese individuals tend to be heavier than previous generations, and the prevalence of obesity is clearly increasing from generation to generation.[67] More than genes appear to be involved in these phenomena.

Three major factors, each influenced to some degree by genes, contribute to body weight—diet, metabolism, and physical activity.[68] Energy intake in the form of calories consumed and the composition of the diet is regulated mostly by the lifestyle characteristics of the family and environmental factors—that is, people learn to eat the foods they eat from associating with family and friends. However, a small part of energy intake, especially that associated with the consumption of fats and carbohydrates—about 20 percent of the variation—can be explained by genes.[69] Influenced to some degree by heredity, these food choices may increase some peoples' inherited susceptibility to obesity.

Variations in resting energy expenditure or metabolism exist between people, and this may contribute to differences in body weight. Genes also partly influence the amount of energy used to process food—known as the thermic effect of food. The level of habitual physical activity, but not exercise participation, may also be partly inherited. Some people just have a greater propensity to be spontaneously active; this is especially the case when both parents were active. Although each of these differences, considered alone, is small, they do factor into the larger picture that results in body weight.

Body weight, body mass, and body shape are the result of the complex interaction of dozens of factors. Certainly heredity plays a part. However, genes define susceptibility—they increase the likelihood of a particular result (e.g., obesity), but they do not determine it. Genes are not destiny. Body weight and mass are the result of interactions between inherited susceptibility and social, environmental, behavioral, psychological, and physiological influences and lifestyle differences.

Hunger and Starvation

An important biological factor that contributes to binge eating is the hunger and starvation that result from fasting and restrictive eating. The influence of hunger and starvation on eating disorders is clearly seen in a study conducted in the 1940s by Ansel Keys.[70] In this study, normal-weight, healthy volunteers were enlisted to undergo a period of starvation followed by a refeeding phase.

One result observed during the starvation and semi-starvation periods, which lasted nine months altogether, was that subjects experienced a dramatic increase in their preoccupation with food. Concentration became more difficult as the subjects were increasingly plagued by incessant thoughts of food and eating. Participants were observed toying with their food and making strange concoctions out of free choice foods. These starving volunteers also smuggled bits of food to their rooms, where they engaged in long drawn-out rituals in which they consumed their stolen morsels. Many became intensely interested in reading cookbooks and menus, even though they had shown no prior interest in such matters. The subjects often reported getting vicarious pleasure from watching others eat or from just smelling food. Much of their day was spent planning how they would eat their food allotment. When they did eat, their total attention was devoted to food consumption. These same behaviors describe a starving anorexic.

The next phase of Keys' starvation experiment involved reintroducing food—the refeeding phase. It provided insight into one origin of binge eating. All of the study participants reported increased hunger, and some experienced intense anxiety and a complete breakdown in control involving binge eating, followed by self-reproach and sometimes self-deprecation. Some lost control all together and ate more or less continuously. Even after twelve weeks of the refeeding phase, many were heard to complain of increased hunger immediately following a meal, and they frequently engaged in snacking after the meal.

Most of the subjects who had experienced periods of severe emotional distress and depression became more severely distressed over the course of the experiment. Mood swings were often extreme, and irritability was common. Anxiety became more evident as the experiment progressed, and many of the formerly even-tempered subjects began biting their fingernails. During the refeeding phase, emotional disturbances persisted, with some people becoming even more depressed, irritable, argumentative, and negativistic.

Keys' study produced some important findings that inform our understanding of eating disorders. First, for some people, starvation and semi-starvation led to binge eating, and this problem persisted for a period of time after free access to food was introduced. The majority of the study participants eventually returned to normal eating patterns and their weight returned to normal as well, but there were emotional consequences throughout the experiment that were associated with both starvation and refeeding.

Symptoms such as those seen in this experiment are also associated with anorexia nervosa and bulimia nervosa. We can conclude from this study that binge eating, which is often a part of the clinical presentation of these two eating disorders, can be the result of undernutrition from starvation and semi-starvation.

Chemical Dependency and Addiction

Binge eating also shares many similarities with alcohol and drug abuse.[71] (Both binge eaters and people with alcohol or drug problems report strong urges or cravings for the substance. Both sets of people experience a loss of control over their behavior, and they often use the substance to regulate their emotional state and cope with stress. Substance abusers and binge eaters frequently continue to use the substance when it is clearly detrimental to their health, and they may desire or make frequent attempts to quit using. Those with certain eating disorders and those who are chemically dependent may frequently deny the gravity of their problem or try to keep it a secret. Some people with an eating disorder also abuse alcohol or drugs.[72]

The Addiction Model of Binge Eating

The addiction model of binge eating and eating disorders assumes that some individuals are biologically vulnerable to certain foods (e.g., sugar) that cause chemical dependence. Recovery requires abstaining from these "toxic" substances or from binge eating, depending on how abstinence is defined. Furthermore, the addiction model proposes the existence of an "addictive personality."[73] Consistent with other Twelve-Step models such as Alcoholics Anonymous, an eating disorder is deemed to be a progressive and lifelong illness that can never be eliminated but only managed. Group support is a key factor in recovery.

Important differences exist between true chemical dependency (addiction) and disordered eating. First, there is no evidence that people with eating disorders experience craving as a direct biochemical result of consuming a particular "toxic" nutrient. As discussed earlier, the popular notion that carbohydrate craving plays a role in binge eating has been discredited.[74] Research evidence suggests that bulimics and binge eaters do not "crave" sugar or even preferentially consume simple carbohydrates during an eating binge. Compared to "normal" eaters, the consumption of carbohydrate by bulimics and binge eaters was basically similar; the major difference between the two groups was that the bulimics and binge eaters consumed more food.[75]

Cravings for either alcohol or food substances are critically influenced by a range of factors, including both biological and psychological factors. Biologically, sweets increase the amount of serotonin in the brain and body, bringing with it calmness, sleepiness, and a decrease in feelings of depression. The person's learned expectations are also an important psychological factor that operates in conjunction with the biological effects of sweets. Eating lots of simple sugar teaches the person to desire it, because sugar is naturally pleasurable. Consumption of processed foods such as ice cream and cookies, which are intensely sweet—much more so than the sweetness available from natural foods like fruits—trains a person to want more. A so-called "sugar addiction" is not born with an individual. In fact, it is a learned, emotional response to sweet taste. Once established, the only way out is to retrain taste buds so that sweets are less desirable. In addition, it is helpful to learn methods for coping with cravings. (See chapter 7 for coping with food cravings.)

Similarly, there is no evidence for an "addictive personality."[76] There are personality types who have more difficulty with controlling impulses. This is especially true for the person with borderline personality organization that was described in chapter 2. Poor impulse control, rather than being a sign of an addiction, points to deficits in self-discipline, which is a learned skill, difficulties containing and managing affect, and a poorly formed sense of self.

Other criticisms of the addiction model of eating disorders are that it ignores the role of dietary restraint and that it encourages all-or-nothing thinking (a core problem for those with eating disorders) by advocating abstinence. Dietary restraint puts the body into a caloric deficit and contributes to poor nutritional status, setting the stage for binge eating. All-or-nothing thinking is characteristic of a perfectionistic style that leaves no room for human error. Such thinking leads to the conclusion that when you aren't perfect, you are a failure and you may as well give up—a thought that often precipitates a binge.

Nevertheless, the addiction model has been helpful to some people in coping with binge eating, largely by providing group support for overcoming compulsive overeating. In addition, it endorses the idea that the substance, in this case, food and eating, serves as a coping mechanism for other problems. To overcome disordered eating, one needs to become a better problem solver.

Notes

1. Wiseman, C. V., J. J. Gray, J. E. Mosimann, and A. H. Ahrens. 1992. Cultural expectations of thinness: An update. *International Journal of Eating Disorders, 11,* 85–89.

2. Stice, E., E. Schupak-Neuber, H. E. Shaw, and R. I. Stein. 1994. The relationship of media exposure to eating disorder symptomatology: An examination of mediating mechanisms. *Journal of Abnormal Psychology, 103,* 836–840.

3. Walsh, T. B., and M. J. Devlin. 1995. Pharmacotherapy of bulimic nervosa and binge eating disorders. *Addictive Behaviors, 20,* 757–764.

4. Strober, M., and L. L. Humphrey. 1987. Familial contributions to the etiology and course of anorexia nervosa and bulimia. *Journal of Consulting and Clinical Psychology, 55,* 654–659.

5. Grigg, D. N., J. D Friesen, and M. I. Sheppy. 1989. Family patterns associated with anorexia nervosa. *Journal of Marital and Family Therapy, 15,* 29–42.

6. Humphrey, L. L. 1987. Comparison of bulimic-anorexic and nondistressed families using structural analysis of social behavior. *American Academy of Child and Adolescent Psychiatry, 26,* 248–255.

7. Humphrey, L. L. 1986. Structural analysis of parent-child relationships in eating disorders. *Journal of Abnormal Psychology, 95,* 395–402; Kog, E., H. Vertommen, and W. Vandereycken. 1989. Self-report study of family interaction in eating disorder families compared to normals. In W. Vandereycken, E. Kob, and J. Vanderlinden, eds., *The Family Approach to Eating Disorders.* New York: PMA. 107–118; Wonderlich, S. A., and W. J. Swift. 1990. Perceptions of parental relationships in eating disorder subtypes. *Journal of Abnormal Psychology, 99,* 353–360; Wonderlich, S. A., M. H. Klein, and J. R. Council. 1996. Relationship of social perceptions and self-concept in bulimia nervosa. *Journal of Consulting and Clinical Psychology, 6,* 1231–1237.

8. Humphrey, L. L. 1989. Observed family interactions among subtypes of eating disorders using structural analysis of social behavior. *Journal of Consulting and Clinical Psychology, 57,* 206–214; Kog, E., H. Vertommen, and W. Vandereycken. 1989. Self-report study of family interaction in eating disorder families compared to normals. In W. Vandereycken, E. Kob, and J. Vanderlinden, eds., *The Family Approach to Eating Disorders.* New York: PMA. 107–118.

9. Johnson, C., and A. Flach. 1985. Family characteristics of 105 patients with bulimia. *American Journal of Psychiatry, 142,* 1321–1324.

10. Wonderlich, S. A., M. H. Klein, and J. R. Council. 1996. Relationship of social perceptions and self-concept in bulimia nervosa. *Journal of Consulting and Clinical Psychology, 6,* 1231–1237.

11. Fowler, S. J., and C. M. Bulik. 1997. Family environment and psychiatric history in women with binge-eating disorder and obese controls. *Behaviour Change, 14,* 106–112.

12. Yanovski, S. Z., J. E. Nelson, B. K. Dubbert, and R. L. Spitzer. 1993. Association of binge eating disorder and psychiatric comorbidity in obese subjects. *American Journal of Psychiatry, 150,* 1472–1479.

13. Gilbert, E. H., and R. R. Deblassie. 1984. Anorexia nervosa: Adolescent starvation by choice. *Adolescence, 19,* 839–846.

14. Golden, N., and I. M. Sacker. 1984. An overview of the etiology, diagnosis, and management of anorexia nervosa. *Clinical Pediatrics, 23,* 209–214.

15. Dittmar, H., and B. Bates. 1987. Humanistic approaches to the understanding and treatment of anorexia nervosa. *Journal of Adolescence, 10,* 57–69.

16. Harding, T. P., and J. R. Lachenmeyer. 1986. Family interaction patterns and locus of control as predictors of the presence and severity of anorexia nervosa. *Journal of Clinical Psychology, 42,* 440–448.

17. Brone, R. J., and C. B. Fisher. 1988. Determinants of adolescent obesity: A comparison with anorexia nervosa. *Adolescence, 23,* 155–169.

18. Vandereycken, W. 1995. The families of patients with an eating disorders. In K. D. Brownell and C. G. Fairburn, eds., *Eating Disorders and Obesity: A Comprehensive Handbook.* New York: Guilford. 219–223.

19. Alexander, N. 1986. Characteristics and treatment of families with anorectic offspring. *Occupational Therapy in Mental Health, 6,* 117–135; Beresin, E. V., C. Gordon, and D. B. Herzog. 1989. The process of recovering from anorexia nervosa. *Journal of the American Academy of Psychoanalysis, 17,* 103–130.

20. Stierlin, H., and G. Weber. 1989. Anorexia nervosa: Lessons from a follow-up study. *Family Systems Medicine, 7,* 120–157.

21. Hall, R. C. W., L. Tice, T. P. Beresford, B. Wooley, and A. K. Hall. 1989. Sexual abuse in patients with anorexia nervosa and bulimia. *Psychosomatics, 30,* 79–88; Kearney-Cooke, A. M. 1988. Group treatment of sexual abuse among women with eating disorders. *Women and Therapy, 7,* 5–21; Oppenheimer, R., K. Howells, L. Palmer, and D. Chaloner. 1985. Adverse sexual experiences in childhood and clinical eating disorders: A preliminary description. *Journal of Psychiatric Research, 19,* 157–161; Root, M. P., and P. Fallon. 1988. The incidence of victimization experiences in a bulimic sample. *Journal of Interpersonal Violence, 3,* 161–173.

22. Pope, H. G., and J. I. Hudson. 1992. Is childhood sexual abuse a risk factor for bulimia nervosa? *American Journal of Psychiatry, 149,* 455–463.

23. Vanderlinden, J., and W. Vandereycken. 1996. Is sexual abuse a risk factor for developing an eating disorder? In M. F. Schwartz and L. Cohn, eds., *Sexual Abuse and Eating Disorders.* New York: Brunner/Mazel. 17–22.

24. Fallon, P., and S. A. Wonderlich. 1997. Sexual abuse and other forms of trauma. In D. M. Garner and P. E. Garfinkle, eds., *Handbook of Treatment for Eating Disorders, 2nd ed.* New York: Guilford. 394–414.

25. Rorty, M., and J. Yager. 1998. Speculations on the role of childhood abuse in the development of eating disorders among women. In M. F. Schwartz and L. Cohn, eds., *Sexual Abuse and Eating Disorders*. New York: Brunner/Mazel. 23–35.

26. Briere, J., and M. Runtz. 1988. Multivariate correlates of childhood psychological and physical maltreatment among university women. *Child Abuse and Neglect, 12,* 331–341; Briere, J., and M. Runtz. 1990. Differential adult symptomatology associated with three types of child abuse histories. *Child Abuse and Neglect, 14,* 357–364.

27. Gilbert, P. 1998. What is shame? Some core issues and controversies. In P. Gilbert and B. Andrews, eds., *Shame: Interpersonal Behavior, Psychopathology, and Culture*. New York: Oxford University Press.

28. Levine, M. P., L. Smolak, and H. Hayden. 1994. The relation of sociocultural factor to eating attitudes and behaviors among middle school girls. *Journal of Early Adolescence, 14,* 471–490; Stice, E., and W. S. Agras. 1998. Predicting onset and cessation of bulimic behaviors during adolescence: A longitudinal grouping analysis. *Behavior Therapy, 29,* 257–276; Stice, E., C. Ziemba, J. Margolis, and P. Flick. 1996. The dual pathway model differentiates bulimics, subclinical bulimics, and controls: Testing the continuity hypothesis. *Behavior Therapy, 27,* 531–549.

29. Hill, A. J., and V. Pallin. 1998. Dieting awareness and low self-worth: Related issues in 8-year-old girls. *International Journal of Eating Disorders, 24,* 405–413; Levine, M. P., L. Smolak, A. F. Moodey, M. D. Shuman, and L. D. Hessen. 1994. Normative developmental challenges and dieting and eating disturbances in middle school girls. *International Journal of Eating Disorders, 15,* 11–20.

30. Pike, K. M., and J. Rodin. 1991. Mothers, daughters, and disordered eating. *Journal of Abnormal Psychology, 100,* 198–204.

31. Hill, A. J., and V. Pallin. 1998. Dieting awareness and low self-worth: Related issues in 8-year-old girls. *International Journal of Eating Disorders, 24,* 405–413.

32. Franko, D. L., and P. Orosan-Weine. 1998. The prevention of eating disorders: Empirical, methodological, and conceptual considerations. *Clinical Psychology: Science and Practice, 5,* 459–477.

33. Bradshaw, J. 1988. *Bradshaw On the Family*. Pompano Beach, FL: Health Communications.

34. Ainsworth, M. D. S. 1989. Attachments beyond infancy. *American Psychologist, 44,* 709–716; Bowlby, J. 1988. *A secure base: Parent-child attachment and healthy human development*. New York: Basic Books; Friedberg, N. L., and W. J. Lyddon. 1996. Self-other working models and eating disorders. *Journal of Cognitive Psychotherapy: An International Quarterly, 10,* 193–203.

35. Friedberg, N. L., and W. J. Lyddon. 1996. Self-other working models and eating disorders. *Journal of Cognitive Psychotherapy: An International Quarterly, 10,* 193–203.

36. Guidano, V. F. 1987. *Complexity of the Self: A Developmental Approach to Psychopathology and Therapy.* New York: Guilford Press; Guidano, V. F., and G. Liotti. 1983. *Cognitive Processes and Emotional Disorders: A Structural Approach to Psychotherapy.* New York: Guilford Press.

37. Guidano, V. F. 1987. *Complexity of the Self: A Developmental Approach to Psychopathology and Therapy.* New York: Guilford Press.

38. Humphrey, L. L. 1986. Structural analysis of parent-child relationships in eating disorders. *Journal of Abnormal Psychology, 95,* 395–402; Humphrey, L. L. 1988. Relationships within subtypes of anorexic, bulimic, and normal families. *Journal of the American Academy of Child and Adolescent Psychiatry, 27,* 544–561; Wonderlich, S. A., M. H. Klein, and J. R. Council. 1996. Relationship of social perceptions and self-concept in bulimia nervosa. *Journal of Consulting and Clinical Psychology, 6,* 1231–1237.

39. Lehman, A. K., and J. Rodin. 1989. Styles of self-nurturance and disordered eating. *Journal of Consulting and Clinical Psychology, 57,* 117–122.

40. Thelen, M. H., J. Farmer, L. McLaughlin, and J. Pruitt. 1990. Bulimia and interpersonal relationships: A longitudinal study. *Journal of Counseling Psychology, 37,* 85–90.

41. Friedberg, N. L., and W. J. Lyddon. 1996. Self-other working models and eating disorders. *Journal of Cognitive Psychotherapy: An International Quarterly, 10,* 193–203.

42. Coovert, D. L., B. N. Kinder, and J. K. Thompson. 1989. The psychosexual aspects of anorexia nervosa and bulimia nervosa: A review of the literature. *Clinical Psychology Review, 9,* 169–180; Garfinkel, P. E., H. Moldofsky, and D. M. Garner. 1980. The heterogeneity of anorexia nervosa. *Archives of General Psychiatry, 37,* 1036–1040; Haimes, A. L., and J. L. Katz. 1988. Sexual and social maturity versus social conformity in restricting anorectic, bulimic, and borderline women. *International Journal of Eating Disorders, 7,* 331–341; Humphrey, L. L. 1987. Comparison of bulimic-anorexic and nondistressed families using structural analysis of social behavior. *American Academy of Child and Adolescent Psychiatry, 26,* 248–255.

43. Canals, J., G. Carbajo, J. Fernandez, C. Marti-Henneberg, and E. Domenech. 1996. Biopsychopathologic risk profile of adolescents with eating disorder symptoms. *Adolescence, 31,* 443–450.

44. Oliver, K. K., and M. H. Thelen. 1996. Children's perceptions of peer influence on eating concerns. *Behavior Therapy, 27,* 25–39.

45. Striegel-Moore, R. H., L. R. Silberstein, and J. Rodin. 1986. Toward an understanding of risk factors for bulimia. *American Psychologist, 41,* 246–263; Thelen, M. H., C. M. Lawrence, and A. L. Powell. 1992. Body image, weight control, and eating disorders among children. In J. H. Crowther, S. E. Hobfoll, M. A. P. Stephens, and D. L. Tennenbaum, eds., *Etiology of Bulimia: The Individual and Family Context.* Washington, DC: Hemisphere Publishers. 81–98.

46. Fabian, L. J., and J. K. Thompson. 1989. Body image and eating disturbance in young females. *International Journal of Eating Disorders, 8,* 63–74; Maloney, M. J., J. B. McGuire, S. R. Daniels, and B. Specker. 1989. Dieting

behaviors and eating attitudes in children. *Pediatrics, 84,* 482–489; Thompson, J. K. 1991. Body shape preferences: Effects of instructional protocol and level of eating disturbance. *International Journal of Eating Disorders, 10,* 193–198; Thompson, J. K., and K. Psaltis. 1988. Multiple aspects and correlates of body figure ratings: A replication and extension of Fallon and Rozin, 1985. *International Journal of Eating Disorders, 7,* 813–818.

47. Cash, T. F., B. A. Winstead, and L. H. Janda. 1986. The great American shape-up: Body image survey report. *Psychology Today,* April 30–34, 36–37.

48. Kanakis, D., and M. H. Thelen. 1995. Parental variables associated with bulimia nervosa. *Addictive Behaviors, 20,* 491–500; Thompson, J. K. 1991. Body shape preferences: Effects of instructional protocol and level of eating disturbance. *International Journal of Eating Disorders, 10,* 193–198; Thompson, J. K., and K. Psaltis. 1988. Multiple aspects and correlates of body figure ratings: A replication and extension of Fallon and Rozin, 1985. *International Journal of Eating Disorders, 7,* 813–818.

49. Desmond, S. M., J. H. Price, N. Gray, and J. K. O'Connell. 1986. The etiology of adolescents' perception of their weight. *Journal of Youth and Adolescence, 15,* 461–474; Levine, M. P., L. Smolak, A. F. Moodey, M. D. Shuman, and L. D. Hessen. 1994. Normative developmental challenges and dieting and eating disturbances in middle school girls. *International Journal of Eating Disorders, 15,* 11–20.

50. Oliver, K. K., and M. H. Thelen. 1996. Children's perceptions of peer influence on eating concerns. *Behavior Therapy, 27,* 25–39.

51. Levine, M. P., L. Smolak, and H. Hayden. 1994. The relation of sociocultural factor to eating attitudes and behaviors among middle school girls. *Journal of Early Adolescence, 14,* 471–490;

52. Stice, E., C. Ziemba, J. Margolis, and P. Flick. 1996. The dual pathway model differentiates bulimics, subclinical bulimics, and controls: Testing the continuity hypothesis. *Behavior Therapy, 27,* 531–549.

53. Heatherton, T. F., and R. F. Baumeister. 1991. Binge eating as escape from self-awareness. *Psychological Bulletin, 110,* 86–108.

54. Leibowitz, S. F. 1995. Central physiological determinants of eating behavior and weight. In K. D. Brownell and C. G. Fairburn, eds., *Eating Disorders and Obesity: A Comprehensive Handbook.* New York: Guilford. 3–7.

55. Ibid.

56. Wurtman, R. J., and J. J. Wurtman. 1986. Carbohydrate craving, obesity, and brain serotonin. *Appetite, 7,* 99–103.

57. Wurtman, J. J. 1983. *The Carbohydrate Craver's Diet.* Boston: Houghton Mifflin; Wurtman, J. J. 1993. Depression and weight gain: The serotonin connection. *Journal of Affective Disorders, 29,* 183–192; Wurtman, R. J., and J. J. Wurtman. 1986. Carbohydrate craving, obesity, and brain serotonin. *Appetite, 7,* 99–103.

58. Lieberman, H. R., J. J. Wurtman, and B. Chew. 1986. Changes in mood after carbohydrate consumption among obese individuals. *American Journal of Clinical Nutrition, 44,* 772–778.

59. Fernstrom, J. D. 1988. Tryptophan, serotonin and carbohydrate appetite: Will the real carbohydrate craver please stand up! *Journal of Nutrition, 118,* 1417–1419.

60. Kaplan, A. S., and D. B. Woodside. 1987. Biological aspects of anorexia nervosa and bulimia nervosa. *Journal of Consulting and Clinical Psychology, 55,* 645–653.

61. Faith, M. S., D. B. Allison, and A. Geliebter. 1995. Emotional eating and obesity: Theoretical considerations and practical recommendations. In S. Dalton, ed., *Overweight and Weight Management.* Gaithersburg, MD: Aspen. 439–465; Heatherton, T. F., and R. F. Baumeister. 1991. Binge eating as escape from self-awareness. *Psychological Bulletin, 110,* 86–108.

62. Woodside, D. B., L. L. Field, P. E. Garfinkel, and M. Heinmaa. 1998. Specificity of eating disorders diagnoses in families of probands with anorexia nervosa and bulimia nervosa. *Comprehensive Psychiatry, 39,* 261–264.

63. Wade, T., N. G. Martin, and M. Tiggemann. 1998. Genetic and environmental risk factors for weight and shape concerns characteristic of bulimia nervosa. *Psychological Medicine, 28,* 761–771.

64. Bouchard, C. 1997. Genetic factors and body weight regulation. In S. Dalton, ed., *Overweight and Weight Management.* Gaithersburg, MD: Aspen. 161–186.

65. Bouchard, C. 1994. Genetics of obesity: Overview and research directions. In C. Bouchard, ed., *The Genetics of Obesity.* Boca Raton, FL: CRC Press. 223–233.

66. Bouchard, C. 1995. Genetic influences on body weight and shape. In K. D. Brownell and C. G. Fairburn, eds., *Eating Disorders and Obesity: A Comprehensive Handbook.* New York: Guilford. 21–26.

67. Lissner, L., L. Sjostrom, C. Bengtsson, et al. 1994. The natural history of obesity in an obese population and associations with metabolic aberrations. *International Journal of Obesity, 18,* 441–447.

68. Weinsier, R. L., G. R. Hunter, A. F. Heini, M. I. Goran, and S. M. Sell. 1998. The etiology of obesity: Relative contribution of metabolic factors, diet, and physical activity. *American Journal of Medicine, 105,* 145–150.

69. Perusse, L., A. Tremblay, C. Leblanc, et al. 1988. Familial resemblance in energy intake: Contribution of genetic and environmental factors. *American Journal of Clinical Nutrition, 47,* 629–635.

70. Keys, A., J. Brozek, A. Henschel, O. Mickelsen, and H. L. Taylor. 1950. *The Biology of Human Starvation.* 2 vols. Minneapolis: University of Minnesota Press.

71. Wilson, G. T. 1995. Eating disorders and addictive disorders. In K. D. Brownell and C. G. Fairburn, eds., *Eating Disorders and Obesity: A Comprehensive Handbook.* New York: Guilford. 165–170.

72. Goodman, A. 1993. Diagnosis and treatment of sex addiction. *Journal of Sex and Marital Therapy, 19,* 225–242.

73. Brisman, J., and M. Siegel. 1985. The bulimia workshop: A unique integration of group treatment approaches. *International Journal of Group Psychotherapy, 35,* 585–601; Brisman, J., and M. Siegel. 1986. Bulimia and alcoholism— Two sides of the same coin? *Journal of Substance Abuse and Treatment, 1,* 113–118; Vandereycken, W. 1990. The relevance of body-image disturbance for the treatment of bulimia. In M. M. Fichter, ed., *Bulimia Nervosa: Basic Research, Diagnosis, and Treatment.* New York: Wiley. 320–330.

74. Faith, M. S., D. B. Allison, and A. Geliebter. 1995. Emotional eating and obesity: Theoretical considerations and practical recommendations. In S. Dalton, ed., *Overweight and Weight Management.* Gaithersburg, MD: Aspen. 439–465.

75. Wilson, G. T. 1995. Eating disorders and addictive disorders. In K. D. Brownell and C. G. Fairburn, eds., *Eating Disorders and Obesity: A Comprehensive Handbook.* New York: Guilford. 165–170.

76. Wilson, G. T. 1991. The addiction model of eating disorders: A critical analysis. *Advances in Behavior Research and Therapy, 13,* 27–72.

Chapter 5

Understanding Binge Eating

Some binges are triggered by hunger precipitated by dieting, and some occur for other reasons. Restrictive dieting, especially the kind that creates self-starvation, sets up compelling conditions for binge eating. Bulimics and anorexics are particularly susceptible to hunger-induced overeating, as are those who skip meals in attempts to cut back on calories. In other cases, negative emotions serve as the trigger for overeating.

Varieties of Binges

Although dieting that leads to hunger and stress—which in turn produce negative emotions—is strongly involved in setting off binge eating, binges are also caused by a variety of other factors. These include feeling deprived, having the opportunity to binge, wanting to extract retribution for wrongs, wanting to feel good, or bad eating habits.

The Hunger Binge

The hunger binge is triggered by physical deprivation. Studies on the effects of starvation[1] have demonstrated that the fasting and caloric restriction typical of anorexics and bulimics produces change in the body and brain. (See chapter 4 for a discussion on how hunger and starvation trigger binge eating.)

Starvation creates a variety of effects, including mood swings and a preoccupation with thoughts of food and eating. Although the combination of food restriction and strenuous exercise can give a false sense of energy, mainly by increasing the production of endorphins, which suppress hunger, this effect is temporary. A hunger binge is likely to result in due time.

The most important means of thwarting a hunger binge is to avoid hunger by eating regularly and adequately throughout the day. Those who think they are saving calories by skipping a meal—usually breakfast or lunch—are setting themselves up for a hunger binge. Anorexics are more likely to experience hunger binges. For the anorexic, other psychological factors often play a role, and these factors must be addressed, in addition to normalizing eating. For example, in Laura's case (see chapter 1), her eating disorder gave her the sense of having some control in the presence of her father's alcoholic behavior.

The Deprivation Binge

Like the hunger binge, the deprivation binge is done in response to restrictive dieting, but, in this case, psychological rather than physical deprivation is the most important factor. Often, the deprivation binge begins with a sense of wanting or needing something but not knowing just what it is that is wanted. In restrictive dieting, certain foods are forbidden, overvalued, or resisted.[2] When foods are forbidden, they become all the more irresistible. As a result, tension builds as "willpower" is used up, and a breaking point is finally reached. It may feel as if an internal rebel takes over and thwarts all intentions to curb eating. The binge brings a relief of the tension that was built up as the result of being vigilant about forbidden foods and focused on monitoring eating. However, the fear of gaining weight causes the reinstitution of vigilance and restrictive dieting, and sets the stage for more binge eating.

Gaby. Sixteen-year-old Gaby would eat only a half bagel for breakfast and she generally skipped lunch. Both of her parents worked, and when she came home from school, Gaby fixed herself something to eat—usually plain white rice. She refused to eat dinner with her parents, claiming that she didn't like red meat, which was usually part of their entree. Later, in her room, Gaby binged on chips and cookies.

An important curative factor in eliminating deprivation binges is to "legalize" formerly forbidden foods. Developing more self-awareness, eliminating restrictive rules for eating, and redefining self-worth are also needed for complete recovery.

The Stress Binge

Stress is experienced when a person's resources for coping are stretched thin or exceeded, endangering his or her well-being.[3] Recurrent interpersonal conflict, unmet expectations, loss, perceived personal failures, unsatisfactory relationships, and disappointments in life are some common sources of stress. Anxiety, depression, anger, loneliness, feelings of insecurity—these emotions and more can result from stress and are at the heart of the stress binge.

The stress binge, sometimes called "emotional eating," serves to alter moods, much as a drug does.[4] Stress eating can produce *dissociation*—a state in which emotion is split off from reality—allowing the person to feel less overwhelmed. Eating numbs out feelings and distracts attention from problems or troubling thoughts. Eating provides the means of day-to-day survival. When food or eating cannot be used to cope, anxiety and tension increase. The psychological discomfort that results eventually brings a return to overeating. The stress binge is an attempt to escape painful self-awareness and to deal with negative emotions, much as the use of drugs and alcohol alters consciousness and substitutes for more adaptive coping. (See chapter 4 for a discussion of how an eating disorder resembles an addiction.)

Mary Ann (see chapter 1) was a stress eater. Holding down a demanding, full-time job as well as carrying out the duties of wife and mother left her with little time to take care of herself. Maintaining her high standards both on the job and at home—the house had to be spotless at all times—and with little help from other family members, Mary Ann felt overwhelmed and exhausted most of the time. Food and eating gave her momentary respite from her many obligations.

To overcome stress eating, two areas need to be addressed— cognition and coping skills. Cognition involves inner "voices" such as that of the Critical Self, which finds fault with both self and others. The Worrier's voice is sure that disaster is just around the corner. The Caretaker puts others' needs before her own. The Rebel Eater is set on disrupting all attempts to eat right. The

Enforcer makes sure that all the rules are followed. These and other inner voices must be identified and challenged to help reduce stress and subsequent binge eating. Likewise, the tendency to use avoidance and denial, rather than problem solving, is a key factor that must be addressed to reduce stress eating.

The Opportunity Binge

Some binges are not triggered by hunger or stress, although they may be a cousin of the deprivation binge. Bulimics are especially vulnerable to the opportunity binge, which occurs when there is high access to privacy, combined with time enough to binge and purge. In some cases, the opportunity binge occurs because of the combination of boredom and unstructured time. In other cases, the opportunity binge provides an escape from having to do chores or bear responsibility. The person who is overly concerned about being productive may use the opportunity binge as an excuse for relaxing.

The likelihood of such a binge happening is increased if the person dwells on thoughts of eating highly preferred but forbidden foods. The thought of being able to get away with something may be an added incentive. Simply realizing that there will be an opportunity to be alone and binge can trigger thoughts about what you want to eat and what you will eat. The expectation of having an opportunity to binge, together with mentally planning what to eat, sets the opportunity binge in motion.

Meredith's story was also introduced in chapter 1. As a nurse, she worked different shifts. At times, she found herself home alone because her husband worked a regular nine to five job from Monday through Friday. On those days she knew she would have the opportunity to binge and purge without any worry of interruption. In addition, she was frequently bored with such free time, and the binge provided an opportunity to indulge herself in forbidden foods. Anticipating eating her favorite binge foods, Meredith planned her opportunity binges well ahead of time. She knew when she would be alone, and she planned and shopped for the forbidden foods she would have during the binge.

Another type of opportunity binge involves socially sanctioned eating opportunities such as vacations, holidays, and celebrations. Any occasion to celebrate can provide an opportunity to overeat. Usually such occasions are associated with positive feelings. However, any change in usual routine—e.g., attending a parent-teacher conference, painting the living room, driving home from a meeting—may provide an opportunity to overeat and possibly binge. These and similar situations often involve a transition from one activity to another, which can pose a particular problem for some people. At such times, when overeating results in the thought, "Well, I've blown it now, so why not go all the way?" a small incident of overeating can trigger a full-blown binge.

The best remedy for the opportunity binge involves managing the environment and planning ahead—deciding how to minimize unstructured time, cope with holidays and celebrations, or deal with transitions. Learning to use the cognitive-behavioral technique of thought stopping (see chapter 7) to redirect thinking away from the potential rewards of eating can be helpful.

Instituting a reward system for reinforcing desired behavior is also a helpful technique. Learning how to prevent a small lapse from turning into a major relapse may prevent a binge as well. Normalizing eating and allowing oneself to eat all foods in moderation is a basic strategy for overcoming all binges.

The Vengeful Binge

Fueled by anger, the vengeful binge is a way of venting hostility. The target is sometimes the binge eater herself, sometimes another person, and sometimes the situation. The body itself may become the target of anger for "letting me down" and becoming obese. Perceived failure attributable to one's own actions or to some accident of fate can also invite self-punishment. Vengeful binge eaters are often people who have been emotionally injured. They must bear a double burden—the original injury plus the choking hatred and disillusionment that has no place to go.

Peter, whose story was introduced in chapter 1, is a vengeful binge eater. He blamed himself for making bad investments that resulted in financial disaster. Initially his binge eating was triggered by the stress of his financial situation. However, as he steadily gained weight, his anger turned on himself—both for his poor money management and for his increasing obesity. His anger turned into self-hatred, which fueled further binge eating.

Likewise, Beth (see chapter 4) punished herself with binge eating for being unattractive and unpopular with her peers. She blamed her body for its shape and she blamed herself for overeating. When dieting attempts failed to alter her shape, she binged.

In other cases, the vengeful binge eater may perceive herself as wronged, slighted, or in some way hurt by another.

Janet. Fifty-three-year-old Janet felt unappreciated at home and at work. Her husband spent most of his free time on the computer ignoring her. Her adult children rarely called or visited. She put in extra hours at work for which she did not get paid. Rather, her co-workers asked even more of her and rarely said thank you. Janet's supervisor seemed not to notice her extra efforts and provided little support. Some of the firm's customers complained that Janet was abrupt with them and hard to work with. Janet's anger at her mistreatment reflected itself in her eating binges, which had a "take that" quality to them.

Sometimes the vengeful binge is instigated by an inner "Rebel" voice, which resents and rejects the authority of good eating habits and takes delight in flaunting poor food choices. The Rebel eschews self-discipline and undermines dieting attempts. The Rebel is often angry about being "different"—having to eat differently from others or having to cope with obesity. Obsession with this unfairness and the wish for revenge prompts the vengeful binge—a symbolic "No"—when there appears to be no other resolution available.

To overcome vengeful binge eating, the underlying anger must be accessed and acknowledged so that forgiveness can proceed. The original injury must be examined, understood, and grieved. Questions must be answered. "Why me?" "What did I do to deserve this?" "How can I forgive?" Underneath the anger there is often deep shame and a conviction of moral failure—one's own or another's, which need to be addressed. Faith in one's own worthiness and the worthiness of others must be restored, and the myth of a fair and just world relinquished. The vengeful binge eater often needs the guidance of a therapist or a spiritual adviser to overcome her or his eating difficulties.

The Pleasure Binge

The pleasure binge is triggered by the desire for stimulation and entertainment. Obese binge eaters are most vulnerable to this type of binge. Often they have few sources of pleasure or satisfaction in their lives, and eating provides a reliable source of reward. Those who succumb to the pleasure binge describe feeling excited by the idea of eating and may spend much time thinking and fantasizing about what they will eat.

To reduce occurrences of pleasure binges, it is important to develop pleasurable nonfood alternatives. Chapter 12 discusses lifestyles that are unbalanced—that have too many "shoulds" and not enough rewards and sources of satisfaction. Some pleasure-giving alternatives mentioned in chapter 12 include getting a massage, going shopping, or visiting a friend. Other possibilities might involve reading a good book, going for a pleasant walk, or spending time on a hobby or pastime you enjoy. Adequate self-nurturing helps reduce the risk of a pleasure binge.

The Habit Binge

The habit binge is the binge that is on automatic pilot—no one seems to be at the controls. Eating involves a basic stimulus/response pattern, with the food being readily available and the response being to eat it without much thinking. Another name for the habit binge might be the grazing binge—continuous, more-or-less nonstop eating without much conscious effort to either control it or feel upset about it. Only later, when the binge eater's consciousness turns to body weight, do negative reactions occur.

Robert (see chapter 3) was a habit binge eater. He ate a reasonable breakfast at home, but every morning on his way to work he stopped at a local fast food restaurant for a second breakfast. At work, he kept a large store of candy bars in his desk drawer, which he snacked on throughout the day. Lunch was eaten out every workday at the same deli across the street, and Robert always ordered the same thing—a tuna melt sandwich, chips, and a large Coke. On his way home from work, he stopped for his first dinner at another fast food restaurant, and after arriving home ate his regular dinner with the rest of his family. Later in the evening, Robert repeatedly drifted into the kitchen to see what might be available to eat. Weekends posed a problem for his habit of continuous eating, because his behavior was more exposed for others to see and make comments about. As a result, his eating habits were generally better on weekends.

The habit binge eater is likely to benefit most from participating in a cognitive-behavioral, weight-management program that provides group support. Self-monitoring, which involves keeping daily records of food eaten and the circumstances under which it was eaten, is the first step for identifying the behavior pattern. It also makes the behavior more available to conscious control and therefore more readily changed. Instituting structured eating, which involves limiting eating only to planned times for meals and snacks, is also important. New behavior patterns can be reinforced with a reward system. An important key in overcoming habit binges is to redefine self-concept so that healthy eating and regular exercise become a part of self-identity. This involves changing beliefs and ways of thinking.

Anatomy of a Binge

Most binges have four stages—tension building, tension release, recovery, and new beginning.

Tension Buildup

A number of factors can contribute to the buildup of tension. When calories are restricted, hunger increases, along with fatigue, irritability, and stress. Tension also results from having to stick to a diet, be vigilant, and guard against succumbing to eating forbidden foods. Stress and the accompanying negative feelings can contribute to tension buildup, as can anger, loneliness, and boredom. Persistent and painful self-awareness of failing to meet high internal or culturally defined standards also contributes to the buildup of tension. The anticipation involved in planning a binge also produces tension, as does the realization that self-imposed rules for eating have been violated. Eventually the tension reaches a point that demands relief, which initiates the next stage.

Tension Release

Binge eating releases tension and reduces anxiety, whether purging takes place or not.[5] In the case of the stress binge, the binge can actually blot out thinking and feeling or provide a source of distraction from problems and negative feelings. The use of compensatory behaviors such as vomiting subsequent to the binge reduces anxiety about weight gain. For the bulimic or anorexic who binges and purges, the purge results in physical exhaustion—often called the "binge hangover." In the case of the obese binge eater, rather than having a definable end, the binge may just peter out, often stopping when the binge eater falls asleep. For some binge eaters, making an appointment to join a weight-management program curtails binge eating, at least for a time, because it instills renewed hope for recovery.

Exhaustion, physical and emotional, initiates the next stage.

Recovery

The recovery stage is a time when energy is below normal and lethargy and fatigue predominate. Many binge eaters say that this phase feels like having a hangover; symptoms can include headache, nausea, diarrhea, fatigue, abdominal discomfort, or a general sense of having "the blahs." Mindlessly watching television or falling asleep are prominent activities during this time. The next stage occurs when energy stores return to normal.

New Beginning

This last stage is brief and for many disordered eaters it is marked by the emergence of hope and renewed resolutions that things will be different in the future. For the obese binge eater, this stage may be initiated when she joins a weight-control program. However, very shortly, tension again starts to build, and the cycle begins again.

Intervening to Prevent Binge Eating

The best stage at which to intervene in binge eating is at the tension buildup stage. Steps need to be taken to identify the sources of stress and tension and to reduce both before they become overwhelming. Although it is possible to avert a binge just before it begins by finding another way to release tension, it is more difficult to do if the tension has built to a high level of intensity. Once begun, it can be very difficult to stop the binge from proceeding. Although the "new beginning" stage would seem to be a time when motivation is highest to turn around binge eating—usually by vowing not to let it happen again—attempts at this stage are often false starts at recovery and a precursor to disappointment. True success is more likely to be achieved by identifying the behavior pattern, including the triggers that elicit the binge and the reinforcers that follow and increase or decrease the likelihood of binge eating occurring again.

Triggers and Reinforcers of a Binge

The occurrence of one or more events can serve to trigger or elicit a binge, and it is important to determine what triggers are most likely to set off a binge for you. An "event" may be something external—perhaps an argument or painful remark. It can also be a decision you make, a thought, a feeling, a physical state, or a reaction to an external circumstance. The following list summarizes some events that typically trigger a binge.

Some Triggers for Binge Eating

- Hunger from restrictive eating
- Anxiety or tension related to external stress and deficient coping skills
- Cravings
- Eating something (anything)
- Breaking a dietary rule
- Recurrent interpersonal conflict and inability to resolve conflict satisfactorily
- Feeling judged, criticized, blamed, rejected, unappreciated, unacknowledged, or taken advantage of
- Thinking that generates negative feelings such as anxiety, anger, sadness, and so forth
- Obsessions and preoccupations with food or eating
- Not living up to one's own expectations; failing
- Boredom from unstructured time
- High access to privacy and preferred binge eating settings
- Thinking about and anticipating eating preferred foods
- Being urged or invited to indulge yourself by eating
- Needing to (or feeling like) rebelling against weight reduction regimen, diet, or external authority
- Transitions from one activity to another
- Worries about money, sex, family, etc.
- Feeling overwhelmed
- Experiencing marital or work-related distress
- Pain, fatigue, negative physical states
- Premenstrual tension
- Drinking alcohol
- Wanting to continue feeling good or pleasant

Reinforcers of a Binge

Most people continue to binge because it "works." That is, the binge provides a means of coping. It provides relief from stress or painful emotions such as anxiety, anger, and loneliness. The binge may temporarily shut out the effects of self-criticism and negative self-talk. It can provide an escape from physical pain, hunger, and fatigue. In some cases, the binge provides a certain amount of satisfaction through the expression of anger or rebellion. A binge provides a reliable and powerful means of nurturing and indulging oneself when there are few other opportunities to do so. All of these events that follow a binge serve to reinforce it—make it more likely to happen again.

Of course, a binge also has its downside. The ingestion of excess calories can produce weight gain. Significant others may become upset about and react negatively to the binge eating behavior. After a binge, most binge eaters feel disgusted, guilty, and ashamed of their behavior. Yet these consequences often do not stop the binge behavior from happening again. The fact that a binge provides an immediate means of coping, even if only temporarily, outweighs most of the negative consequences, which usually occur some time later.

To overcome binge eating, it is necessary to first identify the triggers that elicit binges and the reinforcers that maintain the binge eating behavior, and then plan how to change this pattern and create a new, more desirable one. This begins with assessing the binge eating behavior pattern.

Notes

1. Keys, A., J. Brozek, A. Henschel, O. Mickelsen, and H. L. Taylor. 1950. *The Biology of Human Starvation*. 2 vols. Minneapolis: University of Minnesota Press.

2. White, F. 1998. Treating overeating disorders: A 3 stage nutrition therapy approach. *NEDO Newsletter*. Summer. Tulsa, OK: National Eating Disorders Organization. 1–4.

3. Lazarus, R. S., and S. Folkman. 1984. *Stress, Appraisal, and Coping*. New York: Springer.

4. White, F. 1998. Treating overeating disorders: A 3 stage nutrition therapy approach. *NEDO Newsletter*. Summer. Tulsa, OK: National Eating Disorders Organization. 1–4.

5. Elmore, D. K., and J. M. de Castro. 1990. Self-related moods and hunger in relation to spontaneous eating behavior in bulimics, recovered bulimics, and normals. *International Journal of Eating Disorders, 9,* 179–190.

Part 2

Intervention:
How You
Can Overcome
Disordered Eating

Chapter 6

Assessing Your Binge Eating Behavior

Binge eating doesn't just happen. It is embedded within a context of events, some of which precede and elicit the binge and some of which follow and reinforce the behavior. The preceding chapter referred to the events that occur before the binge as triggers and those that follow as reinforcers.

The ABC Model of Behavior

These before and after events, together with the binge behavior itself, can be better understood using the ABC model of behavior. *Antecedents*, or the "A" part of the model, are the events that come first and, together or singly, trigger the behavior. The binge is the behavior in question and is the "B" part of the model. The *consequences*, or "C," follow the behavior, and are the events that serve to reinforce the "B"—that is, make it more or less likely that the behavior will happen again.

The "Cs" may be desirable, for example, obtaining relief from stress, or undesirable, for example, feeling guilty. Some consequences occur immediately and some occur at some time in the future, for example, gaining weight. Usually several consequences result from a given behavior, some of which are immediate and some of which are delayed. The consequences that matter most in terms of reinforcing behavior are those that take place immediately after the binge. Chapter 5 described a number of types of triggers that can elicit a binge as well as some of the things that serve to reinforce it, such as relief from tension or painful emotions.

There is rarely a single big event or sole antecedent that triggers a binge. More often it is a buildup of a number of small events that includes various thoughts, feelings, and little decisions. Consider the pattern of events that are typical for Mary Ann (see chapters 1 and 5). She leaves work feeling tired and stressed, and stops at the grocery store to pick up something for dinner. She decides to buy a cake because it's on sale. Arriving home, she leaves the cake on the kitchen counter. Later in the evening, feeling bored and lonely, because the kids have gone out for the evening and her husband is watching TV, Mary Ann goes into the kitchen "to see what's there." She spots the cake and tells herself, "I'll just have one piece." It tastes good and eating it makes her feel better, so she has two more pieces. At that point she thinks to herself, "Well, I've already blown it, so I may as well finish it off." A binge is underway.

Notice that Mary Ann's binge started with her feeling tired and stressed—a condition that made her more vulnerable to making poor choices when she stopped at the grocery store. A combination of feelings, decisions, thoughts, and behaviors led to the initiation of a stress binge. At the time these events were unfolding, Mary Ann was not aware that a binge was in the making, and the fact that she would feel bad afterward and possibly even gain weight probably did not enter her consciousness. Or perhaps she dismissed such concerns with a thought like, "I don't care. I deserve a little treat." To overcome her binge problem, Mary Ann must become more aware of her behavior pattern, including the thoughts and feelings that are a part of it, in order to change.

Behavior Chains

One good analogy for a behavior pattern is that of a chain, with one link in the chain hooked to the next. How an eating behavior chain leads to an eating binge is illustrated in Figure 6.1. The first link in the chain is skipping breakfast and lunch. These behaviors set the stage for excessive hunger later, but before the excessive hunger sets in, a number of stress-producing events happen. Hungry and stressed out, overeating at dinner occurs, which is followed by feeling bad and giving up all efforts to make healthy choices. The thought of "already having blown it" facilitates the binge.

Figure 6.2 is an unlabeled chain to help you analyze your own behavior pattern. Think of a recent specific occasion on which you binged. Perhaps it was a stressful time or a situation in which you had the opportunity to overeat. As accurately as you can, label this chain with the events, thoughts, feelings, and decisions you made that led up to your binge. Note that it is usually easier to do this by going backward, one link at a time, starting from the binge link labeled "You overeat." Try to reconstruct from memory the chain of events that led up to the binge. Then go on to record the consequences of the binge in the two succeeding links. Examples of consequences might be "I felt completely disgusted with myself" or "I became exhausted, too tired to move."

Without awareness of the chain of events that set up the binge, you are likely to conclude that you have no control over your eating and that you are addicted to food. However, by tracing the links of the behavior chain, you will begin to understand that in many places along the way, you did have a choice. Knowing this, you may become better able to make better decisions earlier—and to change the course of future events.

Filling in the missing links is a retrospective exercise for identifying the steps that led up to a binge that has already happened. That is, it requires you to recall what happened. Although it is helpful to understand that your control over eating was eroded little by little through seemingly unimportant decisions (e.g., skipping breakfast), you will need a more accurate means of identifying your binge behavior pattern that does not rely on your memory. Self-monitoring provides this means.

Self-Monitoring

The first step in overcoming binge eating is to identify the antecedents and consequences that are operating to elicit and maintain the binge and then take steps to modify the pattern. Although it is sometimes possible to reflect on past binges and recreate events, the best approach is to systematically gather information on the behavior as it happens. This involves *self-monitoring*—keeping a record of when, where, and what you eat, the circumstances that contributed to the eating behavior, whether it was a binge, and your thoughts and feelings at each step of the way.

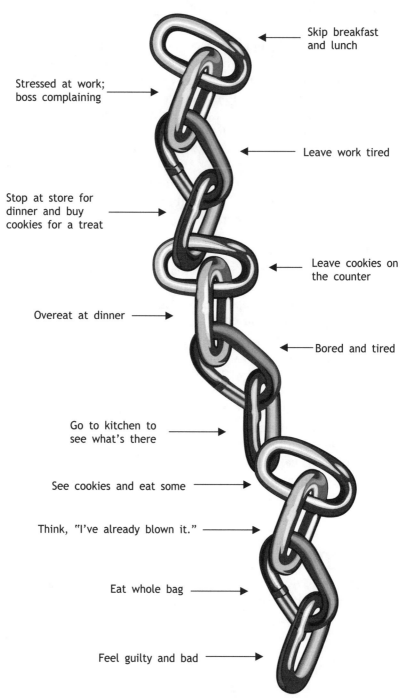

Skip breakfast
and lunch

Stressed at work;
boss complaining

Leave work tired

Stop at store for
dinner and buy
cookies for a treat

Leave cookies on
the counter

Overeat at dinner

Bored and tired

Go to kitchen to
see what's there

See cookies and eat some

Think, "I've already blown it."

Eat whole bag

Feel guilty and bad

Figure 6.1   Chain of Events Leading to Overeating

Instructions: Think of a time when you overate or ate inappropriately. Label each link of this chain with a brief description of the events that you think led up to and followed your overeating. Remember—events can be internal, such as thoughts or feelings, or events can be external, such as something that happens to you or between you and someone else. (*Hint:* It may be easier to work backwards from the "overeating" event to reconstruct the chain of events that led up to your eating behavior.)

Figure 6.2   Chain of Events Leading to Overeating

Concerns About Keeping Records

Some people object to self-monitoring. You may have done it in the past and not found it helpful, or you may feel you already know what triggers your binges. Or perhaps you just don't want to have to put in the effort that self-monitoring requires.

Although you may indeed know what triggers your binges, self-monitoring may add new information that can be helpful. Certainly, keeping records is tedious and time-consuming. However, the process of keeping a record has a big advantage—it helps you become more conscious of your behavior and it aids you in becoming more aware of the thoughts, feelings, and situations that put you at risk for binge eating. In fact, just having to write down what you eat and the circumstances under which you eat helps you to reduce binge eating and improve your eating habits. As some people have reported, "I knew I had to write it down if I did it, so I didn't do it!"

For record keeping to be helpful, you must systematically analyze the records to identify the most relevant and important problems areas so that appropriate tactics for change can be chosen. A means of doing this is included in this chapter.

Recording Your Eating Behavior

Use the Daily Eating Behavior Record provided here to keep track of your eating behavior, including your eating binges, purging, and exercise. First refer to the completed sample of the Daily Eating Behavior Record. Notice that the blank form provides space to record not only what you eat but also other relevant information. Make copies of the blank form provided, and plan to use one form per day, dating each one. You should keep these records for at least two weeks, and longer is better. Carry each day's form with you. Each time you eat something, take out the form and fill in the information. Always record the information as soon as possible, preferably before or during the actual eating. Do not wait until the end of the day to do your recording—by then you may have forgotten what you ate. Besides, having to write down the information immediately teaches you to be conscious of your choices. Instructions for each column follow.

Instructions for Using the Daily Eating Behavior Record

Column	Instructions
Time of Day	Each time you eat anything, record the time of the day you began eating.
Food Eaten	Provide a general description of what you eat and drink. Don't forget little snacks or food eaten "on the run." It is not necessary to record calories or portion sizes. Circle or bracket any food that you consider a meal and label it accordingly—breakfast, lunch, or dinner. Likewise, circle *planned* snacks and label as such. All other food eaten is unplanned snacking and may be part of a binge.
Binge	A binge is anything you consider a binge. Put an asterisk (*) or star in this column when the meal or snack consumed was a binge.
Degree of Hunger: NH, H, VH	Record how hungry you were before you started eating. NH stands for "not hungry," H for "an average or reasonable level of hunger," and VH for "very hungry."
Location/Activity	Indicate where you are eating—in a particular room of the house, in a restaurant, in the car, at your desk, and so forth—and whether you are sitting, standing, walking or otherwise moving around.

Circumstances: Triggers, Thoughts, and Feelings	This is the most important entry of all. Here is where you record any situation that may have influenced your eating behavior. In particular, look for the antecedents that set the stage for or triggered a binge. Record the circumstances of the binge—what happened that set up the binge, interactions with others, your thoughts along the way, and your feelings, especially any negative emotions. Remember, some important events may have occurred well before the binge actually took place. Pay special attention to thoughts such as "I blew it, so why try." If the eating caused you to stop thinking or to push away all feelings, record this fact as well as the feelings that you were trying to avoid.
Purge	If you purge, note this on the record.
Exercise	Briefly record what you did for exercise and how long you did it.

Analyzing Your Behavior

Keeping records is the first step in changing behavior. The next step is to make sense out of the information gathered. It is this step that is often left out or done inadequately, which usually results in concluding that keeping records wasn't worth the effort. In the instructions that follow the forms, you are helped to examine your eating behavior and, in particular, your binge eating behavior pattern. Simply follow the instructions and answer the questions or fill in the requested information based on a review of your Daily Eating Behavior Records.

Sample Daily Eating Behavior Record

M   T   W   (Th)   F   Sa   Su   Date: ___12/10/99___

Time of day	Food Eaten	Binge	Degree of Hunger NH, H, VH	Location/ Position	Circumstances: Triggers, Thoughts, Feelings
7:30 A.M.	Cereal, skim milk, coffee, o.j.		H	Kitchen at table	Sleepy, trying to plan day
10:20	1 peach		H	Office at desk	Anxious, worried. "Can I get this project done?"
12:15 P.M.	Tunamelt, Coke, cookies		H	Cafeteria	"I shouldn't have had the cheese or Cokes." Mad at myself
1:30	Chips		NH	Vending machine, walking back to desk	Bored, tired
3:00	Candy bar		NH	Desk	Tired. "Wish I could leave."
6:00	1 glass wine, wheat thins and cheese		H	Kitchen, walking around	Project didn't get gone. "Why me?"
7:30	Frozen pizza, more wine		NH	In living room watching tv	Bored. "Who cares."
9:45	Popcorn, Coke		NH	Living room	"Wish I were thinner. But I can't do it."
10:15	Milk and cookies		NH	kitchen	"I give up."
10:40	Ice cream (whole gallon) more cookies, Coke, peanuts, chips	★ purge			Not feeling anything

Exhausted |

Time	Exercise, e.g. Walking, jogging	Duration
6:00 A.M.	walk	20 minutes

Daily Eating Behavior Record

M   T   W   Th   F   Sa   Su   Date: _____

Time of day	Food Eaten	Binge	Degree of Hunger NH, H, VH	Location/ Position	Circumstances: Triggers, Thoughts, Feelings

Time	Exercise, e.g. Walking, jogging	Duration

Instructions for Analyzing Records

Examine your records for all instances when you binged.

1. Count the number of days and the number of binges in total. On average, how often did you binge? (Calculate this by dividing the number of binges by the number of days for which you kept records.) _____

2. Overall, what was the frequency pattern of your binges? (Check only one.) Your goal should be to reduce the frequency of binge eating by at least half, if not to eliminate binge eating altogether.

    _____ More than two times per week on average.

    _____ Less than twice a week on average.

    _____ Varied a lot over time—sometimes frequently, sometimes not at all.

3. Was hunger a factor in triggering binges? For each binge, review the Degree of Hunger column. Were you more likely to be very hungry preceding a binge or more likely to be not hungry? (Check one)

    _____ Hunger was *often* a factor in triggering a binge.

    _____ Hunger was *sometimes* a factor in triggering a binge.

    _____ Hunger was *rarely* a factor in triggering a binge.

4. Are you more likely to binge (overeat) during meals or when snacking? (Choose one.) Your answer points to where you need to direct your efforts at change.

    _____ Meals (If yes, which meal?)

    _____ Snacking (If yes, what time of the day?)

5. One at a time, consider each binge that you recorded. Use the blank Behavior Chain shown in Figure 6.2, or construct your own behavior chain to reconstruct as best you can the chain of events that led up to each binge. Review these chains and your records and then answer the following questions:

What *decisions* did you make along the way that led up to the binge? _____

_____

_____

What *thoughts* did you have along the way that contributed to the binge or allowed it to happen? _____

_____

_____

What *feelings* did you experience prior to or at the time of the binge? _____

_____

_____

Rate each of the following statements according to how true each is for you. Circle "1" if the statement is *Not True at All*. Circle "2" if it is *Somewhat True*, "3" if is *Mostly True*, and "4" if it is *Very True*. Those which you rate a "3" or "4" suggest important ways in which binge eating helps you to cope.

Binge eating helps me stop thinking and feeling. 1 2 3 4

Binge eating is a way of expressing anger or
punishing someone.   1 2 3 4

Binge eating provides nurturing that I don't
get elsewhere.   1 2 3 4

Binge eating is my way of rebelling.   1 2 3 4

Binge eating helps me avoid doing other things. 1 2 3 4

Binge eating is exciting, fun, and entertaining.   1 2 3 4

Binge eating (*complete in your own words*):

_____   1 2 3 4

6. What *circumstances* (situations, thoughts, feelings) typically led you to binge? _____

_____

7. What were the immediate *positive* consequences of the binge? (e.g., food tasted good, felt happy, became relaxed, etc.)

_____

_____

8. What were the immediate *negative* consequences of the binge? (e.g., felt guilty, felt bloated, etc.) _____

_____

_____

9. What are your typical binge foods? _____

_____

_____

10. Which of these binge foods are typically avoided or forbidden at other times? _____

_____

_____

11. Is there a particular time of day that is more likely to bring on a binge? If so, what is it? _____

Review the Exercise section of all of your records.

12. Which of the following statements is most true for you? (Choose one.)

_____ I generally don't get much exercise.

_____ Most of the time my exercise is in the healthy range. I expend about 2000 to 3500 calories each week in aerobic exercise, such as running, jogging etc.

_____ I often exercise more than necessary for good health, i.e., expending more than 3500 calories each week.

Review the Food Eaten column of all of your records.

13. When you *aren't* binge eating, which of the following statements is true for you? (Check all that apply.)

_____ I eat pretty much a variety of foods and nothing is really forbidden.

_____ I generally eat a balanced diet, high in complex carbohydrates and fiber, and low in fat.

_____ I avoid fat and fatty foods as much as possible.

_____ I allow myself to eat as much as I want if I buy a nonfat alternative food.

_____ There are only certain foods that I will allow myself eat.

_____ I try to keep my overall consumption of calories as low as I can.

_____ I don't eat in the middle of the day.

_____ I skip some meals.

_____ Sometimes I make healthy choices (i.e. low-fat, high complex carbohydrates, adequate calories to maintain normal weight) but mostly I don't.

14. What foods are your typical *planned*, healthy snack foods?

_____

_____

15. What foods are most likely to be eaten during *unplanned* snacks? _____

_____

16. What foods are forbidden? _____

_____

17. Which meals, if any, do you typically skip? _____

_____

Review the Time of Day column.

18. Do you eat regularly throughout the day, or does your eating cluster at certain times of the day?

_____ No more than 3 or 4 hours elapse between meals.

_____ I eat more or less continuously throughout the day.

_____ My eating clusters at particular times:

Describe times: _____

_____

_____

Review the Location/Position column

19. Where are you when you are eating a meal? Estimate the percentage of time you eat meals in the following places. (Percentages in each column should total 100%.)

	Breakfast	Lunch	Dinner
Kitchen or dining room table or counter	_____	_____	_____
Standing up in or passing through kitchen	_____	_____	_____
In other rooms of the house	_____	_____	_____
At work, on the job	_____	_____	_____
In a car	_____	_____	_____
At a restaurant	_____	_____	_____
At school	_____	_____	_____
Other	_____	_____	_____
	100%	100%	100%

20. What is your body position or action when you are eating breakfast, lunch, or dinner? (Check the appropriate spaces.)

	Breakfast	Lunch	Dinner
Usually sitting	_____	_____	_____
Usually standing	_____	_____	_____
Usually on the run	_____	_____	_____

21. Summarize below what have you learned by keeping these records:

_____

_____

_____

_____

_____

Identifying Behavior Patterns and Problem Areas

You have just completed a systematic analysis of your binge behavior. Using the information provided in your answers to the previous questions, you should now have a better sense of your problem areas and patterns. In particular, you need to determine whether hunger, deprivation, stress, emotions, problem thinking, lack of consciousness, or poor nutrition are playing a role in your binge eating behavior.

Hunger

If you mostly binged when you were hungry, restrictive eating is an important culprit in setting up a binge. One of your goals must be to normalize eating by learning to eat three adequate meals and several planned snacks daily.

Deprivation

Psychological deprivation is the experience of wanting something you can't have and feeling bad about it. When foods are declared forbidden or placed off limits, deprivation can result. Deciding that you are never able to eat another chocolate chip cookie makes them all the more desirable. Having to be vigilant and guard against desires or opportunities to eat such a cookie sets up tension that ultimately can lead to a binge.

Stress

Stress results when more is demanded of you than you can provide without becoming exhausted or distressed. Stress is also generated when your expectations for yourself or others are not met, or your self-esteem or well-being are threatened. Examples of stressful situations might include not being able to meet your deadline for an important project, discovering that your spouse has misspent the latest paycheck, concluding that you look terrible for a party, or having someone make a critical remark about you. The experience of stress can contribute to painful emotions such as anger, anxiety, shame, hurt, sadness, depression, and so forth. Another stress-inducing situation is boredom. When stress and negative emotions are factors in binge eating, it is important to learn how to become a better problem solver and how to be able to reduce stress or cope better with stressful situations. When a stressful situation cannot be averted, it is necessary to learn to cope with the painful emotions without having to engage in avoidance strategies, such as binge eating.

Gratification Seeking

Although overeating is often triggered by painful emotions, it can also happen as the result of feeling good or anticipating pleasure from eating. Some people overeat to prolong happy or good feelings. Others get so excited by the thought of food and eating that they forget all else. Obtaining gratification and pleasure becomes the sole focus, and thoughts about weight or health fall by the wayside.

Problem Thinking

Almost every event is accompanied by self-talk, which is the form of thinking that sounds like your own voice talking to you inside your head. Self-talk can take the form of self-blame and self-criticism or mental pats-on-the-back—self-praise for doing well. Some kinds of self-talk involve excuses and rationalizations that allow you to eat inappropriately, while other self-talk spurs you to try harder and do more. Problem thinking involves either negative self-talk—the kind that makes it harder to overcome disordered eating, or cognitive errors—unrealistic ways of thinking about or perceiving events. Identifying and changing problem thinking is essential for overcoming binge eating.

Lack of Consciousness

If you eat more or less continuously throughout the day with meals and snacks running together, you are probably on automatic pilot and not being conscious of your eating behavior. In all probability, you are snacking out of habit or boredom. Continued self-monitoring will help you to stay conscious and aware of your eating behavior.

Nutrition

Good nutrition is achieved by eating a balanced diet in which 55 to 60 percent of total calories are from complex carbohydrates (i.e., vegetables, whole grains, legumes), less than 30 percent of calories are from fat, and the balance of calories is from protein. Several large survey studies have examined the relationship between diet composition and body weight, and have found that those who eat a diet higher in fat tend to be more overweight.[1] Conversely, those who eat fewer complex carbohydrates, were also more overweight. Good nutrition also means consuming enough calories to maintain weight at a healthy level.

Based on a considerable amount of research, it seems clear that obesity is often associated with consumption of a high fat diet.[2] Many Americans seem to have gotten the message that they need to reduce their intake of dietary fat. However, in their enthusiasm for replacing high fat foods with low fat or non-fat alternatives, they have neglected to control their consumption of total calories.

Portion control is necessary to keep total caloric intake in the moderate range. To achieve weight reduction, energy intake must be less than energy expenditure. The best way to maintain a healthy weight is to consume a low-fat, high-carbohydrate diet of moderate caloric content and to get regular, adequate exercise.

To Weigh or Not to Weigh?

For anorexics or bulimics, the reason for weighing is to prove to yourself that you can eat "normally" and not gain excess weight. For the obese binge eater, decreasing binge eating and learning to make healthier choices may result in weight loss that can encourage you to continue your efforts. Weighing provides feedback that can be encouraging if it is done judiciously.

Some people avoid weighing themselves altogether. Others weigh themselves obsessively, sometimes several times a day. Neither of these approaches is a good idea. It is best to weigh yourself only once a week. Choose the same day and the same time of day. If you become tempted to weigh yourself more often, move the scale to a place that is out of sight (e.g., under the bed) or hard to reach (e.g., on a shelf in the closet). Don't get distracted or upset by small fluctuations in weight. Remember, the scale is not a precise method of determining anything except overall body weight at the moment of weighing. Fluid retention and other factors may cause you to weigh more, and having finished an exercise workout or having had too much alcohol to drink the night before may cause a small drop in weight that doesn't truly reflect changes in fat stores. Rather than reacting to a particular number on the scale at one point, keep track of your weight over time. The overall trend is what counts most.

Notes

1. Colditz, G. A., W. C. Willet, M. J. Stampfer, S. J. London, M. R. Segal, and F. E. Speizer. 1990. Patterns of weight change and their relation to diet in a cohort of healthy women. *American Journal of Clinical Nutrition, 51,* 1100–1105; Dreon, D. M., B. Frey-Hewitt, N. Ellsworth, P. T. Williams, R. B. Terry, and P. D. Wood. 1988. Dietary fat: carbohydrate ratio and obesity in middle-aged men. *American Journal of Clinical Nutrition, 47,* 995–1000; Miller, W. C., A. K. Lindeman, J. P. Wallace, and M. G. Niederpruem. 1990. Diet composition, energy intake, and exercise in relation to body fat in men and women. *American Journal of Clinical Nutrition, 52,* 426–430; Romieu, I., W. C. Willett, M. J. Stampfer, et al. 1988. Energy intake and other determinants of relative weight. *American Journal of Clinical Nutrition, 47,* 406–412; Tucker, L. A., and M. J. Kano. 1992. Dietary fat and body fat: A multivariate study of 205 adult females. *American Journal of Clinical Nutrition, 56,* 616–622.

2. Castellanos, V. H., and B. J. Rolls. 1997. Diet composition and the regulation of food intake and body weight. In S. Dalton, ed., *Overweight and Weight Management.* Gaithersburg, MD: Aspen. 254–283.

Chapter 7

Changing Your
Eating Behavior

To overcome disordered eating you must change both your eating behavior and your use of food and eating to manage emotions and stress. In chapter 6 you examined some of your past binge eating episodes and identified the antecedents that triggered these binges and the consequences that followed. Then you learned to use self-monitoring to gather data and better understand your overall eating behavior, including your current binge behavior. The next step is to normalize your eating pattern. This involves following a structured eating plan and eliminating the dieting behavior that is characteristic of disordered eating.

Dieting and Disordered Eating

Dieting means trying to exercise some type of control over what or how much is eaten, usually for the purpose of losing weight or changing certain health parameters such as cholesterol or blood pressure. Typically in an eating disorder, an elaborate system of rules governs what can or can't be eaten. Eating three meals a day, making healthy food choices most of the time, and keeping calorie intake in the moderate range is generally recognized as an ideal approach to managing eating behavior in a healthy way. Nevertheless, people undertake various dieting efforts that lead to disordered eating and create more problems than they solve.

Three problem dieting solutions are to avoid eating anything whenever possible, to severely limit calories, or to avoid eating certain foods or macronutrients. Protein, carbohydrate, and fat are called macronutrients because they are required in the greatest amount in the body. (Vitamins and minerals are termed micronutrients, because only small quantities are needed by the body.)

Avoiding Eating Entirely

Some people try to avoid eating as much as possible as a means of managing their weight. Sometimes they fast for a day or more because they are under the impression that fasting is good for their health. Others avoid eating for as long as possible during the day. About one in four bulimics and one in twenty of those with binge eating disorder diet this way, as compared to one in 100 in the general population. More often than not, fasting creates a condition of semi-starvation that produces physical and emotional pressures to eat, and excessive hunger from not eating all day often prompts a binge. Therefore, this approach to dieting is not advisable.

Restricting Calories

Another type of dieting involves restricting the overall amount of calories and trying to stay below a specific limit. For bulimics, this limit is often 1000 to 1200 calories per day. Low caloric intake often leads to fatigue, irritability, poor decision making, problems with concentration, malnourishment, and feelings of deprivation—all of which can trigger a binge. Some people who are seriously obese may undertake even stricter caloric limits. Those following a medically supervised liquid fast program may restrict their calories to 500 to 800 a day. Although this usually brings relatively rapid weight loss—much of which is fluid and muscle mass loss—ultimately severe caloric restriction must give way to healthy eating or the weight will be regained. Restricting calories is not a long-term solution to weight management.

Avoiding Certain Foods

Dieting that involves avoiding or eliminating certain foods or macronutrients presents other problems. Many dieters declare certain foods to be "forbidden." Often these foods are sweets, such as ice cream and cookies, or they are foods perceived to be high in fat and calories—such as pizza. Declaring certain foods off-limits usually makes them more desirable, and when they are eaten, it is usually in larger-than-normal quantities.

Likewise, some people avoid or minimize consumption of a certain macronutrient to lose weight or to avoid gaining weight. One example is the recurring fad to blacklist carbohydrates. Every few decades a flurry of popular books is published touting the weigh-loss benefits of a high-fat or a high-protein diet, achieved by limiting carbohydrates in general or certain carbohydrates in particular. At other points in time, the latest diet trend shifts to some other avoidance strategy—e.g., avoiding white foods, avoiding mixing vegetables and fruits in the same meal, avoiding foods that "unbalance" the immune system, and so forth. None of these diets have adequate, scientific research to support them. Rather, healthy eating is obtained by eating a balanced diet in which 55 percent to 60 percent of calories come from complex carbohydrates (vegetables, whole grains, legumes), not more than 30 percent of calories from fat—with an emphasis on mono-unsaturated fats—and the balance of about 15 percent of calories from protein.

Alternatives to Dieting

Other ways used to reduce weight or eliminate calories include abusing laxatives or diuretics, using over-the-counter diet pills, or engaging in more exercise than is healthy.

Laxatives and Diuretics

The trouble with laxatives and diuretics is that they reduce fluid in the body, not fat. By the time food reaches the large intestine, it is too late to significantly reduce the amount of calories ingested. Most of the calories are extracted in the small intestine. Although a few calories are lost in the feces, for the most part all laxatives do is disrupt the system and set the stage for possibly serious health problems later. Laxatives cause decreased gastrointestinal motility, which makes it difficult to function properly without them.

Over-the-Counter Diet Pills

Over-the-counter diet pills were discussed in chapter 1 in the section called "Ineffective Medications." In addition to the drawbacks mentioned earlier, diet pills aimed at reducing appetite don't help much because overeating is frequently not prompted by hunger. In many cases, stress and negative emotions prompt overeating. Side effects of diet pills include headache, anxiety, and irritability. Your best bet is to avoid these alternatives.

Excessive Exercise

Although excessive exercise does burn calories and produce weight loss, it also increases the risk of injury, breaks down the body's health, and negatively impacts the exerciser's social relationships. Cardiovascular health is promoted by expending between 2000 and 3500 calories each week in aerobic exercise— jogging, swimming, bicycling, dancing, brisk walking, and so forth. This can be accomplished with thirty minutes of aerobic exercise a day six days a week, or sixty minutes a day, three days a week. Less strenuous exercise such as gardening or playing with the kids brings health benefits, if not weight loss, when engaged in only thirty minutes a day, five days a week. After 3500 calories are burned in a given week, the health benefits decrease and the risk of injury increases. Often excessive exercise is used as a form of purging unwanted calories, but although exercise is an important part of successful weight management and good health, excessive exercise can be harmful and should be avoided.

Legalizing Forbidden Foods

An important step in normalizing eating behavior is to "legalize" forbidden foods. If you are anorexic or bulimic, it is likely that there are only a small number of foods you feel comfortable eating. On the other hand, you probably have a long list of foods that you regard as "bad" or "forbidden." These are the foods you try to avoid, but if you do eat a food from this list, it can trigger a binge. The paradox is that as soon as a feared food is placed off-limits, it immediately becomes more desirable. It takes energy to be vigilant and guard against eating appealing foods, and if your guard slips, you may easily overindulge.

In chapter 6, you analyzed your Daily Eating Behavior Records and determined which foods are on your forbidden list. Take a moment now to write down all of the foods or types of food that you are afraid to eat or are forbidden for you. After listing all your forbidden foods, rate each one according to how much it is feared. Give a "High" rating to the most feared, a "Low" rating to the least feared, and a "Medium" to foods in between. Try not to give the same ranking to all of your forbidden foods.

Reclaiming Feared Foods

The best way to reclaim feared foods is to introduce them back into your eating plan a little at a time. Start with those with the lowest fear rating. Try to include one or two of these foods with your meals each week. Be sure to do so when you are not unduly stressed or overly hungry. The idea is to prove to yourself that you can eat a feared food in moderation and not have it automatically trigger a binge or cause you to gain weight. Keep in mind that you can always eat that food again on another day, and, therefore, it is not necessary to go overboard now.

Making Better Food Choices

Instead of instituting all-or-nothing, good/bad, forbidden/ allowed rules for food choices, it is better not to declare any foods off-limits but to categorize them along a more flexible continuum— one that allows you to eat any given food without guilt or fear.

To aid consumers in making healthy food choices, the U.S. Department of Agriculture and the U.S. Department of Health and Human Services has provided the "Food Pyramid" shown in Figure 7.1. The Food Pyramid illustrates which groups of food—those at the bottom of the pyramid—should make up most of your food choices, and which should be used sparingly—those at the top.

Based on this model, Table 7.1, "Making Better Food Choices," divides these same food groups into Anytime Choices, Sometime Choices, and Seldom Choices. As you can see, no foods are forbidden, but some foods are designated as best chosen less often than others.

Normalizing Eating

An important key for overcoming disordered eating is to "normalize" your eating pattern. That is, for success, it will be necessary for you to learn to eat in a way that is naturally healthy. By definition, disordered eating is an abnormal and unhealthy pattern that needs to be changed. Natural and healthy eating is regulated by feelings of hunger and satiety, but those with eating disorders no longer tune in to these internal signals, or they confuse them with

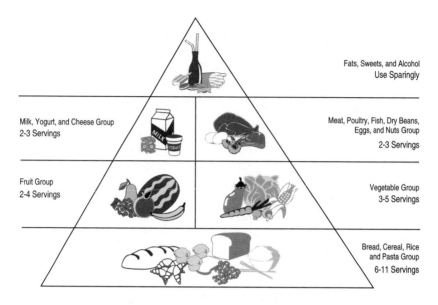

Source: U.S. Department of Argiculture/U.S. Department of Health and Human Services

Figure 7.1   Food Pyramid: A Guide to Daily Food Choices

other feelings. For example, they may interpret anxiety as hunger. Or they may confuse feeling full with being fat.

Misdirected Advice

Some diet books and articles tell you to "eat when you're are hungry and stop when you're full." This well-intentioned advice ignores the fact that the signals for hunger and satiety in those with an eating disorder are disturbed. Restrictive dieting, binge eating, and purging have so disrupted the normal mechanisms that control these sensations that they are no longer reliable guides. You must relearn how to identify these natural signals and learn how to distinguish them from other feeling states. This will occur over time as you maintain a structured plan of eating.

How to Normalize Eating

Normalizing your eating pattern must be done in small steps. The first step is to decide what time each day you will eat

Table 7.1 Making Better Food Choices

Anytime Choices	*Sometime Choices*	*Seldom Choices*
Fats, Oils, and Sweets	**Fats, Oils, and Sweets**	**Fats, Oils, and Sweets**
(Minimize)	olive oil	bacon
Lean Protein	nuts, seeds	butter
	soft margarine	stick margarine
egg white	reduced fat	regular
most fish	mayonnaise	mayonnaise
legumes	**Protein**	**High-fat Protein**
skinless breast of chicken or turkey	most beef	spareribs
beans, lentils	lamb	ground pork
Nonfat Dairy	veal	sandwich meats
	fried fish	hot dogs
skim milk	tofu	sausage
plain nonfat yogurt	whole egg	peanut butter
evaporated skim milk	**Low-fat Dairy**	**Regular Dairy**
nonfat buttermilk	2% milk	whole milk
nonfat cheeses	plain low-fat yogurt	plain yogurt
Fruit, fresh or frozen	sweet acidophilus	goat's milk
	low-fat cheese	cheese
(All)	**Fruit**	**Fruit**
Vegetables, fresh or frozen	apple chips	chocolate-
	cranberry sauce	dipped fruit
(All)	juices	**Vegetables**
Whole grains and cereals	fruit drinks	in sauce
	dried fruit	deep fried
whole wheat bread	**Vegetables**	**Grains and Cereals**
whole wheat pasta	avocado	
brown rice	cole slaw	pies
oatmeal	potato salad	cakes
corn tortilla	potato chips	cookies
barley	french fries	donuts
buckwheat	**Grains and Cereals**	croissants
	muffins	Danish
	biscuits	bread stuffing
	granola	
	fried rice	
	tortilla chips	

Table 7.1 Making Better Food Choices—*Continued*

Food Category:	Servings per Day:	Typical Serving Size:
Fats, Oils, Sugar	Use sparingly	½ tablespoon oils or fats; 2 teaspoons of sugar
Protein	2-3	2-3 ounces cooked lean meat, poultry, fish (½ cup cooked dried beans or 1 egg counts as 1 ounce of lean meat)
Dairy	2-3	1 cup milk or yogurt; 1½ ounces natural cheese, 2 ounces processed cheese
Fruits	2-4	1 medium apple, banana, orange; ½ cup chopped, canned; ¾ cup juice; ¼ cup diced
Vegetables	3-5	½ cup cooked or chopped; 1 cup raw leafy; ¾ cup juice
Grains and cereals	6-11	1 slice of bread; 1 ounce ready-to-eat cereal; ½ cup cooked cereal, rice, or pasta

three meals and two or three planned snacks. You can decide each day what your times will be, and the times may vary from day to day. Or you can decide several days or a week in advance. Adjust your eating times to accommodate your commitments—as long as no more than three to four hours elapse between the times you eat. Once you establish your eating times, you should eat only during those times. Allow yourself only enough time to eat your meal or snack. A meal ordinarily should take no longer than thirty minutes to consume and a snack no more than fifteen minutes. Initially, don't worry about what you eat at each time period. Instead, focus on eating on a regular schedule. Later focus on making healthier food choices. Eat at the planned times, even if you don't feel hungry. Don't skip meals or planned snacks, and try not to eat at other times. If you do slip and eat at an unplanned time or you binge, just get back on track as soon as possible.

At first, this may seem to be impossible to do. Many people who have been used to restricting or who eat most of their calories in the late evening can't imagine eating breakfast. They aren't hungry in the morning, and even the thought of eating breakfast can be repulsive. If it seems too difficult to introduce a planned eating pattern all at once, begin by establishing parts of it. For example, you might begin by eating something small for breakfast and for lunch—just enough to develop the idea of eating at all at these times. Later, after this idea takes hold, you can increase the amount of what you eat or introduce more food choices.

Alternatively, begin by eating lunch, but don't worry about eating breakfast until eating lunch feels normal to you. After eating lunch becomes more comfortable, try eating something small for breakfast and gradually move toward eating a full breakfast. The important thing is to eliminate erratic eating and replace it with regular food intake. The list below summarizes the steps involved in introducing a pattern of regular eating.

Steps for Normalizing Your Eating

1. Establish set times for eating 3 meals a day and planned snacks.

2. Allow no more than 3–4 hours between eating episodes.

3. Initially focus on *when*, not on what you eat.

4. Don't skip meals.

5. Eat only planned snacks.

6. Get back on track as soon as possible if you slip.

7. After you are comfortable eating at pre-established times, begin to introduce healthier food choices.

8. Avoid dieting that involves restricting eating, restricting calories, or restricting specific foods or macronutrients.

Worries About Structured Eating

You may worry that, by adopting a structured eating plan, you will gain weight. You may feel that you are already struggling to keep your weight down and eating more will cause you to gain fat. Or you may be concerned that eating will cause you to feel bloated and uncomfortable. These worries may be especially troubling if, at present, you are severely restricting what and how much you eat.

In fact, eating regular meals and planned snacks will not cause you to get fat. You may even lose weight over time because you will be binge eating less, and binges typically contain large numbers of calories. Even if you purge after binge eating, you do not get rid of all the calories consumed in the binge. Replacing binge eating with regular, healthy eating will, in all likelihood, not increase the number of calories your body absorbs. In fact, eating regularly throughout the day actually improves metabolism and eliminates or reduces wide swings in blood sugar.

However, if you are anorexic or bulimic, eating normally can make you *feel* fat, at least initially. This is because you are not used to the feeling of food in your stomach. Furthermore, beginning to eat again can produce constipation because your system has not been processing food normally for some time. With time, you can overcome the anxiety that accompanies the feeling of food in your system, and eventually your body will adjust and be able to process food easily again.

If you suffer from binge eating disorder, you may have a different worry. Typically, obese binge eaters do not restrict what they eat. Their problem is that obese binge eaters give themselves free access to large amounts of highly palatable food. If you are an obese binge eater, having lots of good food around may provide a sense of security and comfort. The idea of not having lots of good foods available may cause some anxiety. When food and eating have functioned as your primary or only way of coping, not having food available to eat can make you feel vulnerable. Likewise, having been on many diets in the past, usually with poor results, the thought of imposing self-discipline, even if it only requires restricting eating to certain times of the day, is likely to be repugnant to you. If you have never had much success with setting limits on your eating, you may doubt that you can.

Success is built little by little. It is not necessary—or possible—to go from never limiting your eating to being perfect at such limiting. Take it one day at a time, one meal at a time. In a later chapter you will learn to use self-talk to manage anxiety and other emotions. Just tell yourself you'll do the best you can. Each time you succeed at some small goal, for example, limiting one evening's snacking to a predefined time, count that as a success and pat yourself on the back. Analyze what helped you succeed that time, and do more of what works. Keep your eye on the big picture, and don't get distracted by small slips. Remember that the road to success is always under construction.

To help offset any worries you may have about undertaking structured eating, remind yourself of the benefits, which include improved mood and decreased binge eating. This list summarizes the benefits of structured eating.

Benefits of Structured Eating

1. Regular intake of food eliminates hunger and decreases the likelihood of a hunger binge.

2. Because eating is limited to designated times, the likelihood of an opportunity binge, grazing, or unplanned snacking is reduced.

3. Those who avoid eating anything because they fear they will gain weight discover that moderate eating doesn't lead to obesity.

4. Regular eating decreases vulnerability to negative moods.

Coping with Cravings

A *craving* is an intense desire or longing for a particular substance. About 70 percent of bulimics attribute their binge eating to food cravings[1] and about 50 percent of obese binge eaters report cravings—usually for sugary foods.[2] Either hunger or dysphoric mood states can set off food cravings.[3]

When desire overpowers determination, you are in the grips of a food craving. Whether cravings are physiological or psychological is still subject to debate. The desire for sweet, rich foods results from the all-too-human drive for pleasure. It is true that specific body chemicals called opiates determine whether people perceive foods rich in fat and carbohydrates as pleasurable.

However, the psychological component in cravings is strong, and feeling deprived is often at the root. Cravings can be triggered by seeing or smelling the desired food—perhaps in a TV ad—and then thinking about how good something would taste. Or, just feeling hungry can prompt recollections of eating a good-tasting food. The more a person dwells on these thoughts and relives the earlier experience, the stronger the craving becomes. Thinking about eating something good creates a longing for doing it again. In the midst of negative emotions, eating suggests an escape, if only temporary, from the pain of anxiety, sadness, loneliness, or boredom. Food cravings need not lead to binge eating. You can manage cravings by implementing the following tips.

Avoid Becoming Hungry

By following a structured eating plan, you will reduce the likelihood of cravings resulting from hunger. Never go more than three to four hours without eating. Skipping meals intensifies hunger—and food cravings. Satisfy hunger by eating a variety of foods. Include snacks if you need them.

Don't Forbid Certain Foods

Forbidden foods set the stage for feeling deprived—and for a craving for exactly what you "shouldn't" eat. If you do succumb to a "bad" or "illegal" food, you are more likely to binge. Remember that *it is not the type of food but the quantities eaten that adds unwanted weight.* When it comes to weight, total calories count, no matter what their source. It's better to eat a wide range of foods, even an occasional high-fat, high-sugar choice, than to end up feeling deprived because you "can't" have something—which can trigger a craving.

Catch a Craving Early

A craving needs to be interrupted early on, before it gets out of control. You may unintentionally create a craving by seeing or smelling some highly palatable and desirable food, which starts you thinking about having something pleasurable to eat. Or you may start ruminating about a taste experience you have had in the past. If you were to continue thinking about that experience, you could easily become so aroused that your mouth would begin to water. At that point, resisting the craving may be very difficult.

Three techniques are helpful in catching a craving early and stopping it before it gets out of hand—leave or avoid the temptation arena, use thought stopping, and depress the sensory longing.

Leave or Avoid the Temptation Arena

If you should encounter a situation in which you see or smell attractive food, leave or change your course of action. If you are watching TV and an ad for attractive food comes on, switch the channel or leave the room. Go to the kitchen and drink a big glass or two of water or fix yourself some tea. If you walk by a sidewalk café and notice someone eating something interesting, cross the street, remind yourself that you will be eating at your regular time soon, and assure yourself that you too can eat something highly pleasurable at a planned time. Then refocus your thinking on something else. Don't walk through the food court at the mall. Ask the waiter not to bring butter to the table. Anticipate temptations and take action early.

Use Thought Stopping

Thought stopping involves noticing the beginnings of a craving and taking immediate action. As soon as a thought of some tempting food enters your head and you begin to ruminate, tell yourself, "No. Stop thinking about that. Think about something else." Then turn your attention to another topic—a project at work or a pleasant memory that doesn't involve food or eating. Some people even put a rubber band on their wrists and snap it hard or they pinch themselves to get their attention when they are telling themselves to think about something else. The sting of the band or the pinch helps interrupt the food image. You may even have to yell out loud to get your own attention. The key to thought stopping is to immediately turn your attention to another subject. It also helps to get busy on a project and to remind yourself of your long-range health goals.

Depress the Sensory Longing

Another way to make the thought or image of the tempting food item less compelling is to disrupt your own sense of taste or smell. Pop a strong mouth mint and suck on it. Gargle with strong mouthwash. Brush your teeth, or dab some cologne or strong smelling ointment under your nose. This creates competing sensations that make the thought of eating less compelling for a while.

Remember That Cravings Pass

Cravings peak and subside like waves in the ocean. You can "surf an urge" to eat by telling yourself to wait ten minutes before you eat and then decide. In the meantime, get busy doing something else. Urges to eat fade with time, especially if you distract yourself with an alternative activity. If you are following a structured eating plan, check to see how long before your next time to eat. Tell yourself something like, "It won't kill me to wait. I can handle it." Then drink a large glass of water and engage in an alternative activity. Talk yourself into waiting for the next meal or snack time by reminding yourself that cravings do pass and you will be eating again soon.

Have Alternative Activities at the Ready

To help you avoid eating between your planned meals and snacks, you will find it useful to have a range of alternative activities in which you can engage. These might include taking a walk, taking a shower or a bath, calling a friend, playing music, cleaning a closet, or any activity that interests you and can distract you from thoughts of food or eating.

Indulge a Craving with Moderation

If you still feel the urge to eat after delaying and distracting yourself, allow yourself to satisfy the craving, but do so in moderation. Use portion control and have a single scoop of ice cream, for instance, rather than a pint or two. You won't feel deprived and the measured portion is an improvement over the binge that could result if you take an all-or-none attitude toward managing cravings.

Give Up Guilt

Eating one brownie or an occasional ice cream cone won't make you fat, but huge servings of guilt can. Believing you've failed because you ate "just one" can trigger eating the entire ice cream carton. Rather than indulging in self-criticism and generating lots of guilt, remind yourself that eating a favorite food occasionally is not a sign of loss of control.

Use the Five D's

Craving and urges are best kept at bay by using the Five D's: *Delay* at least ten minutes before eating so that you do not impulsively give in to a craving. *Distract* yourself by doing something else that requires concentration. *Distance* yourself from the food or temptation—leave the room, avoid the food court at the mall. *Determine* how important it is for you to eat the food you crave and how much you really want it. Then *decide* what amount is reasonable and appropriate. Eat and enjoy it without guilt.

Tips For Preventing Binges

Although it is useful to have techniques at the ready for interrupting a craving, the best way to prevent a binge is to prevent or reduce the buildup of tension that initiates a binge. (See chapter 5 for a discussion of the tension-building stage in the anatomy of a binge.) One way to avoid tension buildup is to eat regularly throughout the day. This avoids the hunger and deprivation that triggers some binges. Similarly, legalizing forbidden foods removes the temptation to rebel by eating something bad and eliminates the need to be on guard lest a craving overpowers you. This list provides additional tips for preventing binges.

Tips for Preventing Binges

1. Never let yourself become overly hungry. Eat regularly throughout the day.

2. Legalize "forbidden" foods. To avoid feeling deprived, now and then allow yourself some of your highly desired foods.

3. Take time daily to nurture yourself—call friends, do something you enjoy.

4. Monitor your feelings. Problem solve if you can; talk to someone if you can't.

5. Anticipate and, when possible, avoid temptation or plan how to handle it.

6. Postpone the urge to eat for 10 minutes; then decide.

7. Temporarily "ruin" your taste buds—brush your teeth, use mouthwash, or chew a mint.

8. Remind yourself that you have a choice; tell yourself what to do.

9. Don't listen to those internal voices that criticize, worry, or demand.

10. Anticipate situations that make a binge more likely. Avoid them or plan how to handle them better.

Using Self-Reward

As noted in chapter 6, the consequences that follow behavior influence the likelihood that the behavior will be repeated in the future. If the immediate consequences are rewarding, the behavior is likely to happen again. If they are unpleasant, the likelihood of that behavior occurring again is reduced. For example, if eating food made you feel fat, you will try to avoid eating much food in the future. Alternatively, if eating some cookies helped you feel less anxious, cookie eating is likely to happen again whenever you feel stressed.

Rewarding Good Behavior

The best way to increase desirable behavior is to reward it. Simply noticing and commenting on good behavior can be very reinforcing. Attention and approval are rewarding consequences that increase the likelihood that desirable behavior will be repeated. Therefore, giving yourself a mental pat on the back each time you eat at a pre-planned time on your structured eating schedule increases your self-confidence and motivation to continue.

A systematic way of rewarding structured eating involves using a calendar that shows one month at a time. Each time you complete a day in which you ate on your planned schedule, put a metallic star or other colorful sticker onto the square for that day. The star symbolizes your success for that day. Try to get a star as often as possible. Not only is getting a star rewarding, the absence of stars lets you know that you are off-track and need to renew your efforts to normalize eating. This same method can be used to reward yourself for other kinds of behavior such as exercising or making healthy food choices. Be sure to reward behavior and not outcome—i.e., weight loss.

The advantage of the "calendar and stars" method of self-reward just described is that it provides *immediate* reinforcement, which is the most powerful kind. Some people try to use delayed rewards, such as promising themselves they will go to the theater, take a class, or buy something they want once they reach certain benchmarks. Although this can sometimes work, it can backfire. If the benchmark is not reached at the expected time, you may feel punished and deprived because you didn't earn your reward, and you may slip into self-blame. It is much better to reward good behavior as soon as possible after it occurs and to avoid the possibility of feeling punished.

It is also important that the reward *follows* the behavior. It doesn't help to buy yourself fresh flowers this afternoon on the promise that you will exercise this evening, because you might not do the exercise. Of course, treating yourself to fresh flowers is a good way of self-nurturing that can be used without tying it to performance. Technically, this is not self-reward but rather self-nurturing, which is also important in overcoming disordered eating.

Ultimately, the most important reinforcement results from noticing your own accomplishments—for example, getting through a day without binge eating or doing thirty minutes of exercise today—and mentally complimenting yourself. When you give yourself credit for making progress toward your goals, even if that progress is in small steps, your motivation to persevere increases, as does your self-esteem.

Shaping Behavior

Sometimes it is difficult to initiate a new behavior—such as eating at structured times. The solution is to *shape* behavior. This is the method described earlier for introducing structured eating when you have not been used to eating breakfast or lunch. Rewarding successive approximations shapes behavior. The obese binge eater who has been a couch potato all of her life is likely to find it hard to make regular, aerobic exercise a natural feeling part of her life. She must begin by rewarding any small steps that take her closer to her desired behavior pattern. For example, she could give herself a pat on the back and a star for doing a ten-minute walk each day. However, to earn a star after a few weeks have passed, she should increase her goal to a daily fifteen-minute walk. As exercise becomes easier and more rewarding, using the stars as a method of self-reward may no longer be necessary, but many people continue to find it fun and useful.

The Perfectionism Trap

If you tend to be a perfectionist, you may have difficulty rewarding yourself for anything but perfect behavior or a "big" success. Perfectionists set high and often unrealistic goals for themselves and demand that they meet them 100 percent. The way to use self-reward successfully is to choose reachable goals. Create a series of steps that will take you to your goal that are just big enough to be challenging but not so big that they can't be accomplished easily. Then find every opportunity to reward yourself for accomplishing each step.

Making Self-Reward Work

To make self-reward work, you must be willing to play a game with yourself. After all, you are the one who creates the rules, and you must be willing to follow them. Be sure that whatever you choose as a reward is valued by you and readily available. There is no point in planning to reward yourself with a new car if you can't afford it.

This list summarizes the principles for using self-reward to encourage new and more desirable behavior patterns.

Principles for Using Self-Reward

1. Establish realistic, reachable goals for behavior; avoid the perfectionism trap.

2. Reward yourself for behavior, not outcome.

3. To shape behavior, reward behaviors that approximate the ultimate goal.

4. Reward rather than punish.

5. Rewards should be valued and readily available.

6. Be willing to make rewarding yourself a game and stick to the rules.

7. Each time you earn a reward, mentally congratulate yourself.

Notes

1. Mitchell, J. E., D. Hatsukami, E. D. Eckert, and R. L. Pyle. 1985. Characteristics of 275 patients with bulimia. *American Journal of Psychiatry, 142,* 482–485.

2. Bjorvell, H., S. Ronnberg, and S. Rossner. 1985. Eating patterns described by a group of treatment-seeking overweight women and normal weight women. *Scandinavian Journal of Behavior Therapy, 14,* 147–156.

3. Weingarten, H. P., and D. Elston. 1990. The phenomenology of food cravings. *Appetite, 15,* 231–246.

Chapter 8

Challenging Problem Thinking

Have you ever noticed that little voice in your head, the one that keeps commenting on this or that? You know, the one that just said, "What little voice?" That internal voice is part of your thinking process. Simply put, human beings think by talking to themselves, usually silently, but sometimes out loud. For example, have you ever found yourself saying aloud, "Now where did I put those keys? They should have been right here!" Or, have you heard yourself think, "How dare she do that. It's not fair!" That's self-talk—the voice in your head.

When you think, in addition to engaging in self-talk, you draw upon your system of beliefs, attitudes, values, and assumptions to make sense of the world. By focusing your attention on one thing and not another, you select the information inputs to your thinking. You have a store of knowledge that you acquire over the course of your life, and these facts, as well as your implicit assumptions about things, come into play as you try to understand the world around you.

For example, one person may conclude that capital punishment is wrong (a personal conclusion or attitude) by referring to one set of religious teachings (an external belief system) and her personal values (personally held beliefs) that proscribe the death penalty. Yet another person may focus on (attend to) the trauma he observes victims and their families suffer as the result of crime (an observation) and conclude that capital punishment is right and just (a conclusion or belief).

How Thinking Influences Feelings

How you understand an event or a situation influences how you feel about it. As you begin to take your feelings into account, your thinking about the situation can change and your feelings can escalate (intensify). In other words, how you think about something can elicit emotions that then color your understanding of events. The person who does not believe in capital punishment may become upset and angry when a defendant is sentenced to die, while the person who thinks the death penalty is just is likely to feel satisfied that justice is served.

As a different example, if you think that your friend forgot your birthday because you didn't receive a card or a phone call, you might feel hurt or angry. The more you think about how nice you are to her and the more you wonder why couldn't she remember your birthday, the more upset you may become. If later, you hear from your friend that the card she sent was returned for lack of postage, and she only found out about it after returning from a business trip, your hurt and anger are likely to dissipate.

Feelings as Another Way of Knowing

Although thinking influences feelings, emotions can seem to operate as a separate system of understanding that is independent of thinking. Sometimes emotions seem automatic—they just happen, with apparently little or no conscious thought occurring. You may feel uneasy about a particular course of action but be unable to explain why. Some people speak of "the hair on the back of the neck standing up" as an automatic emotional response to threat. In such a case, your emotional sensing system is sending out alarms. Later you may construct a rationale for your alarm.

One woman explained that her intuition told her that to be alone with a particular man would be dangerous. Initially, she couldn't explain exactly why, but in thinking about it later, she remembered that his menacing posture and darting eyes had told her she needed to be careful. Her feelings—intuition—had guided her. Her ability to fully articulate her rationale followed her intuition.

Thoughts, Feelings, and Behavior

Thinking influences feelings, and feelings influence thinking. Which comes first depends on the point at which you observe the sequence. Although, theoretically, emotion and cognition are separable, in nature they are almost always fused. Some experts[1] argue that *cognitive appraisal* (the process of giving meaning to or determining the significance of an event) underlies and is an integral feature of essentially all emotional states. Even when the emotional response is instantaneous and nonreflective, cognitive appraisal is operating at some level. Of course, once emotions have been generated they can affect the appraisal process.

Cognitive appraisal is a continuous process that is often based on partial cues rather than on complete information. When this is so, it may be difficult to articulate a rationale, thus making it seem that emotions precede thinking, when, in fact, both thinking and feeling are united in an ongoing process of monitoring the environment, selecting information to attend to, and giving meaning to events.

Both thinking and feeling influence behavior. How you understand and interpret an event in great part colors how you feel about it, and how you feel about it affects the event's meaning for you. As a result, both affect how you act. In the example of two people with different beliefs about capital punishment, each one had a different reaction to a criminal being given the death sentence. Given their different opinions and emotional reactions to this situation, they are very likely to behave differently as a result of their thoughts and feelings. One might participate in a vigil the night of the execution to protest, while the other might write a letter to the editor of his local paper expressing his approval. In the case of the missed birthday card, you might have told your friend that you were upset she forgot your birthday, but when you learned the card had been sent but not received, you may have apologized for initially being angry.

If you want to change behavior, you need to identify and change your automatic thoughts and feelings. You need to fight back against negative self-talk, and develop healthier and more supportive ways of thinking—not just about food and eating, but just as importantly, about yourself. You also need to develop skills for regulating emotions. Those skills are considered in depth in chapter 10.

Changing Thinking to Change Emotions

It is important to pay attention to feelings without allowing them to overwhelm your ability to cope. Feelings provide needed information for survival. However, sometimes feelings alone are not entirely reliable indicators, and you must assess how you are thinking about the situation. When you have a strong feeling, ask yourself whether the meaning or significance you are giving to the event is causing you to feel this way. Is there reasonable evidence that your feelings are giving you accurate information, or do you need to examine the situation more closely? You may be making cognitive errors that are creating strong but misleading feelings.

Cognitive Errors

Sometimes feelings result from problematic thinking. That is, you may be making errors in your thinking without realizing it. Cognition is another word for thinking, and cognition involves not only *what* you think, but also *how* you think. Cognitive errors are ways of thinking about and perceiving the world that are out of proportion with reality. People with eating disorders frequently make one common cognitive error called dichotomous or perfectionistic thinking. Other cognitive errors include emotional thinking, overgeneralization, catastrophizing, mind reading, and engaging in self-fulfilling prophecy.

Dichotomous Thinking

This type of cognitive error is also known as all-or-nothing thinking, black-and-white thinking, and perfectionistic thinking. Something is either good or bad, okay or forbidden, a success or a total failure. There is no middle ground, no shades of gray. Typically, in this kind of thinking, you hold yourself (and often others) to high standards, and you feel devastated if you fall even a little short of those standards. Even one bite of something forbidden signals total failure. A small indiscretion means total loss of control and abandoning all further efforts. When failure is perceived, self-criticism and self-blame follow. All-or-nothing thinking is a serious hazard for triggering an eating binge and disordered eating.

Emotional Thinking

Emotional thinking is another cognitive error typical of those with an eating disorder. Emotional thinking does not take into account any evidence to the contrary. It relies only on feelings. "If I feel fat, I must be fat." "I feel really bad; that means I'm fat." Emotional thinking is at the core of "body thoughts"—the tendencies to interpret any negative feeling as meaning that you are fat or ugly.

Overgeneralization

In this type of thinking, the meaning of a single event is applied too broadly. Words that designate extremes are tip-offs to this type of cognitive error: words such as "always" and "never," "everyone" and "no one." For example, one lapse in appropriate eating may lead to the conclusion, "I always overeat." If someone criticizes your appearance, you conclude, "Everyone thinks I'm fat." Having a less productive day at work prompts the thought, "They will fire me."

Catastrophizing

Catastrophizing thinking foresees disaster at every turn. This type of thinking embellishes a situation with surplus meaning that isn't supported by objective evidence. The prototypical catastrophizing thought begins with "What if ..." "What if I gain weight?" "What if I fail?" Overeating leads to the conclusion, "If I don't purge, I'll become obese."

Mind Reading

Mind reading means believing that you know what other people are thinking or feeling, and then acting as if this were fact. Examples include: "She thinks I'm fat." "They look at me and think that I'm awful." "He wants me to lose weight." "Everyone is staring at me and thinking I'm fat."

Self-fulfilling Prophecy

Having a negative expectation for the outcome of an event often leads to acting in ways that ensure it will come to pass. This is a self-fulfilling prophecy. Expecting that you cannot control your eating ensures that you won't even try. Concluding that you can't stick to a weight management program means that you probably won't.

Disputing the Evidence

When negative thoughts appear, before assuming they are accurate descriptions of reality, examine and, if necessary, dispute the evidence. What is the evidence that supports your thinking? What is the evidence that argues against your conclusion? For example, one woman frequently became distressed when the thought occurred to her that she had wasted time on the job and not worked productively. The more she thought about her shortcomings in this regard, the more upset and depressed she became. She had to learn to ask herself, "Who has complained about my job performance?" When the answer was, "No one," she then asked herself, "What is the feedback I am getting from my supervisor about my work?" She realized that her supervisor was usually pleased with her performance. Of course, the next question was, "Why am I really so upset?" The answer helped her define the real problem and helped her focus on finding a solution.

Use the following form to help you identify and change your problem thoughts. Use additional forms for each separate problem thought.

Worksheet for Disputing the Evidence

Initial thought: _____

_____

_____

Evidence supporting this thought: _____

_____

_____

Evidence that casts doubt on this thought: _____

_____

_____

Logical conclusion: _____

_____

_____

Self-Talk as Internal Voices

Avoiding cognitive errors or recognizing and correcting them will help to minimize negative emotions. Another way of minimizing negative feelings is to change your self-talk. Self-talk has also been called the "inner dialogue," "automatic thoughts," "verbal thinking," and "stream of consciousness." As stated above, another way to think about self-talk is that it is like an internal voice; and, often there is more than one voice. Under certain conditions, these voices or streams of thought may actually seem to argue with one another. Some people call this "the Committee." People in Twelve-Step programs are generally quite familiar with the Committee and experience it as conflicting thoughts, some of which advocate one way of understanding or acting and others that disagree. All of us have internal voices, but some people worry about what it means to hear their internal voices.

Some people ask, "Don't just crazy people hear voices?" Actually, no. Everyone hears voices in their heads. The difference between the mentally ill and sane people who hear these voices, is that the mentally ill don't realize that the voices belong to them. They think someone has invaded their body, is inserting thoughts into their head, or is whispering behind their back. Learning to notice and identify the voices in your head and to argue back can help you fend off negative emotions and cope better with the problems in your life.

Where Voices Come From

In chapter 4, you learned about how the family and early experiences with caregivers contribute to the formation of our "internal working models" of self and others. That is, you learn what to expect from others and what they expect from you by the way you are treated when you are very young, and these expectations shape who you become, your sense of self, and how you think. What you hear said around you and to you becomes internalized and integrated into your own way of thinking and behaving. Thus, the child who is repeatedly told that she is frail and sickly, and is treated as if she can't manage herself, comes to see herself that way and acts accordingly. Conversely, the child who is told, "You can do it. Get out there and fight for what you want. No one gives you anything. You have to work for what you want," develops a strong work ethic coupled with a fierce independence. How parents and significant others treat a person shapes his or her self-concept.

You internalize the voices of parents and caretakers, and eventually their voices become your own. If a parent is critical, you develop a critical voice. If a parent defers to others and is meek and unassertive, you may develop a caretaker voice. A parent who worries constantly and is fearful can be the source of a worrier voice. The attitudes and concerns of parents and caretakers are internalized by the child and become integrated as the child's own internal voices.

Identifying Your Inner Voices

Most people have more than one internal voice, and it is often possible to name each one based on the kind of things the voice says. The internal voices are all the more compelling when they speak in the first person. In some cases, the internal voice feels as though it has its own consciousness. Some of these voices include The Critic, The Excuse-Maker, The Worrier, The Caretaker, The Victim, The Enforcer, and The Voice of Negativity.

The Critic

The Critic is judgmental, faultfinding, and critical. At times, it may sound like a scolding parent, pointing out your faults and commenting on your shortcomings. It may discount your achievements, attributing your successes to luck, timing, or an accident of fate. The Critic warns you not to feel too pleased with yourself. It is highly moralistic and demanding, and prone to saying things like, "There must be something wrong with you that you're not losing weight." "If it weren't for you, everyone would be a lot happier." "Who do you think you are to complain about being hungry; get off it."

The Critic steals your self-confidence, undermines your self-esteem, and makes you feel demoralized. It promotes shame and guilt. The Critic can cause you to procrastinate or give up your efforts prematurely. At its worst, The Critic can create or exacerbate depression by saying, in essence, "It's you who is the problem. What's wrong with you affects everything you do. Nothing is ever going to change."

The Critic's judgments may extend to others as well, finding faults with their behaviors, ideas, and accomplishments. The Critic may become judgmental of other members of a support group or of a helping professional. "Why do they keep coming to meetings; they aren't losing any weight." "I can't stand the counselor's voice." "She doesn't know what she's talking about."

The Excuse-Maker

The Excuse-Maker develops to help you cope with The Critic. It defends you against the Critic's attacks. "Yes, but . . ." says The Excuse Maker. It too undermines motivation, hinders coping behavior, and is self-defeating, but it works differently from The Critic. The Excuse-Maker says things like, "With my schedule, it's impossible to eat right." "I deserve a little treat now and then." "No one will see me now, so why not?" "I've already blown it, so why not eat what I want to eat."

The Excuse-Maker promotes procrastination with thoughts like "I'll start tomorrow" and "I'm not ready yet." It creates demoralization by thinking, "I've tried before and failed, so why should things be different now?" "No one else really cares, so why try?" The Excuse-Maker shifts blame. "If he didn't keep bringing me candy, I could stick to my diet."

The Worrier

The Worrier is fearful and anxious. It catastrophizes. "What if . . ." is at the core of many of its pronouncements. "What if I gain weight." "What if I don't lose weight for my vacation." "What if they don't like my work." "What if I get fired." "What if I say something stupid." "What if I have a panic attack." By voicing catastrophizing thoughts and worrying about "what if," your Worrier can make you feel upset, anxious, fearful, inadequate, and even panic stricken at times.

Sometimes, The Worrier uses "domino thinking." One thought or event leads to another, like a line of dominos falling. One small slip or problem leads to another and then another, until there is a major catastrophe. One woman with bulimia put it this way. "If I overeat and don't purge, I'll get fat. If I get fat, everyone will see that I'm incompetent. Then I'll lose my job. I won't be able to pay the rent. I'll be out on the street. I have to purge."

The Worrier is hypersensitive to threat, real or imagined, and is often fearful of being ridiculed or shamed. It expects others to be critical and disapproving, and it fears being the target of disapproval, criticism, and rejection. The Worrier compares you and your performance to that of others and worries that you don't measure up. As a result, The Worrier can make you avoid situations in which you think someone will find fault with you or criticize you.

The Caretaker

Most women have a strong Caretaker voice. The Caretaker gives relationships first priority, values nurturing others, and focuses on meeting their needs, often at the expense of her own. The Caretaker tells you that you have no right to put your own needs first—indeed, you shouldn't even have needs—because you are a mother (wife, daughter, friend, etc.). The Caretaker says things like, "I can't ask my children and my family to change their way of eating for me." "It's not right to make others suffer because I need to lose weight." "It's not polite to ask that the hostess cook something on my diet."

The Caretaker tells you that you must be mindful of other people's feelings and take care not to hurt or disappoint them, even if that means you are the one who gets hurt or disappointed. As a result, you may avoid being assertive, even when assertiveness is called for. The Caretaker seeks the approval of others by being nice, polite, agreeable, and undemanding. The Caretaker tells you that you will be liked and loved if you defer to others. When you heed The Caretaker's demands without reservation, you can end up feeling needy and nurturing yourself with food and overeating.

The Victim

The Victim says, "Poor me, why can't I be normal." "It's not fair that others can eat what they want and I can't." "I don't have what it takes to stop binge eating." "People are bored with my eating problems." The Victim dwells on thoughts of being treated unfairly by others or by fate. As a result of listening to the Victim voice, you end up feeling powerless to help yourself.

Sometimes the Victim voice changes from a needy and victimized supplicant to a righteous and angry avenger of past mistreatment. Peter (see chapter 1) saw himself as the victim of his own body's betrayal, and punished himself repeatedly with angry binges. Peter's Victim voice said things like, "I hate myself. I can't control my eating. I'm disgusting. I have a lousy family and a lousy life. What's the point of it all?"

The Enforcer

The Enforcer is a terrible taskmaster. It has a penchant for orderliness, perfectionism, and rigid control. The Enforcer maintains a sense of control by demanding that you pay attention to rules, details, procedures, lists, and schedules. It urges you to set high performance standards for yourself, and work tirelessly toward meeting them, often at the expense of relaxing or having fun. The Enforcer says, "I'm going to exercise every day." "Never again will I touch a chocolate chip cookie." "From now on, I'm not going to overeat." The Enforcer engages in all-or-nothing thinking and tells you that you "should" be perfect in all that you do. It tells you to do more, even when you are already doing too much.

The Enforcer can be self-righteous and inflexible in matters of morals, ethics, or values. In Renee's story, which was told in chapter 3, her Enforcer voice told her that she had to get up every morning to swim and run the highest hills. Doing so made her "special" and "better" than those who were still sleeping in their beds.

The Voice of Negativity

This is the voice that tells you how bad you are, how ugly you are, and how hopeless you are. Although it sounds like The Critic, Negativity focuses exclusively on you—your weight, your shape, your appearance, your future, and your life. It discounts your accomplishments and tells you that you are worthless and undeserving of living. Negativity is often the voice of anorexia. Dora had a particularly nasty Negativity voice.

Dora. At 145 pounds and 5 feet, 10 inches tall, with long blonde hair and green eyes, Dora was strikingly attractive. But she declared, "I'm fat and I'm ugly. I hate my hair. My nose is crooked. My thighs are too big, and I look terrible. It was just a fluke that I graduated from law school and I'll never be a good lawyer. I don't have what it takes. No one could possibly find me attractive and I'm going to be alone for the rest of my life. The only thing that helps me feel any better is my running." Dora is an exercising anorexic who is also seriously depressed.

The Voice of an Eating Disorder

For the person with an eating disorder, there may even be a separate voice that characterizes the thoughts of the eating disorder itself. Sandy provided a good example of this voice.

Sandy. "Anorexia tells me I am nothing without it. I am empty and worthless. Anorexia says it is the only thing that gives my life meaning." At thirty-five, Sandy had been suffering from anorexia since she was a teenager. She spoke of her eating disorder as if it were another entity, but one from which she could not escape. "When I get hungry, Anorexia tells me I'm just whining. It says I have nothing to complain about. I'm just being weak."

Another woman provided another example. "Bulimia gives me something to share. When I meet someone, I can usually tell if she is bulimic too. That gives us something to talk about. We share a special secret that no one else understands. If I didn't have bulimia, I don't know how I could relate to other people."

Still another woman acknowledged that she didn't really want to give up bingeing and purging. This was her "special time" when she indulged herself, and she wasn't convinced that bulimia was all that bad. Only upon closer examination did she realize that this was the Voice of Bulimia talking to her. Her healthy voice reminded her that bulimia was damaging her relationship with her husband, costing money that could be better spent on other things, causing sore throats and swollen glands, and in the long run, jeopardizing her health and the well-being of the children she hoped to have.

Taking Control of Your Self-Talk

Generally speaking, self-talk can be either negative or positive. Negative self-talk is any kind of self-talk or inner voice that keeps you from being happy in life. It is ultimately self-defeating. Negative self-talk can make already painful emotions worse, undermine resolve, and destroy motivation.

In contrast, positive self-talk is a coping thought that facilitates achievement of healthy goals which increase the probability of obtaining greater satisfaction in life. Positive self-talk is characterized by a flexible, accepting attitude toward yourself and others. It focuses on small successes, not just big ones, as in, "This week I increased my walking from ten minutes a day to fifteen." Positive self-talk involves making even-handed evaluations such as, "Overall it was a good week even though I had a few small slips."

Positive self-talk also reflects a problem-solving approach. It helps you to focus on what needs to be done, and keeps you on track. Positive self-talk sometimes takes the form of an instruction, such as, "Don't buy that. If it's not in the house, you won't be tempted to eat it."

It is probably not possible, nor is it desirable, to eliminate all negative self-talk. Some negative self-talk is needed to keep you alert to threats and potential problems. The Critic and The Worrier voices have their place. Rather, it is the overall balance of negative to positive self-talk that matters.

Those with an eating disorder, as well as those with other problems such as depression and anxiety disorders, do too much negative self-talk. Ideally, the best mental health is achieved when there is twice as much positive self-talk as negative self-talk.

When negative self-talk outweighs positive self-talk, or when the voices of The Critic, The Excuse-Maker, The Worrier, The Caretaker, The Victim, The Enforcer, The Voice of Negativity, or The Voice of Eating Disorder are all that are being heard, steps must be taken to overcome this kind of problem thinking. This begins by developing awareness of your inner voices and self-talk.

Developing Awareness

The first step in taking control of self-talk is to develop a greater awareness of how you actually talk to yourself—of hearing which voices are the most salient in your thinking. A good way to begin is to keep a record of what you are saying to yourself, especially related to your eating behavior. One way to do this was introduced in chapter 6 when you used the Daily Eating Behavior Record to track your eating behavior and any associated thoughts and feelings. You should refer back to these records now to help you complete the following exercise. If you don't have these records, start keeping a diary or another record of your self-talk. Every time you look in the mirror, get dressed or undressed, or eat something, inspect your thoughts and listen in to your self-talk.

Using the following write-in lines, try to capture as best you can from your food records or your diary what each of your voices typically says to you related to food or eating. Be aware that not all voices may be present for you, and some are likely to be more prominent than others. After you have written down as much as you can of what your voices say to you, rate on a scale from 1 (very little influence) to 5 (great influence) how much influence each voice has on your feelings and your behavior related to weight and eating. In this way, you can identify the voices that make up your Committee (all of the voices in your head) and take the next step to fight back.

What My Voices Say to Me

The **Critic** says: _____

_____

_____

Very Little Influence   Some Influence   Great Influence
1   2   3   4   5

The **Excuse-Maker** says:

_____

_____

Very Little Influence   Some Influence   Great Influence
1   2   3   4   5

The **Worrier** says: _____

_____

_____

Very Little Influence   Some Influence   Great Influence
1   2   3   4   5

The **Caretaker** says: _____

_____

Very Little Influence   Some Influence   Great Influence
1   2   3   4   5

The **Victim** says: _____

_____

Very Little Influence   Some Influence   Great Influence
1   2   3   4   5

The **Enforcer** says: _____

_____

Very Little Influence   Some Influence   Great Influence
1   2   3   4   5

The **Voice of Negativity** says: _____

_____

Very Little Influence   Some Influence   Great Influence
1   2   3   4   5

The **Voice of My Eating Disorder** says: _____

_____

Very Little Influence   Some Influence   Great Influence
1   2   3   4   5

Programming a Positive Voice

After identifying the voices that make up your Committee, you need to fight back by programming a positive voice that will be on your side and bring some balance to The Committee. This voice is sometimes called the Wise Self voice, your Best Friend voice, or your Coach. If you have ever participated in a sport and had the benefit of a supportive coach, you will see that calling this voice the "Coach" is a particularly good analogy. A good coach is always on your side, never mean or disparaging, willing to show you how to improve, encouraging when things get rough, and able to guide and inspire. Sometimes a coach scolds—but always in a supportive and loving way. Whatever the name of your positive voice, it is supportive, while recognizing the downside. It listens to the rational part of you and at the same time it listens to and validates your emotions.

Characteristics of Positive Self-Talk

Consider the characteristics of positive self-talk that the Wise Self, the Best Friend, or the Coach might use. Positive self-talk reflects flexible thinking. It uses balanced comparisons and makes even-handed evaluations. For example, "Although I've had a few slips this week, for the most part I've succeeded in eating at my scheduled times." Flexible thinking gives credit without discounting or judging, and avoids putting too much emphasis on deviations. Positive self-talk advocates realistic and achievable goals, and maintains confidence and the will to persist. It provides directions for action, focusing on what to do and how to cope with a problem. Positive thinking includes pat-on-the-back thoughts for success, and focuses on accomplishments, progress, strengths, or good qualities. Failure is viewed as a learning experience. Positive self-talk promotes feeling good about yourself and a healthy sense of your own self-worth. Positive self-talk acknowledges and accepts painful feelings for what they are, without trying to talk you out of them. Positive self-talk is hopeful and reassuring, without discounting, disregarding, or invalidating difficulties.

Characteristics of Negative Self-Talk

Negative self-talk undermines self-confidence, depletes motivation, and promotes feelings of shame and guilt. It includes all-or-nothing thinking, perfectionistic goal setting, holding excessive expectations for yourself, and engaging in unflattering comparisons to others or to internal standards. Negative self-talk may reflect an unwillingness or fear of trying to set limits on yourself and to exercise self-discipline, or it may demand perfect self-control and adherence to unrealistically high standards for performance. When these standards are not met, negative self-talk becomes punishing. It engages in self-blame, self-denigration, and excessive self-criticism that demoralizes rather than empowers. Negative self-talk reinforces self-doubt and uses excuses and rationalizations to permit undesirable behaviors. The following list provides a comparison of the characteristics of positive and negative self-talk.

Characteristics of Positive and Negative Self-Talk

Positive Self-Talk	Negative Self-Talk
Builds self-confidence	Steals motivation
Balanced comparisons	All-or-none thinking
Even-handed evaluations	Extreme evaluations
Realistic goals	Perfectionistic goals
Gives instructions	Criticizes
Focuses on problem solving	Generates doubt
Sees failure as opportunity to learn	Attributes failure to self

Reminder Cards

One helpful way of programming the positive voice is to use reminder cards. On separate 5-x-7 index cards write a single positive thought, incorporating the characteristics for positive self-talk given in the list above. These positive thoughts should not be framed as aphorisms, which are short, concise statements of a principle or a general truth such as, "I have much to be thankful for," or "Every day in every way I am getting better and better." Unfortunately, such platitudes are not very helpful because they are often hard to believe. Rather, the positive thoughts that you record should be rebuttals to the negative self-talk used by your Committee.

One person created the following positive statements: "You have finished projects you didn't think you could." (This was a rebuttal to her Critic, which often reminded her that she "never" finished anything.) "Being with friends can be helpful." (She needed a reminder to reach out to friends when she felt over-whelmed.) "Take things one meal at a time." (This thought instructed her to stay focused on immediate choices and not to worry about the future.) "Remember, you no longer eat in the middle of the night." (This pat-on-the-back thought was a reminder of a specific and important accomplishment.)

Begin by creating a few reminder cards. Be sure to put only one thought on a card. Keep the thought as short as possible and positive. Avoid the use of negatives and "don'ts." These positive thoughts should be motivational, inspirational, and believable. Once you have a few cards, keep them in a handy place—your purse or book bag. Every opportunity you get, take out your stack of reminder cards, which can be held together with a rubber band. Read the top card, then move it to the back of the stack. Think about and meditate on the positive thought you have just read.

For example, on getting into your car to drive to or from work, read the top card in your stack. Put the rest away, and while driving, think about what that positive thought means to you. Remind yourself that this is a thought from your positive voice—the real you. Even though the voices of the Committee are your voices too, they say things that don't nurture the real you. The reason for programming a positive voice is to give the real you a chance. The following list provides guidelines for creating reminder cards.

Guidelines for Creating Reminder Cards

1. Write only one thought on a card.
2. Keep the thought short and concise.
3. Be sure the thought is believable.
4. Avoid the use of negatives such as "don't."
5. Create some thoughts that instruct you on how to cope.
6. Create other thoughts that remind you of successes.
7. Assert your personal rights in some thoughts.
8. Add new cards to your stack as often as possible.
9. Carry your stack of cards with you at all times.
10. Take every opportunity to review and think about a thought you have written.

Reducing Negative Thoughts

The objective is not to try to eliminate negative self-talk altogether, but rather to shift the amount to a smaller proportion. Being aware of your shortcomings, lapses, and the needs and feedback of others is useful. The key is to keep negative thinking from becoming overwhelming and disruptive to day-to-day coping. It helps to have some ways of coping with intrusive negative thoughts. The technique of thought stopping was discussed in chapter 7. It provides a means of eliminating from consciousness unwanted and upsetting thoughts or images. For example, one woman found herself ruminating about her appearance and how she didn't compare favorably to others. She needed a way to stop these thoughts from overwhelming her. At first she would say out loud to herself (and later silently think to herself), "No. Don't think about those thoughts. Think about something else." This was her signal to turn her attention to positive thoughts or to distract herself by focusing on different subject matter.

Note

1. Lazarus, R. S., and S. Folkman. 1984. *Stress, Appraisal, and Coping.* New York: Springer.

Chapter 9

Balancing Acceptance and Change

*God, give me the serenity to accept the things
I cannot change, the courage to change the things
I can, and the wisdom to know the difference.*

—Serenity Prayer
Anonymous

The need to find a balance between acceptance and change is a key tenet in recovery from substance abuse and from an eating disorder. This is not because an eating disorder is a progressive disease or because an eating disorder is the result of a spiritual deficit, as alcoholism is assumed to be. It is because there are indeed limits on what can be changed in terms of body shape and weight.[1]

Changes can and should be made in exercise, nutrition, and eating habits; and behaviors that make life more satisfying need to be increased. The latter includes improving skills for interpersonal functioning and for coping with life's inevitable challenges. However, there are limits to the changes that can be made to weight and shape.

Maintaining healthy eating and exercise habits will result in a body weight that is natural and appropriate for your body given your heredity. Shape can be influenced somewhat by weight training, but ultimately shape is also largely determined by genetic influences. Knowing when the limits to healthy change have been reached and learning to accept the results is one of the challenges that must be faced in overcoming an eating disorder.

The Importance of Body Weight and Shape

Excessive concern about body weight and shape is a defining feature of all eating disorders. Body image dissatisfaction and body disparagement are common among anorexics, bulimics, and those with binge eating disorder, as well as others who exhibit other kinds of disordered eating. This dissatisfaction can range from mild feelings of unattractiveness to extreme preoccupation with physical appearance that impairs functioning. Concerns about body weight are fostered in part by images of culturally defined ideal body types and partly by early experiences in the family and among peers. Abnormal attitudes about shape and weight lead to unhealthy dieting, binge eating, and purging.

Members of Beth's (see chapter 4) family criticized her weight and called her names like "Miss Piggy." Later her peers in junior high school also teased her about her shape. Convinced that she was fat and ugly because of a small bulge just above her waist line, she oscillated between stringent dieting and binge eating. Jillian (see chapter 2) was convinced she was ugly despite being strikingly beautiful. Always tall for her age, Jillian was taunted with names like "bean pole" and obliged to stand in the back of all group pictures. When she compared herself to the images of the petite women she saw in the media and all around her, she felt big and fat. Although always slim, Jillian became anorexic in her twenties, which provided her with a means of feeling special.

In addition to great dissatisfaction with body weight and shape, those with eating disorders exhibit a general lack of self-esteem and a tendency toward excessive self-criticism and self-denigration. They define their self-worth in terms of body shape and weight. In part, this may be because appearance, and especially weight, seem more controllable than other aspects of life.

In fact, body shape and weight are far less malleable than is popularly believed. Those with eating disorders often end up trying to change what cannot be changed significantly, and they ignore or avoid grappling with other aspects of their lives that can and should be changed but which may seem more overwhelming or too frightening to tackle. Thus, the preoccupation with weight and shape often serves to mask other psychological and interpersonal problems.

Anorexics severely restrict food intake and through self-starvation force their bodies to become emaciated and dangerously thin, or they exercise at self-destructive levels. Doing so provides a sense of control and a substitute for a fully realized self-identity.

Bulimics skip meals, avoid forbidden foods, and alternate between restricting and binge eating. Their binge/purge behavior serves primarily as a means of tension release, but their frequent failures in the struggle for self-control result in shame and self-blame.

Those with binge eating disorder frequently lose control and eat too much, or they give up efforts to control their eating at all. Eating helps to temporarily distract attention from distressing problems and associated negative emotions, but the resulting obesity brings guilt, shame, self-criticism, and self-blame.

For all of these eating disorders, a main goal of treatment is to establish a regular pattern of eating characterized by flexible rules, moderate caloric intake, and nutritionally sound food choices. Likewise, extreme exercise habits—either exercising too little or too much—need to be normalized and brought into the healthy range. To accomplish these goals, problematic thinking and behavior must be changed. Steps must also be taken to improve body image and reduce dissatisfaction with and lack of acceptance of physical appearance.

Acceptance and Change

The desire to be thinner is characteristic of those with an eating disorder. Both body weight and body shape are changeable only within strict limits usually defined by heredity. Once a pattern of flexible, healthy eating combined with sensible exercise has been adopted, the body will settle naturally to a weight which, at that point, is largely controlled by genes.

Similarly, the distribution of body fat is under powerful genetic control.[2] Women generally tend to accumulate body fat in the hips and thighs, and weight loss does not alter this pattern significantly. Increasingly cosmetic surgery is being sought as a means of altering genetically determined patterns of fat distribution, although this, too, has its limitations and potential hazards.[3]

What can change are your attitudes and behaviors regarding your weight and your shape. To effect such a change you begin by realizing that bodies come in a variety of shapes and sizes, and that being thin does not promise happiness. Don't let your body define who you are. Practice appreciating those parts of your body that you do like, and realize that those who are perfectly happy or content with every aspect of their appearance are very rare. Some body dissatisfaction is normal and such dissatisfaction need not cause undue unhappiness or lead to excessive efforts to change.

Explore other aspects of your personality that make you special and wonderful—your personal qualities (such as being a caring or honest person), your skills and capabilities, and your spiritual side. Rather than pursuing the "perfect" body or image, focus on developing your personal strengths and supportive interpersonal relationships. Remember that attractiveness comes from within; feeling better about yourself will affect how others view you. Find ways to pamper yourself—by getting massages, smoothing lotion on yourself, indulging in manicures and pedicures—and treat your body with the respect it deserves.

Be aware of your own prejudices and judgments about weight and appearance. Guard against judging or criticizing others, even if only in your own mind. When you are critical of others, you are likely to be critical of yourself as well. Remember that what society views as "beautiful" changes over time, and that pursuing this fleeting ideal is like chasing a rainbow. Although there are benefits to being beautiful, there is no pot of gold at the end.

The Benefits of Beauty

More and more people are dieting and trying to improve their appearance. A 1985 survey on body image that included 30,000 American adults found that 34 percent of men and 38 percent of women were generally dissatisfied with their looks, and these numbers are increasing daily.[4] By contrast, a similar study done in 1972 found that 15 percent of men and 23 percent of women were discontent with their appearance. Often there is no objective foundation for this dissatisfaction. The 1985 survey also found that 47 percent of women and 29 percent of men who were actually of normal weight felt that they were overweight.

Being physically attractive has significant personal and social rewards, especially for women. Looks do count, at least in initial encounters. A mountain of research evidence finds that physical attractiveness is important for both men and women. The "beautiful people" are seen as possessing a wide variety of positive personal qualities. They are assumed to be more sociable, outgoing, popular, likable, happy, confident, and well-adjusted. Attractive men are seen as more masculine, and attractive women as more feminine.

In addition, beautiful people generally are given preferential treatment on the basis of appearance alone. From preschool to adulthood, being attractive brings added benefits. Attractive babies are cuddled, kissed, and looked at more, and parents, teachers, and peers prefer attractive children. Attractive adolescents and young adults have more dates with the opposite sex and report greater satisfaction in social interactions. Even attractive criminals get off easier with more lenient sentences, and attractive mental patients get more therapy than unattractive ones. Thus there is truth to the conviction held by those with an eating disorder that body weight and shape do count importantly in society.

Obstacles to Acceptance

The reality that looks do count and that this society values a thinner, fitter body is one obstacle faced by those with an eating disorder to accepting the reality that they may not be able to force their bodies to fit society's ideal.

Another obstacle, however, is that those with eating disorders, unlike most other people, have only one standard for evaluating their self-worth—their appearance. Because they do not measure up, in their own eyes, on this single criterion, they see themselves as defective and less worthy. Their resulting low self-esteem either leads them to exert great efforts to achieve an ideal weight, or they give up in despair at any efforts at self-control.

Weight and shape come to be seen as either entirely under their personal control, or completely out of their control. This self-defeating belief becomes the fulcrum upon which life revolves. Weight and shape become issues of being in control or out of control—all or nothing. Finding a middle ground—the ground of self-acceptance—can be difficult.

This is especially true for anorexics, who may receive substantial social support for their thin appearance, at least in the early stages of the disorder. Friends envy their appearance, and even health professionals may compliment their success in managing their weight. By the time they reach dangerously low levels of weight, their perception of their body has become so distorted that they see them selves as fat, even though others are becoming alarmed by their appearance.

Body Image

Body image is the picture of the body as seen through the mind's eye. It consists of perceptions, images, thoughts, feelings, attitudes, emotions, and concepts about the body. Body image also includes the physical experiences of body posture, size, weight, volume, location in space, tactile and inner sensations, and the emotional significance of various body parts and the body as a whole.

A negative body image involves dissatisfaction with the body in general or some body part in particular, and this dissatisfaction causes significant psychological distress. Concern about some perceived defect in appearance can become so severe that it occupies a person's thinking much of the time, causes serious emotional distress, or interferes with relationships. Jillian, as mentioned previously, believed herself to be fat and ugly, even though others saw her as quite attractive. Although unwarranted on an objective basis, her distress about her appearance made Jillian depressed and anxious, and it interfered with her ability to create relationships.

How Body Image Develops and Changes

Influenced by interpersonal, environmental, and temporal factors, one's body image begins to emerge in infancy and continues to develop and change throughout the life cycle. Over time, each person organizes and constructs his or her body image through the integration of many perceptions and experiences over a lifetime. Body image becomes part of the internal working model of self that was mentioned in chapter 4.

Although body image continues to evolve throughout life, adolescence is a particularly difficult time. Adjusting to rapid physical changes and the accompanying impact of these changes on body image is a major psychological task. Surveys of young adolescents confirm high degrees of anxious body preoccupation and dissatisfaction—fertile ground for an eating disorder to develop. Generally, girls are more dissatisfied with their weight and shape than boys. The recent epidemic rise in eating disorder symptoms, which are associated with body image dissatisfaction, and the spread of dieting behavior into grade school indicates that body image is a great source of turmoil and a big stumbling block in adolescent development. At this point peer influences, such as teasing and critical comments about appearance, which may be aggravated by negative parental reactions to a teenager's physical changes, can foster body dissatisfaction and trigger dieting and eventually a full-blown eating disorder. Beth's story, told in chapter 4, is a good example of this. At fourteen, she was failing in school and had already attempted suicide because of her unhappiness with her appearance and her inability to curb her binge eating.

Body image is complex and dynamic. Although it usually reaches a level of stability by adulthood, small fluctuations and changes can and do occur over short periods of time. Even during a single day body image can vary. For example, after strenuous exercise a person may "feel thin" for a while and then, a few hours later, after eating a meal may feel "bloated and fat." This very often happens to anorexics who exercise, as well as to bulimics, who may interpret these temporary and natural fluctuations in body image as permanent or as signs of impending obesity. For the eating disordered person, the solution appears to be to lose weight.

The reality is that weight loss may bring a temporary reduction in anxiety, only to be followed by renewed body dissatisfaction and more anxiety. Losing weight does not necessarily guarantee a "normal" body image, even among obese individuals, and the available research evidence suggests that nonsurgical weight reduction is not an effective treatment for a negative body image.[5] Body image dissatisfaction is a problem independent of weight status. To improve body image—and overcome disordered eating—negative attitudes about body weight and shape, as well as self-defeating beliefs about self-worth, must be changed and the unalterable aspects of physical appearance must be accepted.

Changing Negative Body Thoughts

The first step in changing problem thinking that contributes to a negative body image is to understand what influences contributed to the development of your body image and what conclusions you made about yourself as a result of these influences.

Complete the following Body Image History form to help you identify these influences. For each of the periods listed, describe your body in terms of whether you were underweight, overweight, or normal for your age. Also describe other aspects of your shape and appearance—were you taller or shorter than most others your age, did you wear glasses, did you have crooked teeth or bad skin, did you develop earlier or later than others, or were there other characteristics that made you self-conscious? At that period, how did others treat you? Were you teased, criticized, or rejected because of your weight, shape, or appearance? Or did your appearance attract positive attention that made you uncomfortable? Did participating in a sport play a role in your feelings about yourself? What messages did you get about your body and your appearance? Finally, what conclusions did you reach about yourself?

Body Image History

Early Childhood (up to eight-years old)

Describe your body: _____

_____

_____

How did others treat you? _____

_____

_____

What messages did you get about your body or your appearance?

_____

_____

What conclusions did you make about yourself? _____

_____

_____

Later Childhood (age eight to twelve)

Describe your body: _____

_____

_____

How did others treat you? _____

_____

_____

What messages did you get about your body or your appearance?

_____

_____

What conclusions did you make about yourself? _____

_____

_____

Early Adolescence (age twelve to sixteen)

Describe your body: _____

_____

_____

How did others treat you? _____

_____

_____

What messages did you get about your body or your appearance?

_____

_____

What conclusions did you make about yourself? _____

_____

_____

Later Adolescence (age sixteen to twenty-one)

Describe your body: _____

_____

_____

How did others treat you? _____

_____

_____

What messages did you get about your body or your appearance?

_____

_____

What conclusions did you make about yourself? _____

_____

_____

Early Adulthood (age twenty-one to twenty-nine)

Describe your body: _____

_____

_____

How did others treat you? _____

_____

_____

What messages did you get about your body or your appearance?

_____

_____

What conclusions did you make about yourself? _____

_____

_____

Adulthood (Age thirty to your present age)

Describe your body: _____

_____

_____

How did others treat you? _____

_____

_____

What messages did you get about your body or your appearance?

_____

_____

What conclusions did you make about yourself? _____

_____

_____

During the Past Year

Describe your body: _____

_____

_____

How did/do others treat you? _____

_____

_____

What messages did/do you get about your body or your appearance?

_____

_____

What conclusions did/do you make about yourself? _____

_____

_____

After completing the Body Image History form, it should be evident to you what the influences were that helped to form your current body image as you were growing up. Your actual physical self at various stages, how others treated you at each stage, and the messages you got about yourself from others and society led you to certain conclusions about yourself. These conclusions helped form your body image. In order to feel better about yourself and your body now, you may need to challenge whether these conclusions are still warranted or change the decisions you originally made.

Body Talk and Avoidance Behaviors

In chapter 8 you learned that self-talk and your internal voices contribute to painful emotions. Some of your self-talk, especially that coming from The Critic, The Worrier, and The Voice of Negativity, relates to your appearance and promotes dissatisfaction with your body. Examples of negative body talk might be, "My rear end is disgusting." "They think I'm fat and ugly." "I hate my looks." "They're laughing at me." "I'll never be attractive." Some of the negative self-talk about appearance relates to self-worth, for example, "I'm so fat I'll never have a relationship," or "I'm too ugly to ever get married," and "No one can ever love me."

Such thoughts may prompt dieting efforts or they may lead to avoidance behaviors. You may start wearing baggy clothes so that others can't see your body, or you may avoid being with friends or entering into situations in which you might be subject to being scrutinized or receiving negative comments by others. In other cases, you may check your weight obsessively by getting on the scale several times a day. Or you may avoid mirrors whenever possible.

Renee (see chapter 3) was a twenty-four-year-old woman who exercised excessively, refused to eat in the presence of other people, and generally restricted her eating but sometimes succumbed to an eating binge. No one could discern Renee's shame or whether she was overweight, although her face and neck appeared tiny and delicate. That was because she wore layers of baggy clothing and skirts that went down to her ankles, revealing only her dark hose and heavy shoes. All that was visible were her small hands and head. Renee never looked in a mirror, wore no makeup, and arranged her hair without the benefit of seeing her reflection. She was so threatened by knowing her weight that her personal trainer weighed her backwards on the scale and did not tell her what she weighed.

Use the following worksheet to identify negative body thoughts and distressing situations that you are currently experiencing. You may wish to refer back to your Daily Eating Behavior Records for clues. Or, you could begin keeping a journal of these thoughts and situations as they occur.

Negative Body Thoughts
I often find myself saying the following about my body or my appearance:

_____

_____

_____

_____

_____

Distressing Situations
The following situations are distressing to me because of my appearance:

_____

_____

_____

_____

_____

Fighting Back

A certain amount of body dissatisfaction is normal, especially in this culture. It is very painful to feel that you aren't as pretty or as good or as popular as others are. However, you have to work with what you have. Berating yourself for not measuring up to socie-ty's standards only makes things worse. Self-acceptance does not mean you will abandon all restraint, eating whatever you might desire, and totally forgetting about controlling your weight. Rather, self-acceptance implies developing a healthy self-concept that includes taking responsibility for your thoughts, feelings, and behavior—including your eating and exercise behavior.

To fight back against negative body talk and body dissatis-faction, you need to do several things. First, you need to identify negative thought sequences and challenge the erroneous assump-tions and misguided conclusions that underlie your domino think-ing patterns. Next you need to create and use neutral or positive body talk. Finally, you need to make friends with your body.

Domino Thinking

You may recall from chapter 8 that "domino thinking" is a sequence of thoughts or events that act much like a line of dominos—one thought or event triggers another, which leads to yet another, until an extreme conclusion is reached. When domino thinking is used for thinking about appearance, it can go like this: "I look fat. Other people notice and care that I look fat. They think it's awful that I am so fat. Being fat proves that I'm not okay. I am worthless."

It is important to challenge the assumptions implied in each of these thoughts and examine the evidence that each is true. Some of the erroneous assumptions buried in this sequence of thoughts are as follows:

- that you are indeed fat (you may not be fat by some standards)

- that other people notice that you are fat (most people are too concerned about themselves to take much notice of others)

- that other people care (this is an assumption based on mind reading)

- that other people judge extra weight as awful and terrible (some do, some don't)

- that being overweight means you are not okay (this is an overgeneralization; there is other evidence that you are okay), and

- that overweight is proof of lack of self-worth or that you are unlovable, stupid, lazy, weak, incompetent, immoral, disgusting, unfeminine, and so forth (another overgeneralization as well as all-or-nothing thinking)

Domino thinking can be triggered by stress and negative emotions. Just having a "bad day" can lead to the conclusion that you are "too fat." A good example of this is the woman who spent the first session with her therapist complaining about how her boss was mistreating her and how her co-workers weren't doing their fair share of the work. When the therapist asked what the woman thought needed to happen, the woman replied, "I need to lose ten pounds." Like many people with an eating disorder, this woman translated feeling bad and having difficulties in her relationships into a conclusion about her weight. In fact, she needed to focus on improving her relationship skills.

One frequent assumption embedded in domino thinking is that you have to be perfect—perfectly beautiful, perfectly shaped, perfectly treated, perfectly appreciated, and so forth. This is an important assumption to challenge. There are lots of less-than-perfect people who are considered attractive, who are loved, who are valued, and who succeed. Can you think of any? How about someone in your family whom you love and admire but who isn't physically or even intellectually perfect? Do you have any friends whom you like and who like you who aren't perfect? The I-must-be-perfect-or-I'm-nothing assumption creates pain and perpetuates an eating disorder.

Using the three columns in the following worksheet, write out the thought sequences that you go through when you are engaging in domino thinking related to your weight or body shape. You could do this retrospectively by examining the past week, or you may want to create a record of the next few days. Put each domino thought on a separate line. Then go back and consider, what is the evidence that the assumption underlying this thought is actually true? What facts suggest it may not be true—what is the evidence against the assumption? Finally, in the last column, write a "fight-back" thought—a thought that refutes the assumption in the domino thought, or that refutes the conclusion you reached when using domino thinking. Repeat this sequence for as many separate thought sequences as you can identify. Take a moment to review the sample form to better understand what you should do.

Positive Body Talk

In chapter 8 you began to program your positive self-talk voice to be more supportive by using reminder cards. Now you need to add some new reminder cards to your stack. These should focus on positive aspects of physical appearance or reflect greater self-acceptance. Some examples of positive body talk might include: "My family loves and accepts me the way I am." "True friends judge me on who I am, not on my weight or shape." "I am more than my weight or my shape." "I may not be perfect, but I do the best I can."

Remember that these examples of positive self-talk are not affirmations in the usual sense of the word. They are not simply nice ideas you aspire to. Create a positive thought that is true and that you can believe. Positive thoughts can be reminders of your positive qualities. They can be directives that tell you what to do. They may serve to refocus your attention in a positive direction.

Many people who have eating disorders regard their body as "the enemy." They don't trust it. They dislike it. They are afraid of it. They punish or fight with it. And they reject it. To overcome disordered eating, this war between the Self and the Body must end. You need to find a way to make friends with your body—not conditionally, as in "when it reaches a certain weight or achieves a certain shape"—but now, today, just the way it is. This can begin by engaging in peace talks with your body.

Making Friends with Your Body

This is a difficult exercise for many people, but it is worth trying. The idea is to open a dialogue—peace talks, if you will—with your body. In the privacy of your room, face yourself in the mirror, preferably without wearing any clothing. Inspect your body carefully. Talk to it about what you like and what you don't like, what you would like to change and what you know you have to accept. Thank your body and its different parts for what it and they do for you. Apologize to your body for having mistreated it—for having starved it, put it on restrictive diets, denied it good nourishment, pushed it to exercise too much or exercised it too little for good health, for having ignored it or criticized it, for rejecting it and hating it. Ask your body for forgiveness, and ask what it needs from you now.

Fighting Back Against Domino Thinking
(Sample Form)

Domino Thought	Evidence For or Against	Fight Back Thought
I look fat.	When I look in the mirror, I see a bulge over my waist.	I may not like what I see, but I'm doing the best I can with my eating and my exercise.
Other people notice and care that I look fat.	I don't really know if they notice. I just imagine that they care.	Stay focused on doing the best I can under the circumstances.
Others think it's awful that I'm so fat.	Some people do judge others based on weight or appearance, but no on has actually said anything to me.	I need to be less concerned about what others might think and remember that I'm doing my best.
Being fat proves I'm not okay.	A lot of people worry about being too fat, but that isn't proof that they are good or bad people. Besides, my body fat is actually within the normal range. When I feel bad about other things, I start thinking about being fat.	When I start to "feel fat," I need to focus on what is really bothering me and what to do about that.
I'm worthless.	My boss says I do a good job. I have friends and family who like and love me.	My self-worth is best judged on the basis of my relationships and my accomplishments, not my weight or body shape.

In your imagination listen to what your body says. Write down your body's response so you can reread it as needed. If you cannot do this exercise actually standing in front of a mirror, try to do it first in your mind's eye, in your imagination. Repeat the exercise until you are relatively comfortable seeing yourself in a mirror. As you make friends with your body, you will be better able to face it in the mirror and experience greater self-acceptance.

Fighting Back Against Domino Thinking
(Sample Form)

Domino Thought	Evidence For or Against	Fight Back Thought

Coping with Distressing Situations

Anxiety is a common component of an eating disorder, and it can trigger binge eating. Anxiety also leads to avoiding situations in which it is feared the body will be exposed to criticism or evaluation by you or others. Avoiding mirrors or reflective surfaces so that you do not encounter your own image is one type of avoidance behavior. (Conversely, repeatedly inspecting your body in the mirror or repeatedly weighing yourself is an attempt to reduce anxiety about appearance or weight, even though such behaviors usually bring about increased anxiety.) Camouflaging your body in baggy clothes, avoiding going to the gym or the beach for fear that others will see your body shape, or declining social invitations are still other examples of avoidance behaviors. Even the thought of encountering such situations can be stressful. Take a moment now to review the different situations listed below and check off all those that you avoid because of anxiety about your body. Add your own, additional distressing situations where indicated.

Distressing Situations I Avoid Because of My Body

☐ Seeing myself in mirrors

☐ Shopping for clothes

☐ Being seen in public

☐ Engaging in sports or public exercise

☐ Engaging in sexual relations

☐ Being seen in a bathing suit

☐ Wearing tight-fitting clothing

☐ Wearing pants

☐ Getting a massage

☐ Having a medical exam

☐ Other: (Describe)

_____

_____

Overcoming Avoidance

By continuing to avoid distressing situations, you reinforce the idea that your body is unacceptable or even repulsive to others. By engaging in, rather than avoiding, such situations you are likely to discover that your body is not as unacceptable as you think. The anxiety that you feel at the very thought of encountering these distressing situations is prompted by the fear that you will be criticized, scorned, or rejected. This fear needs to be confronted and overcome. By doing so, you will move closer to self-acceptance and greater confidence in yourself. Using the following technique of stress inoculation can help.

Stress Inoculation

Positive self-talk is a powerful technique for managing stress. When you know that a potentially distressing or stressful situation is in the offing, you can use stress inoculation to help you overcome the stress and to not engage in the avoidance behaviors you typically use. Stress inoculation involves preparing and using positive self-talk at key stages of the encounter. In addition, you mentally rehearse how you will feel and act during the distressing situation.

Begin by breaking down a potentially distressing situation into stages. The Before Stage occurs when you are thinking about and preparing for the encounter. At this point, you experience anticipatory anxiety. The During Stage is when you are actually in the situation trying to cope. The After Stage, of course, is after the encounter is over and you must deal with residual arousal and stress.

Before the situation is to take place, imagine what you think will happen. Plan what you will say to yourself mentally at each stage. Be sure to include instructions that will help keep your anxiety under control. For example, "Stay calm. It will be all right." Also include congratulatory thoughts in the After Stage.

First write out the scene for each stage and the positive self-talk you will use to help yourself cope successfully. Then, using your imagination, visualize and imagine yourself going through the entire situation from start to finish. Stay calm and relaxed during this mental rehearsal, repeating it in your imagination until you can do it without feeling overly anxious or distressed. Start with one of the less distressing situations you noted earlier and move to more distressing ones as you succeed. The sample Stress

Inoculation Planning Worksheet provides an example of one such situation. Make copies of the blank worksheet and use these to plan how you will cope with each of the situations you checked earlier.

Enhancing Self-Esteem

Self-esteem is the product of a comparison process. When you compare yourself to some standard—perhaps your own internalized picture of an ideal body or what you think you should look like or be like—or to some external standard—a friend or person you see whom you admire, your self-esteem can go up or down. The further away you are from your "ideal" or your standard of comparison, the lower your self-esteem is. The closer you are to your standard of comparison, the higher your self-esteem.

Self-esteem depends, in part, on the standard of comparison you use and, in part, on how you evaluate yourself compared to it. If the standard of comparison is out of reach, say, looking like one of the super-thin runway models, or being perfect at everything you do—you are likely to experience decreased self-esteem. The gap between what you want to be and what you are is too great. It behooves you, therefore, to choose more attainable and realistic standards of comparison.

Bombarded with media images of beautiful bodies and apparently successful people, it is easy to forget that technology—not real bodies—has created these images. Computers are used to erase undesirable lines and even slim down the images of already too-thin models. Likewise, if the media are to be believed, sex and drugs make young people happy. No matter that so many celebrities die of drug overdoses or suicide. The standards that people are urged to accept are not only unrealistic, they can be deadly.

How you make comparisons counts as well. Too often what is in your mind when you make a comparison is not the whole picture. You focus on your shortcomings but forget about your strengths. If you happen to be feeling bad or fat at the time you see someone who seems to have a lot going for him or her, you feel even worse and may conclude that you'll never be attractive or successful. All of this is made worse if you are feeling criticized or rejected because of your appearance. Your self-esteem can fall to an all-time low, and you can become depressed.

Stress Inoculation Planning Worksheet
(Sample Form)

Distressing Situation: Going to the gym in my exercise clothes

Before Stage

What do I imagine will happen?	What do I need to say to myself?
I'll drive up to the gym and get out of the car with my gym bag in my hand. I'll go into the locker room to change clothes. There will be all sizes of bodies there.	"I can handle this. Stay calm. Just take some deep breaths and relax. No one cares about my weight. They are there for themselves. This is for me."

During Stage

What do I imagine will happen?	What do I need to say to myself?
I'll put on my exercise clothes and go out to the floor. Both men and women will be there. I'll do some stretching and then I'll get on the treadmill. Then I'll do some weight training. When I'm done I'll go back to the locker room and take a shower. It is an open shower with no doors. I'll get dressed and leave the gym.	"I'm doing fine. Need to stay calm. Don't worry about them. Stay focused on what I need to do. Relax. Just ignore any looks. No one will say anything. Why should I care? This is for me. Focus on counting. This shower feels good. I'm okay. Be friendly. Say something nice."

After Stage

What do I imagine will happen?	What do I need to say to myself?
I'll get into my car to drive home.	"I did it! It was okay. I'm proud of myself. As soon as I get home I'm going to call some friends and brag."

Stress Inoculation Planning Worksheet
(Sample Form)

Distressing Situation: _____

Before Stage	
What do I imagine will happen?	What do I need to say to myself?

During Stage	
What do I imagine will happen?	What do I need to say to myself?

After Stage	
What do I imagine will happen?	What do I need to say to myself?

Not only do you have to constantly challenge the standards you use to make comparisons, you have to keep in mind all that you do have to offer. (Better yet, stop comparing yourself with others altogether.) You need to expand your definition of self beyond appearance. You are not just your body. You are much more than that, and long after age has taken its toll, your important qualities will remain.

To help you get in touch with these qualities, and to expand your definition of self beyond just physical qualities, create a Personal Inventory. On a separate sheet of paper, list at least five of your strengths and positive qualities separate from your shape and weight. More is better. Count qualities you might consider "mundane," such as keeping a clean house, and don't overlook off-beat ones, such as "I do a good imitation of Dino the Dinosaur." Keep this Personal Inventory in a place you can easily find and review it. When you are feeling down on yourself, get out this inventory and reread it.

Remind yourself that even if you could be the ideal weight and shape, this would not fix everything. Satisfaction and a happy life require much more that just a pretty face or body. Those who have a chance to get to know you judge you on who you are and how you treat them, more than on how you look. You are more than your physical appearance, your weight, or your shape.

Notes

1. Wilson, G. T. 1996. Acceptance and change in the treatment of eating disorders and obesity. *Behavior Therapy, 27,* 417–439.

2. Bouchard, C. 1995. Genetic influences on body weight and shape. In K. D. Brownell and C. G. Fairburn, eds., *Eating Disorders and Obesity: A Comprehensive Handbook.* New York: Guilford. 21–26.

3. Nash, J. D. 1995. *What Your Doctor Can't Tell You About Cosmetic Surgery.* Oakland, CA: New Harbinger Publications.

4. Cash, T. F., B. A. Winstead, and L. H. Janda. 1986. The great American shape-up: Body image survey report. *Psychology Today,* April, 30–34, 36–37.

5. Rosen, J. C., P. Orosan, and J. Reiter. 1995. Cognitive behavior therapy for negative body image in obese women. *Behavior Therapy, 26,* 25–42.

Chapter 10

Improving Your Coping Skills

The story of Donna and her husband Eric was introduced in chapter 2. You may recall that Donna was an overweight woman in her forties who overate more or less continuously throughout the day when Eric wasn't home. Eric was a very self-centered man whose own interests and needs always came before Donna's or their two daughters'. Eric complained frequently about Donna's weight and made numerous attempts to get her to lose weight, including enrolling her in Weight Watchers, hiring a personal trainer for her, and finally insisting that she see a therapist that he chose. Donna agreed that she should lose weight, but she was unable to curb her eating.

In therapy, Donna came to realize that her secret binge eating throughout the day was fueled by her anger with Eric for his selfishness and neglect of her and the family, for his criticism and belittling of her appearance, and for his intrusiveness and violation of her autonomy. At first, Donna was unwilling to address these concerns with her husband, fearing that he would become angry and possibly even divorce her. Eventually, with the therapist's support, Donna began to assert herself and insist that Eric be more considerate of the family's needs, and stop criticizing her and intruding on her weight and eating issues.

Eating Disorders and Coping

Donna's story demonstrates how a person with an eating disorder can use food and eating to cope inappropriately with a stressful situation. Donna used secret binge eating as a way to avoid dealing with her feelings about Eric's treatment of her and the family. Her fear of being abandoned led her to suppress her anger and eat in secret, rather than attempt to resolve the problems in her relationship.

Coping refers to any cognitive or behavioral effort made to cope with stress. Stress has been defined as "a particular relationship between the person and the environment that is appraised by the person as taxing or exceeding his or her resources and endangering his or her well-being."[1] Stress is not the result of events themselves. Rather, stress is the product of how a person evaluates and copes with events that occur.

Eric behaved in ways that were upsetting and stressful to Donna. She felt she was unable to change his behavior, even though she also felt it was hurtful to her and the children. She coped by giving herself free access to food at times when she knew Eric could not control her. In so doing, she achieved some temporary relief and at the same time avoided having to deal with what seemed like a problem without a solution.

Appraising Stress

According to Richard Lazarus and Susan Folkman,[2] experts in the field of stress and coping, stress involves a process of appraisal that occurs at two stages. The *primary appraisal stage* focuses on whether a threat exists. When confronted with an event or stressful situation, you must decide what that event means and whether it poses a threat to your physical or emotional well-being. Threats to self-esteem—such as a failure experience, being rejected or unappreciated, or the breakup of a relationship—are particularly stressful. Too often the eating disordered person identifies a threat to self-esteem in terms of presumed defects in body shape or appearance.

For example, when Eric criticized Donna's weight, she became upset. She believed that his criticism meant that she was not attractive. This made her feel ashamed, and her self-esteem fell. Donna assumed that her weight was actually the problem, and overlooked the possibility that the real problem had to do with her relationship with Eric. His complaints about her weight kept her busy trying to please him by keeping a nice house and by not asking too much of him.

The *secondary appraisal stage* has to do with evaluating the options for coping. Because Donna believed that her weight made her unacceptable, she tried repeatedly and unsuccessfully to curb her eating and lose weight. She also kept quiet about her dissatisfaction with Eric's role in the family for fear he would become angry if she conveyed her needs to him. Donna suppressed her frustrations by eating, and her distress with Eric by using an avoidance strategy—binge eating.

Whether an event is experienced as stressful involves the following three aspects of any situation[3]:

1. The degree to which the event is evaluated by you as potentially harmful, threatening, or challenging—the more harmful, threatening, or challenging, the greater the stress.

2. The options you think you have for coping—the more options, the less stress.

3. The coping strategies you use to deal with the event—the more adaptive the strategy, the more likely that stress will be reduced.

Coping Strategies

A coping strategy refers to the way in which you manage a stressful situation or the emotional reactions that arise as a result of that situation. Coping strategies are either problem-focused or emotion-focused. There are several types of emotion-focused strategies, some of which are adaptive (i.e., make you better able to adjust to new or difficult circumstances), and others that are not. Poor emotion-focused strategies include avoidance, distancing, or discharge. Better emotion-focused strategies include eliciting the relaxation response, seeking the support of others, changing dysfunctional thinking, and learning to cope better with painful emotions.

Problem-Focused Coping

Problem-focused coping involves problem solving and other active attempts to change a problematic event or stressful situation. It is best used when a situation can be influenced in some way. Research has found that women with bulimia are much less likely to use problem-focused coping than are women without an eating disorder.[4] Women with bulimia also tend to endorse the belief that it is better to avoid problems than to confront them directly.[5] The failure to use problem-focused coping resulting in binge eating is exemplified in the following description of Karen's experience.

Karen. Bulimic for over ten years, Karen binged and purged when she felt overwhelmed by stress. Although Karen had managed not to binge/purge for several months, she suddenly had four days in a row of doing so. At first, she could explain it only by saying she had had a terrible week. Further exploration revealed that she had calculated her taxes, which were due to be paid within the next two weeks, and had found to her surprise that she owed money to the IRS. On a tight budget, Karen didn't know how she could pay her taxes. In addition, she had several overdue projects at work, and had just had a fight with her mother about sending a graduation gift to a distant relative she hardly knew and didn't particularly like. Feeling unable to cope and not wanting to face the unpleasant reality of her tax situation, or work, or her mother, Karen escaped into binge eating and purging.

With the help of her therapist, Karen eventually was able to more accurately specify her different problems and to think of alternatives for taking effective action. For example, Karen's initial formulation of the tax problem was "I don't have enough money." Deeper examination revealed that Karen wasn't sure she had calculated her taxes correctly because she didn't know how to handle the accounting for stock she had cashed out. She needed to get more information to be sure that her calculations were correct, and if they were, she realized that she could ask for an extension, so that she could save the necessary money for paying the taxes, or obtain a loan. Karen also needed to bring problem-solving skills to her work environment and to her interpersonal difficulties.

The infrequent use of problem solving by those with an eating disorder may be attributed to a lack of adequate or accurate information about the problem, or to the belief that the problem has no ready or easy solution. Eating disordered individuals tend to think simply and concretely. As a result, they tend to miss important cues and information that suggest what the problem really is and that there may be a solution within reach. Thoughts such as, "I don't want to hurt his/her feelings," or "What if he gets upset," may prevent taking effective action. If the decision is made that the situation is beyond their control or influence, those with an eating disorder simply give up and turn to some means of escaping their unpleasant feelings. As a result, the eating disordered person is less effective in coping with stressful situations.[6]

Emotion-Focused Coping

When it appears there is little means of changing or influencing a stressful event, coping behavior focuses on mitigating the negative thoughts and feelings that result. Those with eating disorders tend to rely most on strategies that allow them to avoid or escape the distressing situation and the attendant negative feelings.[7]

Avoidance strategies include excessive eating or drinking, smoking, gambling, spending, using drugs, and so forth. These behaviors serve to divert attention from either the problem and its associated thoughts and feelings, or both. Distancing is an emotional escape strategy that involves emotional detachment or denial. With this strategy, the person stops caring or insists that there really is no problem at all.

Emotional discharge strategies are verbal and behavioral expressions of unpleasant emotions that serve to reduce tension temporarily. Yelling, swearing, hitting, and throwing things all serve to discharge emotions, especially anger. Engaging in compensatory behaviors, especially self-induced vomiting, is a discharge strategy that serves to reduce tension and anxiety in bulimics.[8] Likewise, excessive exercise may be used to discharge anxiety.

These strategies may temporarily reduce negative affect by diverting attention from painful feelings or by providing the appearance of a solution to a problem, but in the long run they usually make the problem worse, and they do nothing to change the existing stressful situation. Avoidance interferes with accurate assessment of the problem, causes the person to overlook possible negative consequences of such avoidance, and delays or prevents the use of more adaptive coping strategies.

Those with eating disorders rely on avoidance strategies for several reasons. One problem is that they often have difficulty knowing what they are really feeling.[9] In particular, they have difficulty differentiating between hunger cues and other aversive sensations and feelings. For example, anxiety may be confused with feeling hungry and needing something to eat. Even if they can identify their emotions, they may feel overwhelmed by them and not know how to cope effectively.

In addition, those with eating disorders perceive themselves as having unsatisfying interpersonal relationships.[10] Compared to those without eating disorders, both bulimics and anorexics are less likely to seek emotional support from others in times of stress.[11] Although they value and seek the approval of others, they do not reach out to them.[12] Without adequate social support to count on, they resort to using less adaptive strategies involving avoidance, distancing, or discharge.

Colleen. At the age of seventeen, Colleen started bingeing and purging subsequent to an incident that made her the subject of gossip and nasty rumors in her high school. An older male employee of the store where she worked had seduced her into a situation in which he molested her. Hurt by the gossip that went around the school, Colleen quit high school and retreated into an eating disorder. Life had been difficult as an adolescent in any case. For years, her parents had fought frequently and openly. Colleen recalled huddling on the sofa with her siblings, trying to take comfort from each other while the parents fought. Her parents had finally separated about a year before the molestation. Since their separation, her siblings had taken to fighting among themselves and were no longer supportive of each other. Colleen felt alienated from her peers and from her family. She finally began to overcome her eating disorder when she joined a church group that provided the caring and nurturing support she needed to cope with her situation.

Adaptive Coping

Adaptive coping involves using good problem-solving skills when these are appropriate to the situation. This includes adopting an attitude toward all stressful situations that starts with assessing the situation accurately and deciding what can be done. To take effective action may require setting aside thoughts that inhibit effective, problem-focused coping. When negative emotions are generated in a stressful situation, adaptive coping involves using emotion-focused strategies that do not include avoidance.

Coping Style

Coping style refers to the pattern of strategies used across situations. Most people use a combination of problem-focused and emotion-focused coping strategies in the face of stressful events. An adaptive coping style is flexible and uses problem-focused strategies when faced with a controllable situation or one that can be influenced to some degree. An adaptive coping style also uses effective emotion-focused strategies—those that do not involve efforts to escape or avoid negative affect—to deal with negative emotions. A maladaptive coping style is inflexible and relies primarily on avoidance, distancing, or emotional discharge strategies. Such an ineffective coping style can instigate and maintain an eating disorder.

Eating Disorders and Appraisal

Eating disordered persons may fail to accurately appraise whether and to what degree something is threatening—thus demonstrating a deficit in the primary appraisal process. Or they may fail to evaluate all the options for coping, which signifies a deficit in the secondary appraisal process.

Deficits in Primary Appraisal

Those with eating disorders tend to be more sensitive to stress, experience more types of situations as stressful, and cope less well with stress than do those without disordered eating.[13] They tend to appraise many situations as threatening, even when they are not. For example, many people with an eating disorder are convinced that others are judging them silently and negatively. Any social occasion—a work-related cocktail party, going out to dinner with friends, a high school reunion—can be seen as threatening.

Similarly, those with an eating disorder tend to attribute the cause of a stressful situation, such as being criticized at work, to their weight or shape. One woman who was having difficulty with a colleague at work concluded that if she lost weight, the situation would improve. Another woman was convinced that the breakup with her lover was due to her weight, even though further questioning revealed that they had stopped sharing interests or having a sexual relationship long before she started gaining weight. Those with an eating disorder tend to think narrowly and look for the "One Thing" that is the cause of all their problems, and they usually conclude it is their weight or shape.

Deficits in Secondary Appraisal

Eating disordered individuals often fail to evaluate their options adequately for coping. If they do accurately assess the situation, they may believe that there is little they can do about it, or the range of coping strategies they can call on may be so limited that their efforts are in vain. More often, their misunderstanding of the problem causes them to choose coping strategies that are ineffective or off target. For example, Donna half-heartedly pursued her attempts to lose weight to please her husband, not understanding that even if she were to be successful in losing weight, she would still be carrying the major responsibility for the family's welfare and not getting her own needs met.

Eating disordered individuals often lack confidence in their ability to influence a problem situation or cope effectively. Because they think they have less control and are not very effective, especially with other people, they have low expectations for success. For them, the best solution is to avoid or deny problems and hope they go away or get better on their own. Binge eating provides a means of escape, if only temporarily, from their troubles. Many people with an eating disorder skip trying to figure out why they are feeling bad and go directly to the binge or binge/purge to "numb out" their feelings.

Improving Your Coping Skills

To overcome disordered eating, you need to become a better problem solver and improve your coping skills. In particular, you need to shift from making inaccurate appraisals and using avoidance-based coping to making accurate appraisals and employing the appropriate use of problem-focused and adaptive emotion-focused coping strategies.

Improving Problem-Focused Coping

Problem-focused coping involves assessing and defining the problem, generating alternative solutions, deciding which to try first, and evaluating how effective your choice was in influencing the situation.[14]

Defining the Problem

Formulating the problem correctly is a crucial part of good problem-solving skills. This involves seeking out all available facts, describing these facts clearly, separating facts from assumptions, and identifying obstacles and conflicts. Like others who suffer from an eating disorder, you may have difficulty defining the problem because of a tendency to describe problems in overly vague, general, exaggerated, or negative terms. Or you may lump several problems into one, leading you to feel overwhelmed or unable to find a solution. In fact, feeling overwhelmed should be your first clue that more than one problem is at hand, and you need to avoid jumping to a "One Thing" explanation. Focus on defining the problem in such a way that it suggests a solution. For example, instead of saying, "I'll never overcome my eating disorder," which is demoralizing and frightening, try to reformulate this more positively, as in, "I need to develop the necessary skills for overcoming my disordered eating."

Self-monitoring can be helpful in defining a problem. This technique was introduced in chapter 6 as a means of gathering information about behavior patterns. Self-monitoring can also help in problem definition and formulation. Eating disordered persons are often very poor in recalling or identifying the source of negative emotions. As such, you are likely to need assistance in accurately identifying the circumstances that lead to your negative feelings. Earlier you learned that certain events precede and elicit a binge. These events may be thoughts, other feelings, stressful interactions with others, or actual unpleasant events, such as getting a bad grade on a test.

Brainstorming Alternatives

Brainstorming involves generating ideas without screening or evaluating them negatively. This invites creativity and encourages seeing the problem in different ways. After coming up with a list of alternative solutions, you can evaluate each one for its merits. For example, Karen generated the following alternative solutions to her problem of calculating her taxes: 1) Contact a friend or student who understands accounting and tax preparation and get them to review her calculations. 2) Have a professional such as H&R Block review her calculations for a price. 3) Call the IRS telephone hot line and ask for help. 4) Get on the Internet and see if the IRS has a website that answers tax questions.

Implementing a Solution

Having generated a number of possible solutions, consider how practical as well as how effective each alternative is likely to be. Then choose one and try it out. In some cases, implementing more than one alternative may be feasible and appropriate. Be sure to give the alternatives you try a fair chance to work. If an alternative brings partial success, consider how you might improve on this, or whether partial success is good enough. Be sure your expectations are realistic. For example, if you try brushing your teeth as a way of interrupting a binge and it works some of the time but not all of the time, this is still a good strategy to use. If the solution you try doesn't work at all, try another. If nothing works, consider the possibility that you have not defined the problem adequately. Go back and start again. Following is a summary of the steps involved in problem solving.

How to Problem-solve Effectively

1. Treat "feeling overwhelmed" as a signal that several problems are involved.

2. Identify in concrete and specific terms each of the problems involved.

3. Formulate each problem in such a way that it suggests a solution.

4. Brainstorm as many possible solutions as you can think of.

5. Choose one and try it out.

6. Evaluate the effectiveness of the solution you have tried; be sure you have given it a fair chance.

7. Review the results. If the solution didn't help, try another and repeat steps 4 through 7.

8. If none of the solutions you try work, go back and reformulate the problem.

Improving Your Adaptive Emotion-Focused Coping

As noted earlier, emotion-focused coping is most adaptively used for situations that are largely unchangeable and for the emotions that accompany any stressful situation. Adaptive emotion-focused coping, which does not involve the use of avoidance strategies, reduces emotional overarousal that may interfere with active problem solving. Adaptive emotion-focused coping may involve eliciting the relaxation response, using imagery or self-hypnosis, seeking social support, and identifying and changing dysfunctional beliefs or thoughts. The latter might involve beliefs regarding the need for approval, expectations for high performance, projected misfortune, or anxiety and fear about others' evaluation, disapproval, or criticism of your weight, shape, or eating behavior.

Eliciting the Relaxation Response

Stress and the negative emotions that accompany stress are often the precursors that elicit binge eating. Eliciting the relaxation response to deal with stress, together with rewarding yourself for good nutritional habits, can lead to a reduction in the desire to binge and in the frequency of binge episodes.[15] Using relaxation to cope with urges to binge is effective. In addition, learning to be more relaxed in general, not just when the urge to binge is present, helps to reduce overall frequency of binge urges and binge episodes.[16]

Relaxation training begins with progressive relaxation. This forms the basis for learning to use deep breathing, which is a shorter method for eliciting the relaxation response. Deep breathing, combined with positive self-talk, can be very effective in reducing arousal from stress. Imagery is another means of coping with emotions that also involves eliciting the relaxation response.

Progressive Deep Muscle Relaxation. If you do not know how to concentrate on relaxing, progressive deep muscle relaxation is useful. It helps you learn the difference between muscle tension and relaxation in three phases: first, tensing a muscle and noticing how it feels; second, releasing the tension and paying attention to that feeling; and third, concentrating on the difference between the two sensations.

To try this, find a quiet, relaxing place where you will not be disturbed for at least fifteen minutes. Then sit or lie down, removing contact lenses or glasses, and loosening tight clothing.

Start with your hands. Make a fist with one hand and notice how it feels. Your muscles will be taut and strained, maybe even trembling. (Never tense so hard that it hurts.) Hold the tension for a few seconds, and then let go. Relax your fist, and let the tension slip away. Repeat the tensing and relaxing stages one or two times, and notice the difference between the two. Does your hand throb or feel tight when tensed? Does your hand tingle or feel warm when relaxed?

Now progress to the other muscles. Move up the arm to include the forearm, then the whole arm. Completing that arm, do the same sequence—hand, hand and forearm, whole arm—with the other arm. Then focus on your legs, one leg at a time—first the feet, then the feet and calves together, then each whole leg. (Do not include your arms when you are tensing and relaxing your legs.) After each tensing and each relaxing, pay attention to the difference in feeling.

Alternately tensing and letting go, continue moving up your torso with your buttocks, abdomen, chest, and shoulders. For your head, tense and relax first your jaw, then all your facial muscles. Finally, tense and relax your whole body at once, including arms and legs. Pay attention to the difference between feeling tense and feeling relaxed.

After you have completed the entire exercise, allow yourself to enjoy total relaxation for a few minutes before continuing with your daily activities. The feeling of warmth and relaxation tells you that you have elicited the relaxation response. Remember what this feels like and remind yourself that you can achieve this state of relaxation again whenever you choose.

Deep Breathing. To elicit the relaxation response through deep breathing, simply inhale slowly and deeply through your nose and allow your lungs to breathe in as much oxygen as possible. Let your abdomen relax and expand, so that you take in as much air as possible. Once you have filled your lungs, hold your breath for a few seconds. Then exhale slowly through your mouth, focusing on letting go of muscle tension as you do so, until your lungs feel almost empty. Pause again, and then inhale as before. Recall the sensation of relaxation you had when you did the progressive deep muscle relaxation exercise. Repeat the deep breathing cycle several times until you feel relaxed. Remind yourself that you can attain this state of relaxation again, anytime you choose to do so.

Imagery. Imagery can be used to evoke the relaxation response and improve mood. Doing imagery simply means allowing yourself to "see" in your mind's eye imaginary scenes or actions, as in a movie. Everyone has the ability to call up mental images, even though they may think they don't. Dreams are one example of unbidden "mental movies." Visualizing how to get to some place is an example of a consciously directed imagery process. The idea behind using imagery to evoke the relaxation response is to visualize a pleasant or relaxing scene, which can be a memory of some place you have actually been, or a place you invent in your own mind. The steps for doing imagery follow:

1. *Get relaxed.* Find a private place where you will not be interrupted for a period of time—usually for at least fifteen to twenty minutes, although you could do this anywhere (e.g., a park bench, or on a bus) for whatever time you have available. It helps to get comfortable. Then close your eyes and using the deep breathing technique described previously, allow yourself to relax. Turn your focus inward, and allow imagery to arise without trying to control it or "do it right." There is no right or wrong way to do imagery, and with practice it becomes easier.

2. *Mentally picture a relaxing scene.* Allow a relaxing or pleasant scene to come to mind. For example, imagine walking on a lovely beach, sailing on a sunny lake, hiking on a picturesque trail, or lying in the green grass of a quiet meadow. Direct your attention to the sensory details—the sounds, colors, smell, touch, temperature, and motion. Notice the enjoyable aspects of the scene and give yourself permission to become more involved and relaxed.

3. *When you are ready, bring the imagery to a close.* Continue until you have enjoyed the mental imaging sufficiently and are feeling relaxed and satisfied. Tell yourself you can return to this enjoyable scene anytime you wish, simply by taking several deep breaths. Without opening your eyes, allow your mental images to fade. Then gently bring your consciousness back to the present. Open your eyes, stretch your muscles, and continue your day with an improved perspective.

4. *Consider writing out or recording your relaxing scene ahead of time.* You may find it easier to do imagery if you carefully write out the details of the scene that you want to imagine. Then record it on an audiocassette tape to play back while you are relaxing. When you are recording your scene on tape, take care to speak slowly and in a relaxing tone of voice.

5. *Practice doing imagery.* Do imagery at least once a day, repeating steps 1 and 2 each time, until you feel confident in your

ability to improve your mood by using imagery. If you wish, try different kinds of images to alter your mood.

Seeking Social Support

Effective use of social support is another important and adaptive emotion-focused coping strategy. Such coping involves contacting others to obtain information, advice, and emotional support when feeling emotionally overwhelmed. In the face of stress, those with an eating disorder tend not to reach out for support, possibly because they do not trust that support will be forthcoming. Indeed, family and friends often do not understand disordered eating and may be quite critical of the person. Or they may provide unsolicited and off-target advice, or engage in well-meaning but misdirected efforts to coerce the person into getting treatment.

Often the first step in obtaining effective social support is to reveal the eating disorder to significant others and to educate them, not only about the eating disorder, but also about what the eating disordered person needs from them—that is, how significant others can be most helpful. It can also be useful for the eating disordered person and her significant others to meet together with a qualified therapist to address the issue of support and to educate the significant others about the central role of self-esteem in an eating disorder.

One of the main barriers to seeking social support is the fear of disapproval or criticism. When the eating disordered person thinks she is worthless due to her eating disorder, it seems logical to conclude that others will think the same. The person with an eating disorder must be able to tolerate her approval fears in order to seek help. Learning how to tolerate distressing emotions is addressed later in this chapter.

Changing Dysfunctional Thinking

Chapter 8 addressed the role of dysfunctional thinking in eating disorders. In particular, those with an eating disorder tend to be anxious and overly invested in gaining the approval of others or in avoiding their disapproval. They catastrophize— "What if . . . ," accelerating their anxiety and creating their own sense of fear and of being overwhelmed. Eating disordered people compare themselves to others or to their own internal and unrealistic standards for weight or shape, ending up short in the comparison. They often impose on themselves high expectations for their performance, or feel that they are the helpless victims of past injuries and injustices. As eating disordered people learn and adopt healthier ways of thinking—i.e., reducing cognitive errors and using more positive self-talk—they find that they are less likely to be overwhelmed by painful emotions.

One useful means of coping with painful emotions is to step back from your feelings and choose to understand them differently. Instead of deciding that it is terrible and awful that you feel this way—which leads to wanting to escape, usually through bingeing or purging—tell yourself that the stress you are experiencing is a means to personal growth and greater awareness of self. It is also helpful to remind yourself that emotional arousal follows a predictable pattern if you allow it to takes its natural course, rather than trying to suppress it.

Emotional arousal builds up in intensity and peaks, after which it waxes and wanes in intensity until arousal completely resolves. No one ever died from their emotions, although people have died or been hurt trying to escape their emotions. A better approach is to learn how to modify the intensity of emotional reactions or to discover that you can tolerate the distress of negative emotions. (It may be helpful to enlist the aid of a therapist for learning how to cope more effectively with painful feelings.)

Coping with Painful Feelings

Marsha Linehan has developed and tested various techniques for helping those who have difficulty with emotional distress learn to manage it more successfully.[17] She first teaches mindfulness skills, which she regards as the basis for balancing rational thinking—the "reasonable mind" in her terms—and emotional experiencing—the "emotional mind." According to Dr. Linehan, the Wise Mind is that part of you that holds both reason and emotion at the same time and draws wisdom from both. (Notice that the Wise Self voice introduced in chapter 8 is similar to the concept of Linehan's Wise Mind.)

Mindfulness skills lay the foundation for becoming better able to tolerate emotional distress and cope with painful feelings.

Mindfulness Skills

Mindfulness involves learning to observe, to describe, and to participate with awareness. It also means taking a nonjudgmental attitude, focusing on only one thing at a time, and doing what works best. *Actively observing* means attending to events, emotions, and other behavioral responses, even if the emotions are distressing, without trying to avoid or escape in any way. To do this, you must reserve a part of your consciousness to step back from the event itself and act as an observer of whatever is happening. This "observer" part of you is alert and watching whatever is going on without getting caught in the experience or reacting to it.

Describing is a mindfulness skill that involves putting into words what is happening, including your responses to the situation, without evaluating or judging. When a feeling or thought arises, or you do something, the observer acknowledges it and describes it. For example, the observer might say in your mind, "I am feeling fat today" rather than "I'm fat." The observer describes what is happening—as in, "I am worried about that project, and I feel like bingeing so I don't have to deal with it" rather than "I should be further along on that project than I am, and that's terrible." Applying verbal labels not only to the events as they happen but also to your thoughts, behaviors, and feelings, helps you maintain self-control. Learning to describe the situation nonjudgmentally helps you not to take your emotions and thoughts too literally.

Participating with alertness and awareness, but not self-consciously, means staying present in the moment, without separating yourself from what is happening. Continuing the example, participating requires staying conscious and aware of the anxiety and worry associated with the project at work, and asking yourself what can be done to influence the situation. That is, the focus is on what needs to be done in the situation you are in, rather than thinking of some other situation that would feel better—i.e., having an eating binge.

Dr. Linehan distinguishes between three "What" skills of mindfulness—attending, describing, and participating—and three "How" skills—nonjudgmental attitude, which involves foregoing making judgments about what is happening, staying present in the moment, and focusing on what works.

Forego judgment. Instead of evaluating the situation as good or bad, or yourself or someone else as worthwhile or worthless, simply observe what happens and the consequences that follow. Watch but don't evaluate.

Stay present in the moment. Don't become distracted by attending to past or future events, intruding thoughts or worries or feelings not related to the present. For example, it does not help to think obsessively about the last time you were late with a project and how bad you felt. You must learn to focus on one task or activity at a time, the one at hand, and engage in it with alertness and awareness.

Focus on what works. Consider what is needed in the situation. Do what needs to be done. Avoid thoughts about "should" and "should not," "good" and "bad," "fair" and "unfair." Do the best you can to meet the needs of the situation you are in, and don't be distracted by thoughts of other situations you wish you were in or that are more comfortable than the present situation.

By implementing these mindfulness skills, you will be better able to stay focused on the present, stressful situation, and decide whether the use of problem-focused coping is called for, or whether adaptive, emotion-focused coping is needed.

Distress Tolerance Skills

The ability to tolerate and deal effectively and appropriately with distress is necessary for good mental health. The reality is that stress and pain are a part of life and cannot be avoided or removed. Furthermore, personal growth and change inevitably bring some pain and suffering, at least over the short run. Distress tolerance involves being able to accept, in a nonjudgmental fashion, both yourself and your current situation. It is the ability to perceive your environment without demanding that it be different, to experience emotions without attempting to escape them, and to observe your own present-moment thoughts and action patterns without attempting to stop or control them. However, acceptance of reality does not mean approval of reality. The reality may be that you are 100 pounds overweight, but you need not approve of this. It does mean accepting this fact as it is in the moment and focusing wisely on what needs to be done.

There are a number of techniques that can be helpful for tolerating painful events and emotions. One involves distracting yourself by engaging in healthy activities, preferably those that provide the opportunity to experience positive emotions—joy, happiness, satisfaction. Examples might include reading a book, going to a movie, listening to music. Another technique might be to do something nice for someone else or do volunteer work.

Another group of techniques for tolerating painful events and emotions involves being able to self-soothe by engaging one or more of your five senses—sight, touch, taste, smell, or hearing. Buy yourself some flowers. Light a scented candle. Go to an art museum. Sing a happy song. Apply perfume or lotion. Fix a cup of herbal tea. Take a bubble bath.

Earlier in this chapter you learned how to elicit the relaxation response and how to use imagery to modify your emotional mood. Additional ways of improving the moment include engaging in prayer, if you are a spiritual person. Or trying to see the beneficial aspects of a stressful situation. When life serves up lemons, make lemonade. Become your own cheerleader. Tell yourself over and over, "I will make it out of this," and "I'm doing the best I can." Focus on your long-term goals, and try to recall the times when you felt at peace and without pain.

Emotion Regulation Skills

Like distress tolerance, the ability to manage emotional responses to everyday events requires the application of mindfulness skills. It is most important that you remain nonjudgmental when you are observing and describing your current emotional responses. By becoming more mindful of your own emotional experiencing, you become less vulnerable to the effect of your emotions. Dr. Linehan describes a number of specific emotion regulation skills. These are as follows:

1. *Identifying and Labeling Emotions.* The first step is to identify and label ongoing, current emotions. Many people with an eating disorder have never learned to differentiate one emotion from another. Some people lump all negative emotions together and translate the entire mass into a single thought about the body, such as, "I'm fat." Other people can identify only one emotion—usually anger, but lump all the rest into an undifferentiated mass they call "feeling bad." They are like artists who have only one or two colors to work with, instead of an entire palette.

   Having a whole palette of emotions is necessary for good mental health. Being able to identify and label a range of emotions and emotional responses is important. You can learn to identify an emotional response if you can observe and describe the events that prompt the feeling, the meaning or interpretation associated with the feeling, where in the body you experience the emotion, and how you express it. These are all discussed in greater detail later in this chapter.

2. *Identifying Obstacles to Changing Emotions.* Emotions work. They function to get the person something she wants. That is, there

are certain "payoffs" for various emotions. To change emotional behavior, it is first necessary to identify the functions and reinforcers of a particular emotional behavior. Generally, emotions function to communicate to others and to motivate one's own behavior. They also can influence or control the behavior of others, and they validate our own perceptions and interpretations of events. Beth (see chapter 4) would rage at her parents for not buying her the diet pills or other weight control products that she wanted until they finally gave in to her demands. She believed that she was right and that her parents were being unfair to refuse her demands. Beth's anger served to coerce and control her parents, to communicate the depth of her misery, and to validate her own beliefs.

3. *Reducing Vulnerability to Stress.* Stress makes most people more emotionally reactive. Those with an eating disorder are hypersensitive to threat and unusually reactive to stress. Learning to cope more effectively with stress by becoming a better problem solver is important. In addition, taking care of yourself physically, by eating properly and getting adequate exercise and sleep, is also important. By engaging in restrictive dieting and either overexercising or not exercising at all, eating disordered persons increase their vulnerability to stress.

4. *Increasing Positive Emotional Events.* People feel bad for good reason. Peter (see chapter 1) was angry with himself and ashamed for having made poor investments that had sabotaged his financial health. He punished himself by working two jobs and isolating himself from social support. By doing so, he virtually eliminated any opportunities for positive daily experiences. Without these, he sank deeper and deeper into anger, depression, and shame. To get out of this predicament and lift the weight of negative emotions, Peter needed to increase the number of positive events in his life and to make life changes so that more positive experiences could occur. To overcome your negative emotions, you too need to find ways to increase positive experiences and to notice and take advantage of any when they do occur.

5. *Increasing Mindfulness to Current Emotions.* To increase mindfulness to current emotions, it is necessary to experience painful or distressing emotions without judging them or trying to inhibit them, block them, or distract yourself from them. If you feel

angry but decide you shouldn't be angry, you are likely to feel guilty as well as angry, which makes the distress more intense and tolerance more difficult. It is better to observe, describe, and enter into your anger and the distressing situation, without judging, getting distracted, or losing sight of what is the most effective course of action.

6. *Taking Opposite Action.* One way to change or moderate an emotion is to act in a way that is inconsistent with the emotion—for example, doing something nice for the person you are angry with, or engaging in a social situation that generates anxiety for you. Jillian (see chapter 2) was convinced that no one could find her attractive. As a result, she avoided going to social events where she might meet someone. Avoiding social events only reinforced her belief that she was fat and ugly. At her therapist's urging, Jillian went to one social event with another friend. She was surprised to discover that several strangers engaged her in conversation. This was a beginning step in overcoming her anxiety about her appearance and served to undermine her firmly held belief in her unattractiveness.

7. *Applying Distress Tolerance Techniques.* It is important to be able to tolerate painful emotions without trying to avoid or escape them. Earlier, a number of techniques were given for tolerating distress. By using these, you will discover that the intensity and duration of your negative emotions fade sooner than you expected.

Expanding Your Emotional Palette

Eating disordered persons frequently have restricted emotional palettes; they fail to recognize or make distinctions between various emotions. They may also confuse physical sensations, such as hunger or pain, with emotional experiences. Therefore, it is important to improve your emotional intelligence.

Begin by listing various emotions, such as anger, sadness, fear, anxiety, shame, guilt, boredom, joy, and love. Write the name of each emotion on a separate piece of paper. For each emotion, first list all the words you can think of that indicate or refer to that emotion. For example, words that convey some level of anger would include annoyance, frustration, fury, hostility, irritation, rage, wrath, and so forth. Words associated with sadness might include depression, despair, gloom, grief, hurt, sorrow, and woe.

Words associated with joy could include happiness, pleasure, gladness, euphoria, rapture, satisfaction, and so on.

Next, list the events that trigger or evoke each emotion in you. For example, anger may be prompted by not getting what you want, being threatened, or being criticized. Sadness may result when things turn out badly, or your best friend gets upset with you. Being successful at a task, receiving a nice surprise, or being with people who love or like you could prompt joy.

Then, write down on the same sheet of paper, the thoughts or conclusions that prompt a particular feeling. Believing that you are "right" and the other person wrong may prompt anger. Feeling that you are worthless may bring feelings of sadness. Knowing that you are loved and appreciated can bring joy.

Finally, describe how you experience and express each emotion. Where do you feel it in your body? What are the physical signs of the emotion? How do you behave when you are in the grip of the emotion? For example, anger may cause your face to flush and your fists to clench. Perhaps you yell or pound something when you are angry. Sadness may make you feel empty inside. There may be a pain or hollowness in your chest or gut. You may cry, lose your appetite, or feel dizzy. Joy probably brings a smile to your face and a feeling of excitement or pleasure. You may talk in an excited voice, laugh, or hug people.

Learning to differentiate between emotions and becoming more familiar with their signs and symptoms will help you to cope more effectively. You will better understand your own experience and be less afraid of being overwhelmed. Developing a full palette of emotions is important. Although all sorts of painful emotions can be involved in disordered eating, one emotion in particular is most relevant for those with an eating disorder—shame.

Shame: A Core Emotion in Eating Disorders

At the core of an eating disorder is the emotion of shame. Shame was first mentioned in chapter 4. The threat of shame is an unseen regulator of behavior that helps society function. However, internalized, toxic shame is a wound to the self and is at the root of many emotional problems.[18] Gershen Kaufman[19] was one of the first to expose shame as an emotion common to those seeking psychotherapy.

The Emotion of Shame

Shame feels like unexpected exposure, like suddenly being revealed as less than another or less than what you should be. The self feels exposed to view, as if impaled under a magnifying glass, but the watching eyes belong to you.[20] Feeling exposed to judgment—your own or another's—is inherent in the experience of shame. Its affective, cognitive, and interpersonal signs characterize shame.

Affective Signs

Shyness, embarrassment, discouragement, self-consciousness, and guilt are signs of shame. Depression and anger can both have shame as a component. Often the inner experience of shame is misconstrued as anxiety. When any of these emotions is present, shame is often an underlying dynamic. Although shame can be a passing experience, as in momentary embarrassment or shyness, it is most toxic when it manifests as chronic shyness or enduring feelings of inferiority.

Cognitive Signs

Low self-esteem, diminished self-concept, and negative body image are other ways in which shame is manifested cognitively. Thinking or talking about oneself in self-defeating ways, as stupid, inferior, unattractive—or fat—are cognitive signs of shame. Some people who experience shame as a core affect see themselves as worthless or unlovable. They may feel acutely inferior, deeply inadequate, or like born failures. For others, there is a sense of inner deficiency, of something being vitally wrong with themselves. They may complain of feeling empty inside or feel that there is no real self within. They may speak of feeling different from others or of being an outsider among their peers. Some just feel "crazy."

Interpersonal Signs

The person for whom shame is a core emotion may attempt to control others as a way of maintaining the illusion of power. People for whom shame is a central emotion may be contemptuous and put others down as a means of negating their own shame. Competitiveness, or the constant need to draw attention to one's positive aspects, is also symptomatic of shame. When shame is activated, the shamed person may become angry and even fly into a rage. They may blame or find fault with others in their efforts to shift the experience of shame from themselves. Sometimes feeling shamed results in a shut-down personality, in which the real person remains hidden from view, unavailable to friends or even family. Demanding absolute perfection of oneself, and striving unrealistically to excel, improve, or be more perfect, points to underlying shame. Being perfect and above reproach is an attempt to avoid criticism and judgment that might activate core shame. Sarcastic or self-deprecating humor—making fun of oneself or others—can also be signs of core shame.

Attempts to Escape from Shame

Shame is so painful and deleterious to the self that it must be avoided or escaped at all costs. Some people attempt to avoid shame by compensating for what they believe to be their inferiority by aiming to reach high standards. They work hard and develop perfectionistic standards that they hope will put them beyond criticism. Others avoid asserting themselves or their needs to avoid another's ire or rejection. Shame can also be avoided by withdrawing from those situations where it might be experienced. Thus, avoiding reaching out to others for help, avoiding socializing, avoiding sex, avoiding competing—are all examples of dealing with potential shame by never putting yourself in situations where shame could arise.

The pain of shame may be partly escaped by hiding it with another emotion. Anger and even aggression can substitute for shame—the person who is criticized or has her mistakes noted or commented upon may become angry as a defense against feeling shamed. Avoidance behaviors, such as binge eating, purging, excessive exercising, abuse of drugs or alcohol, compulsive spending, gambling, or nonrelational sex (i.e., sex without emotional involvement) can also be used to escape from the experience of shame.

Another way to deal with shame is to keep it a secret. Such secrecy can be personal or at the level of families or even organizations. Secrets such as rape, incest, molestation, alcoholism, physical abuse, infidelity, discrimination, or harassment can contribute to personal difficulties that may be expressed through an eating disorder. The secrecy of bulimia is fueled by the desire to avoid feeling shamed. Shame that is kept secret and never acknowledged cannot be worked through or alleviated.

Tolerating Shame

Shame can be likened to growing mushrooms. Mushrooms grow best in the dark or heavy shade and in dead or decomposing material. Opened to the bright sunlight, mushrooms wither.

Likewise, to be healed, shame must be aired openly and given direct expression. You need to become fully conscious of your shame, able to recognize when you are experiencing it, and able to identify its sources. To do this, you must become better able to tolerate the emotion of shame and cope with it when it is activated.

Refocusing Attention

When shame is generated, attention turns inward and the focus is intensely on the self. A tool for releasing shame is *refocusing attention*.[21] Although not a means of healing or resolving toxic, internalized shame, refocusing attention allows you to cope with debilitating shame whenever it becomes reactivated in the present without having to resort to using avoidance behaviors such as binge eating and purging.

By intentionally and with effort shifting your focus from yourself to outside yourself, shame is temporarily dismissed. This can be accomplished by becoming immersed in external sensory experience, particularly visual and physical. This is especially helpful for interrupting *shame spirals*—the experience of feeling more and more shame and being unable to escape from it.

Jillian (see chapter 2) believed she was fat and ugly, despite being strikingly attractive. She rode the bus every day to work, during which time she compared herself to every other woman on the bus. If the woman was attractive, Jillian faulted herself for being less attractive or focused on the features of her own body that didn't measure up. If the woman was unattractive, Jillian tortured herself with thoughts of how she too would one day look like that. If an attractive man entered the bus, Jillian told herself that he would never be interested in anyone as unattractive as she, and that she was likely to live out the rest of her life alone. By the time Jillian got off the bus, she would be overwhelmed by shame. Jillian was held prisoner by her shame spirals.

Deliberately refocusing all of one's attention outside oneself by becoming visually and physically involved in the sensory world outside breaks the shame spiral and allows shame feelings and thoughts to subside. Jillian's therapist instructed her to focus her attention on the buildings the bus passed. She was to notice the color, the trim, the types of windows, how many stories, the doors, and so forth. If her attention turned to someone entering or leaving the bus, she was to deliberately and through sheer effort of her will, refocus her attention back to the buildings. A fall-back strategy, in case she became overwhelmed, was to simply close her eyes and not look at whoever was on the bus. By refocusing her attention, Jillian had a tool for managing her experience of shame, which also enhanced her mastery over it. Turning your attention outward interrupts the shame spiral. It also allows the creation of positive affect. Jillian eventually found enjoyment in focusing her attention on interesting architecture.

The essence of shame involves focusing attention inward upon the self, which, for the eating disordered person, may be triggered by the appearance of some attractive person or by catching a glimpse of herself in a reflective surface. At that point, the self feels excruciatingly exposed. When we feel shame, suddenly we are observing and evaluating ourselves. This inner scrutiny, this torment of self-consciousness, creates shame's binding, paralyzing effects, and the pain that demands escape or avoidance.

Using the technique of refocusing attention takes practice, and mastering it can be difficult. Although it provides a reprieve from shame as long as an external focus is maintained, self-consciousness can return quickly. However, continued use of the procedure will eventually provide leverage over the experience of shame. An important aspect of making it work is to focus on creating or finding new, positive-affect scenes. Enjoyment and peace must become associated with scenes that previously triggered the shame. Jillian had to teach herself how to make riding the bus an opportunity to enjoy the scenery, rather than a sentence to engage in painful comparison of herself with others.

Repair of Shame

Ultimately, the repair of shame involves forgiveness of the self and learning to accept and trust the forgiveness of others. Self-forgiveness means reducing harsh, internal self-attacks and focusing on your positive qualities. For those with an eating disorder, repair of shame means accepting yourself with whatever flaws you think you have, while owning your strengths and positive qualities. It also involves being able to tolerate that some people may judge you negatively, but most people, if given a chance, are caring and accepting.

Repair of internalized, toxic shame also involves returning shame to its interpersonal origins. The original shame wounds and their present-day manifestations, or *governing scenes*—the psychological "black holes" into which you are sucked when shame is triggered—must become conscious and recognized. These scenes can involve the family, peer group, or school setting, and constitute the early wounds that set shame in motion. The power of the governing scenes is that they can synthesize ever-new repetitions of the same scene, using present-day interactions.

Consider Carol from chapter 1. Carol suffered from exercise anorexia, and whenever she felt criticized at work, she would slip into a shame spiral. Her thoughts focused on what a bad job she did at work, what a bad mother she was, what a bad wife she was, how ugly and fat she was, and so forth. Eventually she became so overwhelmed by shame she had to escape by leaving work to go for a punishing run. Although Carol was not initially aware of it, her present-day shame was linked to her experiences as a young girl when her parents repeatedly shamed her for eating too much and for being overweight.

Shame wounds are often inflicted in early relationships, especially when the needs to be loved, wanted, or valued are involved. Therapy is one means of identifying and working through these early wounds. Another is writing or keeping a journal. By observing your inner experience and then writing in a journal about it, you may be able to identify early shaming experiences and see how they are being triggered again in the present. This means learning to observe yourself and your reactions immediately preceding binge eating and also after purging. The roots of shame and how it influences eating behavior can also be identified by using self-monitoring, which was introduced in chapter 6. Through these means, you can learn how to distinguish and accurately name your feelings and your needs, and begin to repair your shame and overcome your disordered eating.

Notes

1. Lazarus, R. S., and S. Folkman. 1984. *Stress, Appraisal, and Coping.* New York: Springer. 19.

2. Ibid.

3. Christiano, B., and J. S. Mizes. 1997. Appraisal and coping deficits associated with eating disorders: Implications for treatment. *Cognitive and Behavioral Practice, 4*, 263–290.

4. Etringer, B. D., E. M. Altmaier, and W. Bowers. 1989. An investigation into the cognitive functioning of bulimic women. *Journal of Counseling and Development, 68*, 216–219; Janzen, B. L., I. W. Kelly, and D. H. Sakolfske. 1992. Bulimic symptomatology and coping in a nonclinical sample. *Perceptual and Motor Skills, 75*, 395–399.

5. Mizes, J. S. 1988. Personality characteristics of bulimic and non-eating-disordered female controls: A cognitive-behavioral perspective. *International Journal of Eating Disorders, 7*, 541–550.

6. Christiano, B., and J. S. Mizes. 1997. Appraisal and coping deficits associated with eating disorders: Implications for treatment. *Cognitive and Behavioral Practice, 4*, 263–290.

7. Neckowitz, P., and T. L. Morrison. 1991. Interactional coping strategies of normal-weight bulimic women in intimate and non-intimate situations. *Psychological Reports, 69*, 1167–1175; Soukup, V. M., M. E. Beiler, and F. Terrell. 1990. Stress, coping style, and problem-solving ability among eating disordered patients. *Journal of Clinical Psychology, 46*, 592–599; Troop, N. S., A. Holbrey, R. Trowler, and J. S. Treasure. 1994. Ways of coping in women with eating disorders. *Journal of Nervous and Mental Disease, 182*, 535–540; Troop, N. S., A. Holbrey, and J. S. Treasure. 1998. Stress, coping, and crisis support in eating disorders. *International Journal of Eating Disorders, 24*, 157–166.

8. Leitenberg, H., J. Gross, F. Peterson, and J. C Rosen. 1984. Analysis of an anxiety model and the process of change during exposure plus response prevention treatment of bulimia nervosa. *Behavior Therapy, 15*, 3–20; Rosen, J. C., and H. Leitenberg. 1990. Bulimia nervosa: Treatment with exposure and response prevention. *Behavior Therapy, 13*, 117–124.

9. Barrios, B. A., and J. W. Pennebaker. 1983. A note on the early detection of bulimia nervosa. *The Behavior Therapist, 6*, 18–19; Bruch, H. 1988. Disturbed concepts of food, body, and self. In D. Czyzewski and M. A. Suhr, eds., *Conversations With Anorexics*. New York: Basic Books. 114–152; Garner, D. M., M. P. Olmstead, and P. E. Garfinkel. 1983. Does anorexia nervosa occur on a continuum? *International Journal of Eating Disorders, 2*, 11–27.

10. Casper, D., and D. Zachary. 1984. The eating disorder as a maladaptive conflict resolution. *Individual Psychology Journal of Adlerian Theory, Research, and Practice, 40*, 445–452.

11. Steiner, H., P. Rahimzadeh, and N. B. Lewiston. 1990. Psychopathology in cystic fibrosis and anorexia nervosa: A controlled comparison. *International Journal of Eating Disorders, 9*, 675–683; Troop, N. S., A. Holbrey, R. Trowler, and J. S. Treasure. 1994. Ways of coping in women with eating disorders. *Journal of Nervous and Mental Disease, 182*, 535–540.

12. Butterfield, P. S., and S. LeClair. 1988. Cognitive characteristics of bulimic and drug-abusing women. *Addictive Behaviors, 13*, 131–138; Teusch, R. 1988.

Level of ego development and bulimics' conceptualization of their disorder. *International Journal of Eating Disorders, 7,* 607–615.

13. Christiano, B., and J. S. Mizes. 1997. Appraisal and coping deficits associated with eating disorders: Implications for treatment. *Cognitive and Behavioral Practice, 4,* 263–290.

14. D'Zurilla, T. J., and M. R. Goldfried. 1971. Problem solving and behavior modification. *Journal of Abnormal Psychology, 78,* 107–126.

15. Mizes, J. S., and J. M. Lohr. 1983. The treatment of bulimia binge-eating and self-induced vomiting : A quasi-experimental investigation of the effects of stimulus narrowing self-reinforcement, and self-control relaxation. *International Journal of Eating Disorders, 2,* 58–65.

16. Mizes, J. S., and E. L. Fleece. 1986. On the use of progressive relaxation in the treatment of bulimia: A single-subject design study. *International Journal of Eating Disorders, 5,* 169–176.

17. Linehan, M. M. 1993. *Cognitive-Behavioral Treatment of Borderline Personality Disorder.* New York: Guilford.

18. Karen, R. 1992. Shame. *The Atlantic Monthly,* February, 40–70.

19. Kaufman, G. 1989. *The Psychology of Shame.* New York: Springer.

20. Ibid.

21. Ibid.

Chapter 11

Increasing Interpersonal Effectiveness

An eating disorder does not happen in a vacuum. It develops and is maintained within an interpersonal context consisting of family, friends, peers, and significant others. Both the person with the eating disorder and those who form the interpersonal context reciprocally influence one another. Cultural norms and values in turn influence and are influenced by the existing social environment. Improving interpersonal functioning is an important goal for coping with stress and emotions and for generally increasing satisfaction in life. (See chapter 4 for a discussion of the various cultural and interpersonal factors that affect disordered eating.)

Interpersonal Psychotherapy (IPT) is a specific treatment originally developed by Gerald Klerman and his associates to treat depression.[1] It has since been adapted and shown to be effective in the treatment of bulimia[2] and has been used successfully to treat obese binge eaters.[3]

Although cognitive-behavioral therapy (CBT) makes the assumption that dysfunctional thinking is what maintains an eating disorder, IPT assumes that relationship issues are at the heart of an eating disorder. Difficulties associated with the interpersonal context produce stress and painful emotions, and an eating disorder functions as a means of coping. According to IPT thinking, relationship issues are grouped into four categories. These include *grief* resulting from relationship losses, *interpersonal role disputes* involving unmet expectations, *role transitions* occurring as the result of a specific life event (e.g., going away to school) or changes in circumstances (e.g., financial loss, physical illness), and *interpersonal deficits* such as shyness, a poorly developed sense of self, and so forth.

Both IPT and CBT produce decreases in binge eating, purging, and general psychological distress, as well as improvements in social functioning, although there is a difference in the timing of these improvements.[4] Cognitive-behavioral therapy produces quicker results, but IPT catches up and may provide extra benefits in the long run. It has been suggested that both the interpersonal focus and the cognitive-behavioral focus are helpful in ameliorating eating disorders, although they work in different ways. Some experts have suggested that neither approach provides a fully adequate conceptualization of eating disorders, and that a "higher order," more inclusive conceptualization that embraces both concerns is needed.[5]

This chapter briefly addresses grief, role transitions, and interpersonal deficits, but focuses primarily on how to increase interpersonal effectiveness for resolving interpersonal role disputes. To this end, particular attention is given to the roles played by anger, communication, conflict management, and assertiveness.

Grief and Eating Disorders

Loss or the break up of a relationship can trigger an eating disorder. In normal grief, a person experiences sadness, disturbed sleep, agitation, and decreased ability to carry out day-to-day tasks. These symptoms tend to resolve without treatment in two to four months as the person comes to grips with the loss and begins to reinvest in other relationships. When symptoms do not resolve, when grief reactions are overwhelming, or when grieving is delayed, counseling can be helpful. The goals of such counseling are to remember the associated events and to explore related feelings.

After the break up of a four-year relationship with her high school sweetheart, one young woman went into a deep depression that lasted several months. During that time she lost nearly thirty pounds, taking her weight down to 115 pounds on her 5 feet, 8 inch frame. With increasing weight loss, her periods became more irregular and eventually ceased. However, as her weight dropped, she started receiving more and more compliments, particularly from strangers and recent acquaintances, although her family and longtime friends were becoming alarmed. With her self-esteem at an all-time low from her boyfriend's recent rejection, this young woman was flattered and encouraged by the admiration for her low weight. She began consciously to restrict her eating, losing even more weight, and she rejected her family's efforts to get her to eat more or to seek treatment. Her anorexia gave her a sense of control and power that she had not had before. Treatment focused first on the grief work that had not been completed at the break-up of the relationship and then on her underlying control and self-esteem issues.

Role Transitions and Eating Disorders

Similarly, role transitions can elicit an eating disorder. At any given time, most people have multiple roles. For example, your current roles may include those of parent, adult child, spouse, breadwinner, community activist, town resident—to name a few. These roles help define your sense of who you are and where you fit. A role transition involves changing roles, losing one or acquiring another. Moving, changing jobs, leaving home, becoming a parent, retiring from work, becoming ill are all examples of role transitions.

The developmental process that involves changes tied to maturation determines some role transitions. The transition from childhood to adolescence and reaching the menopause are two examples of developmental transitions. Marriage, divorce, a job promotion, and moving to another location are examples of transitions associated with social or cultural patterns.

Any change in role requires that adjustments be made and new skills acquired. A role transition can result in the loss of familiar social supports or attachments. Graduating from college and taking a job in a faraway city means leaving behind familiar friends and places. Painful emotions such as anger, anxiety, sadness, or fear may occur. When a person has difficulty making the necessary changes or is not satisfied with the new role or its status, depression and anxiety can result, along with diminished self-esteem.

Leaving home to go to college is a role transition that is frequently associated with the emergence of an eating disorder. For the first time, the young person is on her own, making more of her own decisions than ever before, and having to leave behind old friends and family. Feeling homesick and unsure of herself, not knowing how to cope with feelings such as loss and the fear of failure, the eating disorder provides an escape from painful emotions and a distraction from a problem without an apparent solution.

Achieving a successful role transition involves evaluating and grieving the loss of the old role, including understanding and accepting the feelings associated with this loss. Leaving behind a familiar role can cause you to idealize its benefits and minimize the negative aspects. It is important to acknowledge the difficulties of the old role, while remembering its positive aspects. When a valued or familiar role is lost, grief is a normal reaction. Even when change is desired and sought, giving up an old role may be experienced as a loss. Mourning its loss is appropriate.

Successful role transition also involves acquiring new skills needed for the new role and developing new interpersonal relations, attachments, and supports. Talking about and planning ahead for an anticipated role transition can be helpful. Parents should encourage their college-bound children to think and talk about what they expect it to be like to be away from home, and how they expect to handle feelings of homesickness. The stresses involved in making a move—whether to a new job, across town, or to a new city—should be anticipated and talked about with friends or family. Going through a realistic assessment of your assets and skills for managing a transition to a new role, and examining your assumptions about the anticipated role, can be helpful. Think about how you will meet and get involved with others in order to form new, supportive relationships.

Interpersonal Deficits and Eating Disorders

Shyness is one example of an interpersonal deficit that can be associated with an eating disorder. Shyness, which is fueled by worries and anxiety about whether others will be critical or rejecting, causes the shy person to pull back and avoid certain social situations. Shy people are usually uncomfortable in groups, preferring one-on-one interactions or being left alone. As a result, shy people become increasingly isolated and lonely. They may have few friends and, often, food becomes their best friend.

Good social functioning includes having close and supportive relationships with family and significant others, maintaining satisfying but less intense relationships with friends and acquaintances, and developing positive relationships with co-workers or peers. Those who are shy or socially reserved may lack relationships in one or a combination of these areas.

Sarah. Fifteen-year-old Sarah (see chapter 4) was a perfectionist who got good grades in school, but she had few friends. She regarded herself as a "dork" and not one of the "in group." Her shyness kept her from trying to make friends and discouraged others from engaging her. Sarah also had difficulties in her relationship with her mother, who was frequently angry with various family members. When she wasn't doing homework, Sarah escaped into elaborate fantasies of being admired for rescuing oppressed peoples in faraway places. Sarah's anorexia served to allow her to feel special and powerful, to escape from her mother's moods, and to cover up her loneliness.

Overcoming social isolation is a primary goal in the treatment of shyness. The help of a skilled therapist is often needed to encourage the shy person to overcome anxiety, take interpersonal risks, and to develop the skills necessary for creating and maintaining relationships. Sarah had to be taught and encouraged to make new friends at school. She had to learn other ways of enduring her mother's emotional outbursts without becoming overwhelmed and fearful. To this end, Sarah was helped to focus on the positive relationship she had with her aunt, which provided hope that relationships can be validating and safe.

Interpersonal Role Disputes and Eating Disorders

Interpersonal conflict occurs for many reasons. Klerman and his colleagues[6] cite *nonreciprocal role expectations* as an important factor in interpersonal role disputes. That is, at least one person holds expectations about the relationship that are not shared or met by the other. For example, a wife who expects her husband to be the financial provider but who must hold a job for the family to pay its bills has an expectation of her husband that is not being met. Another example would be that of a mother who expects her teenage daughter to confide fully the details of her friendships, while the teenager expects to keep some things private.

Other factors can incite conflict in relationships. When one person breaks a promise, is intolerant of another's shortcomings, or acts in such a way that the other person's self-worth is threatened, anger and conflict can ensue. Misunderstandings, often resulting from poor or inadequate communication, can also lead to disputes. Likewise, when one or both parties act unfairly or are deliberately hurtful, conflict may result.

Conflict involves disagreement, argument, opposition, resistance, and hostility. It can generate aggressive behavior such as verbal or physical abuse. Conflict is usually disruptive, uncomfortable, and painful. Sometimes conflict is unnecessary and unwarranted. At other times conflict can be positive and growth producing. It can clarify issues, strengthen relationships, and lead to problem solving.

Unproductive and unnecessary conflict is generated by any number of factors—blaming, criticizing, cross-complaining, denying responsibility, failing to listen, invalidating the other person's feelings, acting as if the other person is incompetent or worthless, stonewalling (withdrawing or refusing to communicate), failing to negotiate clear agreements, and so forth. Disputes that occur repeatedly and are not resolved can cause demoralization and the loss of hope. Binge eating provides a momentary escape from a situation that appears beyond influence.

Productive conflict provides resolution in disputes and results in an improved sense of self-esteem for both parties. Productive conflict involves listening and being willing to be influenced by the other's point of view while maintaining respect for one's own needs and opinions. Inevitably, people have conflicting needs and wants in any relationship. Necessary conflict involves negotiating compromises so that each person gets some of his or her needs met. Resolving interpersonal conflict begins with understanding the factors that generate conflict.

Unmet Expectations and Conflict

Interpersonal disputes and conflicts occur when one or more people hold different expectations about their relationship or how each is to behave. Anger can result when one fails to act in accordance with the expectations of the other. Claire's conflict with her boyfriend (see chapter 2), provides a good example of how unmet expectations play a role in interpersonal disputes. Claire and her boyfriend had many arguments because she wanted and expected him to pay more attention to her, and he felt she was making unreasonable demands. Sometimes, their arguments would escalate to threats of ending the relationship, but nothing was ever resolved. Often Claire became so upset after an argument that she binged and purged. When there is a gap between what is expected and what actually occurs, anger, hurt, frustration, and disappointment result. An eating disorder can provide the means of pushing aside those feelings.

Examining Expectations

To improve your relationships and be able to manage conflict better, you first need to identify and become fully aware of your expectations. You are quite likely to have expectations about the other person that influence the way you feel, think, and act. Likewise, there is no doubt that the other person has expectations for you and your behavior. Such implicit expectations can wreak havoc in a relationship, and you both need to clarify what your expectations are.

Sometimes expectations are inherent in certain roles. Parents expect their children to do what they are told, follow the rules, and be respectful of their elders. Children expect parents to be predictable, reliable, supportive, understanding, and caring. Friends expect each other to be fun, interesting, supportive, tolerant, appreciative, and trustworthy. Spouses generally expect each other to be loving, respectful, understanding, accepting, trustworthy, supportive, and monogamous. Employers expect employees to be reliable and do a good job. Employees hope to be treated fairly, given timely reviews, and rewarded for good work.

Although some expectations are defined by roles, others are arbitrary. Allowances may be made for a particular person's idiosyncrasies or special needs. The rules (expectations) that govern any relationship usually develop early and are difficult to change. In Claire's relationship with her boyfriend, she realized that he was a workaholic and that, despite her desires to the contrary, he would devote some of their shared time to work-related activities. However, Claire and he never discussed how to balance his need to get work done with her need for affection and attention.

Another factor in examining expectations is to ask whether they are realistic. Sometimes what you want from the other person is not possible, given the circumstances. In fact, Claire wanted her boyfriend's undivided attention, and she interpreted any time he devoted to his work as a rejection of her.

Stress results from the failure to clarify expectations and to obtain a clear agreement. It is critical for each person in the relationship to understand and agree to what the other expects. To avoid disputes, begin by talking with the other person about what you want and how you want to be treated in the relationship. Be sure to listen to the other person's expectations as well. Try to negotiate an agreement that you both can live by. Remember that simply communicating what you want does not ensure you will get it. Both parties need to arrive at a mutual agreement. This involves communicating effectively and assertively. Both of these skills are discussed in greater depth later in this chapter.

Broken Promises and Conflict

Interpersonal conflict can also result from broken agreements and unkept promises. Sometimes the terms of a promise or agreement are not clear, or one person has a different understanding of what was agreed to than the other does. One couple ended up in an argument because he understood her suggestion that they continue talking about a particular course of action to mean that it was okay for him to proceed. Her expectation was that before proceeding they would discuss it further.

When making an agreement, be sure each of you understands and agrees to terms that are specific and concrete. For example, instead of saying, "Let's get together this weekend and do something," say, "Are you up for going to the seven o'clock movie on Friday?"

Negotiating Agreements

Never make an agreement you do not intend to keep or that you have reservations about keeping. If necessary, qualify your promise as in, "I'll go to the movies with you on Friday if I don't have to work." Once you make an agreement or a promise, do all you can to keep it. If you find that you must break a promise, take responsibility for doing so and make amends. When you break promises and agreements, you not only increase the risk of interpersonal conflict, you also undermine the other person's trust in you.

If someone breaks a promise to you, try to ascertain why this happened and what you should do. Perhaps the agreement was too vague and left room for misunderstanding. Try renegotiating and this time be more specific. Perhaps something unexpected occurred that legitimately interfered. Is the explanation offered for breaking the agreement reasonable? Should you negotiate a new agreement? Or is the broken agreement yet another in a pattern of broken promises? If so, you may need to accept that you cannot trust this person's promises and probably ought not to count on them. Continuing to make agreements with a known promise-breaker is a setup for anger and hurt.

Fourteen-year-old Beth (see chapter 4) often became infuriated with her mother, who repeatedly made promises and then went back on her word. Explaining why she was breaking the promise she made, Beth's mother would say to Beth, "I just said that to get you off my case." Beth's inability to trust her mother's word and the high level of conflict this engendered was a major contributor to Beth's binge eating.

Intolerance of Shortcomings

People who have a low tolerance for small frustrations can find themselves chronically angry. As a result, they may precipitate conflict with others, either by openly criticizing them or by passive-aggressively expressing anger. They may use sarcasm to communicate their displeasure or try to cloak their criticism in humor by following their criticism with statements like, "Oh come on, I was only kidding." Or they may withdraw into an angry silence when things don't go their way.

People with a low tolerance for frustration generally hold high expectations for themselves and others, and they want things to be easy, smooth, and hassle-free. When things do not go well, these people get frustrated, annoyed, irritated, and angry. They often pride themselves on getting things done efficiently and in an orderly fashion, and they expect others to work hard and efficiently, as well. When something goes amiss, they get upset. If someone else doesn't do things the way they think they should be done, or if another person doesn't understand or agree with their point of view, they become irritated. When there are discrepancies between their beliefs about how things should be and how things really are, or when someone commits a transgression of the "rules" as they understand them, they get angry. Such people are convinced they know the *right* way, and they shouldn't have to put up with other people's shortcomings. As a result, they are prone to getting angry, which may result in open conflict with others.

Increasing Tolerance

Such people need to identify and challenge the anger-engendering beliefs and self-talk they use. A good clue that such beliefs are present is the use of words such as "always," "never," "every," "should," and "shouldn't." Rigid thinking needs to be replaced with an attitude that is more accepting and forgiving of self and others.

Threats to Self-Worth

Threats to self-worth can trigger interpersonal conflict. Some people believe that their self-worth depends on what others think of them and on how successful they are in gaining the attention, acknowledgment, acceptance, or love of others. When the actions of others are interpreted as rejecting or critical, their self-worth is threatened, and they may become angry. Claire's anger with her boyfriend's lack of attention was mentioned earlier. When her boyfriend did not pay sufficient attention to her, she became upset and angry, interpreting this as meaning that he did not love her and that she was not good enough for him. She needed his attention to validate her self-worth. Threats to her feelings of self-worth, triggered by unreasonable expectations for his behavior, fostered ongoing conflict with him.

Avoiding Threats to Self-Esteem

Identifying expectations and negotiating realistic ones help to avoid the threats to self-esteem that can result in relationships. It is also important not to take things personally, as Claire did. When others don't treat you well or are rejecting or critical, think about how to deal with the situation appropriately. Later in this chapter you will learn how to handle another's criticism of you in a way that will protect your self-esteem.

Misunderstandings and Inappropriate Behavior

Misunderstandings can result from making assumptions without checking them out, but most frequently misunderstandings occur because of poor or inadequate communication. Inappropriate behavior can be intentional, as in deliberately making a promise you do not intend to keep, or unintentional, such as forgetting to do something you promised to do. All of these can trigger anger and conflict. Acquiring better communication skills helps in the resolution of disputes that are the result of misunderstandings or insensitive behavior.

Anger and Interpersonal Disputes

Anger is an understandable reaction to perceived interpersonal slights, transgressions, or injustices, and it can prompt interpersonal disputes. Anger may range in intensity from mild irritation and annoyance to fury and rage. Muscle tension, a flushed face, increased heart rate, and changes in breathing are some of the signs that point to the physical arousal that accompanies anger. Anger-engendering thoughts or beliefs can stimulate anger and cause it to escalate. Sulking, glaring, yelling, cursing, pushing, hitting, avoiding eye contact, falling silent, leaving, making snide or sarcastic comments are some of the behaviors that may occur as the result of anger.

How Anger Is Avoided or Expressed

Many people do not know how to express anger appropriately or how to use it effectively. As a result, they generally become either anger avoiders or anger expressers. Both styles of expression are found in people with eating disorders.

Anger Avoiders

Many people—especially women—try to avoid, ignore, or suppress anger or its expression. They have learned that in our society anger is not a "nice" emotion for women to show. Furthermore, they may fear that becoming angry or showing their anger will result in hurting someone's feelings, damaging the relationship, or causing retaliation. Anger avoiders do not recognize that they have rights in relationships. As a result, they do not stand up for themselves or assert their own needs.

Anger avoiders seldom notice the early signs of anger in themselves, even though others may be aware of their anger. When anger avoiders do get angry, they try to keep it to themselves. If angry feelings emerge, they get confused about what to do or feel too paralyzed to take any action. Often anger avoiders just give in to others instead of standing up for themselves. At times, they act on their internalized anger by engaging in passive-aggressive behaviors, such as "forgetting," being late, procrastinating, making sarcastic remarks, punishing someone else (the kids, the dog), or "accidentally" damaging things that belong to the person who has angered them.

At other times, internalized anger is expressed with a vengeful binge, which was discussed in chapter 5. Occasionally anger avoiders lose control and let loose with an outburst of anger. When they do openly express anger, they feel guilty and often end up apologizing and taking back their anger.

Anger avoiders usually try hard to please others and to win their approval. If someone gets angry with them, anger avoiders assume it was something they did or said that caused it. Anger avoiders assume they are the ones who are illogical, too sensitive, overly emotional, negligent, stupid, or incompetent. Often they end up feeling bad, wrong, or "less-than." Anger avoiders often "stuff" their feelings by eating.

Overcoming Anger Avoidance. Anger avoiders need to recognize and own their own anger. They must confront problems sooner than later, rather than postponing conflict in the hope the problem will go away. Anger avoiders need to learn that they have certain rights in relationships. Some of these include the rights to be treated with respect, to ask for what they want or need, to refuse requests, to experience and express feelings, to say no and not feel guilty, and to make mistakes without being demeaned. Then, anger avoiders need to assert these rights, while respecting the fact that others also have these same rights. (Later in this chapter, the section on assertiveness discusses in greater depth personal rights in relationships.)

Anger Expressers

At the other end of the spectrum are those who anger easily and express their anger openly. Such people may be overly sensitive to real or imagined interpersonal slights or transgressions. They respond quickly to even minor provocations, sometimes exploding with impulsive and exaggerated reactions. Anger expressers assume more rights than they really have in relationships. They often justify irresponsible behavior by blaming others for provoking them or by blaming "anger," as in, "I did it because I was angry." They tend to brood over past insults and slights, while remaining hypervigilant for new insults. As a result, they never really let go of their anger, which makes them especially sensitive to the next provocation. Eating helps temporarily to suppress the physical arousal that accompanies their chronic anger.

Some anger expressers believe that they should vividly and freely give voice to their anger, sometimes by yelling and shouting, slamming doors, or kicking furniture. At times, such expressions of anger escalate to pushing, shoving, hitting, or blocking the other person's exit. Or anger expressers may simply withdraw into an angry silence. Some anger expressers try hard to cover up their irritation and frustrations with others, only to "lose it" periodically and fly into a rage, which is often triggered by the proverbial "last straw."

Often seeing themselves as the injured party and their anger as righteous and warranted, anger expressers use anger to solve problems, to try and gain control of a situation, or to obtain temporary relief by venting. Displaying anger increases their feelings of anger because it reinforces their belief that they are justified in being angry. Because anger often succeeds in intimidating others or causing them to stop or change what they are doing, at least temporarily, anger avoiders receive reinforcement for expressing their anger.

Anger expressers can refrain from expressing anger if they think showing their anger will hurt their position or incur some cost to them. In such cases, they may displace their anger onto someone or something else. Or they may binge or purge.

Getting Control of Anger. Before disputes can be resolved and conflict engaged in productively, anger expressers must get control of their own anger. This begins with their being willing to examine their expectations as well as their anger-engendering beliefs and self-talk. They need to understand that no one has the right to use anger as a means to control or bully others. Furthermore, no one has the right to mistreat others just because he or she is in a bad mood. And no one has the right to insist that others behave the way they think they "should" or adhere to their philosophy about how things "should" be. Anger expressers need to catch anger as it rises and take steps to de-escalate. To this end they need to learn to identify the physical cues—tension in certain parts of the body, change of voice tone, clenched teeth or jaws, and so forth—that tell them they are becoming angry. Then they must use one or more of the emotion-focused coping skills outlined in chapter 10.

Using Anger Productively and Appropriately

Anger, used productively and appropriately, serves as a signal that something is wrong and points to the need for some kind of corrective action. Anger is often a cover for other emotions—for example, shame, fear, or anxiety. When anger is used to cover up another emotion, it is as a defense against feeling vulnerable. At these times, the underlying emotion needs to be identified and addressed. At other times, anger arises because needs are not being met. Some needs are personal, such as the need to feel competent and in control. Often the unmet needs involve interpersonal relationships, such as the need to feel accepted or be respected. The first question that should be asked once anger arises is, "What is the problem?"

Sometimes anger is triggered when a current situation taps into anger associated with much earlier experiences. For example, one woman felt angry every time she went on a diet. Eventually she realized that dieting triggered old anger she felt toward her mother, who had forced her to diet or participate in various weight reduction programs as a child. Finally, angry thinking can trigger anger. To use anger well, it should be used as a signal, and not as a solution.

Anger tells you to identify the problem and decide if it is trivial and can be ignored or if it is significant and needs to be addressed. Choose carefully the issues on which you will take a stand; pick your battles. If you decide action is warranted, express yourself clearly, tactfully, and without blaming or labeling others. Be sure to take responsibility for your feelings and use "I" statements. (See the following section on communication skills.)

Don't allow yourself to get hooked into someone else's anger. Manage your own feelings and physical arousal by pausing and taking several deep breaths. Share your perceptions, feelings, and wants as assertively as possible. Be willing to make conciliatory gestures and admit your responsibility. Ignore verbal abuse, and don't take it personally. Avoid escalations in anger. If necessary, take a "time-out"—that is, call a temporary halt to the discussion. Try to create a win/win situation, allowing the other person to save face, instead of pursuing a win/lose solution in which one person ends up one-down and feeling wrong or blamed.

Remember that the goal is the solution of the problem in a manner that respects both parties involved. Once the problem is resolved or an understanding is reached, you need to let go of your anger and avoid carrying grudges.

Communicating Effectively

Effective communication involves sending a message in such a way that the other person understands what you meant and is enabled to act. Miscommunication happens when the sender's intent and message do not correspond to what the receiver gets. Sometimes miscommunication results from basic differences between the sender and the receiver. Those who have different cultural backgrounds or who have large age differences may experience more communication problems. Gender differences in communication are probably among the most common sources of miscommunication.

Gender Differences in Communication

Recently, quite a number of books have been written on how men and women communicate differently. The underlying thesis of all of these books is that women are relational while men are competitive and hierarchical. That is, women are concerned about protecting and promoting relationships, while men are more focused on getting the job done and being on top relative to other men. These different orientations produce differences in the way men and women communicate.

Men hear women's complaints and sharing of feelings as a problem that must be solved. Their inclination is to figure out what the problem is and then offer solutions. Men want to get to the bottom line, and they are not interested in a lot of details, usually regarding them as boring or irrelevant. Their basic attitude is that trivial problems aren't worth discussing; "just make a decision and be done with it." Men regard questions as requests for information. They believe in being rational and logical and insist that complaining about feelings doesn't help. Men assume everything is fine when there is no talking, and they demonstrate their feelings with actions.

Women, on the other hand, experience sharing feelings and talking about problems as a relief and a way to be close and supportive. They often become frustrated with a male's "fix-it" attitude. Details aid understanding a situation, and talking about a problem shows that you think the person is important, even if the problem isn't. Questions are asked to make others feel comfortable in expressing their opinions; also asking questions is a good way to show your interest in the other person. Logical analysis and rational arguments can drive some women to tears. If no one is talking, women assume something is wrong. Women want their partners to say how they feel in words, not just actions.

Of course, this summary of the gender differences that can affect communication consists of generalizations, not all of which apply to every individual. Some men are more relationship-oriented and exhibit a more female style of communicating, while some women have a more masculine style. Some people can flexibly adjust their style to the situation.

Blocks to Conflict Resolution

In addition to gender differences, there are other blocks to effective communication. Four processes in particular—criticizing and blaming, being defensive, acting contemptuously, and stonewalling—are destructive to relationships[7] and block the resolution of conflicts. Although everyone engages in the "terrible four" from time to time, it is best to avoid or minimize doing so if conflict is to be resolved productively.

Criticizing and Blaming

Criticizing and blaming are different from making a complaint or disagreeing. For example, a husband might complain that his wife had not balanced their joint checkbook (an expectation in their relationship) by saying, "The bank called today about two bounced checks, and I was very embarrassed." In this situation he specifies what happened and how he feels about it. Contrast such a complaint with the following example involving criticism and blame, as well as other blocks to resolving the conflict: "As usual, you screwed up our checkbook. You're no rocket scientist, but at least you could learn to do simple arithmetic. You don't care about anything except your own needs." In this situation, the husband engages in blaming (you screwed up), labeling and name-calling (you're no rocket scientist), sarcasm (at least you could learn to do arithmetic), and character assassination (you don't care about anything except your own needs). What makes this attack so destructive is not the husband's anger but his derision and gratuitous insults. His message is that his wife not only made a mistake, she *always* makes mistakes and is stupid to boot.

Notice that in the first example of a productive complaint, the husband used an "I" statement, whereas in the example of destructive criticism, he used "you" statements. When you use "I" language to describe feelings, needs, expectations, and actions, you take responsibility for these, rather than shifting the blame for your feelings, unmet needs or expectations, or actions onto the other person. "You" language is the language of blaming and attacking, and it causes others to become defensive.

Being Defensive

Criticism and blaming invite defensiveness. This may involve counter-attacking with a cross-complaint, interrupting, gunnysacking, denying responsibility, or offering excuses.

Cross-complaining. *Cross-complaining* means responding to the other person's complaint with a complaint of your own. "Oh yeah? Well what about when you bounced a check for the insurance and we lost our coverage? At least when I bounce a check, it's for store merchandize and not something really important." Alternatively, adopting the innocent victim posture is another way of being defensive. "How can I help it? You don't give me enough money to cover the household expenses."

Interrupting. Another way of being defensive involves *interrupting* the person who is trying to state a point of view or describe a situation. The interruption may start with "Yes, but . . ." and serve to derail the point being made. The person who interrupts may disagree with what is being said or fear that he or she will not get a chance to argue his/her point. "That's not the way it happened. I can tell you what really happened." Or the person may feel that what is being said is irrelevant and not worth listening to, and that he is not interested in hearing what is being said. "This is going nowhere. Let's focus on what's really important."

Interrupting often goes hand in hand with cross-complaining, and frequently serves to block another's complaint before it is fully aired. It stops the other person in mid-argument and distracts attention to another issue. "Yes but, you should know I'm not like that. How many times have I stepped in and taken charge of a problem?" At times, the cross-complaint may invalidate the other's feelings. "You shouldn't feel that way." Interrupting is usually an attempt to dominate the discussion. The person who gets interrupted ends up feeling frustrated, angry, and hopeless, and convinced that the other person does not listen.

Gunnysacking. This involves storing up unspoken complaints, which are then either dribbled out one at a time, or dumped all at once during an argument. Gunnysacking is akin to *kitchen sinking*, in which discussion about one issue eventually winds up dragging in previously discussed problems, which may or may not have been resolved. The argument ends up including "everything but the kitchen sink." Before there is a chance to reach resolution on one concern, one or both parties introduce other gripes that may or may not be related to the issue at hand. The intention is to add weight to the current complaint and get the other person to take corrective action. The actual effect is to cloud the issue and distract attention from the problem at hand. Pretty soon both parties feel overwhelmed and angry, and the dispute becomes like a tangled knot, impossible to solve. Stored-up complaints and the introduction of old gripes perpetuate interpersonal conflict and seriously interfere with conflict resolution.

Denying Responsibility. When there is conflict, it is easy to feel that the other person is at fault, especially when the situation is seen from only one point of view—yours. Although it may feel better and give you the sense of being right to attribute the problem entirely or even principally to the other person, failure to take responsibility for the role you play in the dispute blocks resolution of the conflict. Both parties must "own" the problem—i.e., be accountable for their part in it—and take responsibility for their individual thoughts, feelings, and actions without offering excuses.

Acting Contemptuously

Contempt involves speaking or acting as if the other person is incompetent or worthless. It usually involves *character assassination*—turning a complaint about the other person's behavior into a global judgment of him or her as a person. Contemptuous treatment hurts others and sows the seeds of destruction in a relationship. Those who engage in character assassination may get initial relief from their angry feelings, but in the long run they hurt themselves and their relationships. Those treated with contempt are less likely to respond constructively to legitimate complaints because the message is filtered through their hurt feelings. Contemptuous treatment may trigger its own barrage of contemptuous counteraccusations, causing the two people to trade attacks until one or the other simply withdraws.

Stonewalling

Stonewalling involves removing oneself emotionally or physically from the dispute. One person may refuse to answer or look at the other, or may storm out of the room. Stonewalling can go on for days or weeks, eventually fading away without ever leading to a resolution of the conflict. Stonewalling causes disputes to simmer and never reach closure. Because of stonewalling, unresolved complaints from the past remain available to be dragged into current disputes that have little or nothing to do with the previous problems.

Communicating by Listening

Lack of skill in communicating is at the heart of many interpersonal problems. Active listening is one of the most important communication skills you can learn. It is a sure way to maintain friends, create good impressions, and minimize interpersonal problems. When there is a dispute and the other person feels that you have truly heard and acknowledged their complaint or point of view, even if you don't agree with what they say, they are often willing to compromise.

Active Listening

To be a good listener, you must listen with the intention of hearing and understanding what the other person is saying, and suppress the tendency to focus on what your response should be. Instead of focusing on what the other person is saying, the poor listener is busy figuring out how to defend himself, how to convince the other person of his point of view, or how to get the other person to understand the facts as he knows them. The poor listener focuses on the countercomplaint he wants to issue, his excuses, or the angry feelings that arise as a result of what the other person is saying. To listen well, you must set aside your own agenda and suspend judgment. True understanding won't take place if you tune in merely to confirm your expectations or beliefs. Try to put yourself in the place of the other person and understand what is true for them, even if it is not true for you.

Active listening also involves using congruent nonverbal behavior. Be sure to validate the other person by making good eye contact, nodding, and maintaining an open body posture, all of which "tells" the other person that you are paying attention. If the other person is emotional, acknowledge her or his feelings without trying to fix them. A pat on the hand or a gentle response such as, "I understand," can help.

Another important component of active listening is paraphrasing and asking for clarification. *Paraphrasing* means repeating back to the other person what you understood him or her to say. This gives the speaker an opportunity to elaborate or clarify. It also lets the other party know you are listening, and gives you a chance to check out your assumptions. People often react to what they think they heard, and this is often quite different from what actually was said or meant. *Clarification* involves asking questions and paraphrasing what you hear until you are clear about the other's experience or point of view. Do not assume you know what is meant; check it out by asking.

Active listening involves setting aside your own beliefs and suspending judgment so that you can truly hear and understand what the other person is speaking as their "truth," even though your "truth" may differ from theirs.

Managing Conflict

Some people seem to spend most of their lives embroiled in conflict. They argue with friends or family members, berate their subordinates, and seem unable to get along with bosses or coworkers. They always seem to be finding fault with and disapproving the actions of others. Such people tend to generate unnecessary conflict by being critical of others.

Although a certain amount of conflict is useful in clarifying issues, strengthening relationships, and solving problems, sometimes conflict is not only unproductive but also destructive. Assumptions, expectations, wrong judgments, and insensitive or inappropriate behavior produce most unwarranted conflict. Managing conflict productively involves skill in communicating. Learning to cope with criticism without becoming hurt, angry, overwhelmed, or devastated is an important coping skill. Likewise, knowing how best to issue criticisms can avoid unproductive conflict.

Coping with Criticism

Criticism often precipitates interpersonal conflicts. Criticism hurts and, for most people, accepting criticism graciously is not easy. Many people try to avoid criticism by anticipating what the other person might want and then acting on what they suppose is expected of them. In so doing, they may or may not avoid a dispute, but often this is at the expense of suppressing their own wants or needs. Others fight back by issuing their own criticisms or by getting angry. Two ways to cope with criticism from others include acknowledging justified criticism and using "clouding" as a means of coping with unfounded or hurtful criticism.[8]

Acknowledging Justified Criticism

Sometimes criticism is warranted, in which case it behooves you to acknowledge your mistake. In some cases the criticism may call your attention to an error or a problem that you were unaware of and which does need your attention. In other cases, you already know what the problem is, and the other person, for his or her own reasons, is letting you know you did something wrong. When you receive criticism with which you can agree, even if it is an unnecessary reminder, it is best to simply acknowledge it and move on. For example, "You're right. I should have checked with you on this first. Next time I'll be sure to do so."

Clouding

Clouding is a means of dealing with criticism that has no basis in fact, is an exaggeration of the truth, or is meant as a putdown. When you use clouding, you find something in the critical comment to agree with, while inwardly maintaining your own sense of what is true for you. By seeming to agree with the criticism, you can turn the conversation to more productive means or reduce your exposure to the critic by simply ending the conversation. In either event, you are less emotionally vulnerable, because you have asserted control in the face of your critic's aggressiveness. There are essentially three ways of clouding—agreeing in part, agreeing in principle, and agreeing in probability.

Agreeing in part involves finding some part of the other person's criticism that you can agree with, and acknowledging that they are right about that part. For example, when Eric complained to Donna that her housekeeping was not perfect, she said, "It's true that my desk in the kitchen is a mess. I'm the only one who uses it, and I'm okay with it being that way. I do go to great effort to keep the rest of the house clean and neat, and I think I do a pretty good job with that." Agreeing in part has the effect of defusing the other person's criticism, because it provides a balanced statement about how you are partly right and the other person is partly right. In the example just given, Donna also asserted her right to keep a messy desk as long as it didn't infringe on anyone else's rights.

Agreeing in principle often takes the form of an if/then statement. It appears to show agreement, yet does not really require giving ground. When Eric complained to Donna, "It's all your fault that our son has problems in school. If you would only make him do his homework, things would be different. I have a difficult job and you can't expect me to oversee his homework." Donna's agreeing-in-principle reply was, "If you believe it's none of your responsibility to help our son with his homework and that I should do it all, no wonder you blame me for his bad grades. I have a different point of view about the situation." By agreeing in principle, Donna gains some emotional distance from Eric's criticism so that she is not overwhelmed by it. At the same time, she uses an "I" statement to assert that she has a different point of view. She does not tell him he is wrong but suggests that each of them as a different "truth."

Agreeing in probability is the approach to use when there is some chance your critic is right. Even if it is highly unlikely that the critic is right, you can make replies such as, "It could be true that . . ." or "You might be right . . ." When Eric faulted Donna for not helping their son enough with his homework and thereby causing him to get bad grades, her reply might have been, "You could be right that there was more I might have done to help."

Issuing Criticisms to Others

Criticizing others is a habit some people find difficult to break. Sometimes criticisms are issued openly; at other times criticism and disapproval can be communicated nonverbally with a certain look or tone of voice. Criticizing others can make you feel good temporarily, because it allows you to feel righteous, superior, and justified, but it can produce unnecessary and unproductive interpersonal conflict. To avoid this, consider the following alternatives:

Before you criticize, stop and think. Take a few moments to decide if your expectations are unreasonable or unrealistic. Consider whether this is a matter that must be addressed. Ask yourself what you will gain from issuing criticism and what you stand to lose.

Examine your intent before you criticize. What do you want to accomplish? Are you trying to get someone to change his behavior or are you just trying to inflict hurt? Are you lashing out because of your own frustration? What is the best way to deal with the situation, and how can you phrase your concerns so that the other person can hear what you are saying without becoming defensive?

Most importantly, *describe the problem or situation without a value judgment attached or implied.* For example, say, "It's time to leave now" instead of "Aren't you ready yet?" Similarly, try, "I notice you are eating a third piece of cake" rather than "You shouldn't eat that." Make an observation and state the facts, rather than criticizing or attacking.

If you must give criticism, *include some good news along with the bad news.* For example, "You have done a good job cleaning your room. Now I'd like to see you organize your closet rather than just dumping the clothes on the floor of the closet."

Assertiveness

Acting assertively means standing up for your legitimate rights and expressing what you believe, feel, and want in direct, honest, and appropriate ways without violating the rights of others.[9] Assertiveness involves active listening and being open to negotiation and compromise, but not at the expense of your own rights and dignity or that of others. It also involves using "I" statements to express what you think, feel, and want.

Lack of assertion, or nonassertiveness, involves taking no action to remedy an unpleasant or unacceptable situation. You don't directly express your feelings, thoughts, and wishes, but may communicate them indirectly with a look or a tone of voice. Or you may find fault with yourself and take responsibility for someone else's thoughts, feelings, or behaviors. This passive style involves ignoring your feelings and desires in order to avoid conflict with others, but results in your feeling helpless, exploited, angry, and disappointed with yourself. You may also lose the respect of others and, most importantly, you can lose respect for yourself.

If you are a person with an aggressive style of communicating, you say outright what you think, feel, or want, but often at the expense of others' rights. You may humiliate others with sarcasm or humorous put-downs or go on the attack when you don't get your way. You may use aggression to get what you want through intimidation or coercion. You openly criticize, blame, and call names. When you speak, your favorite word is "you," and you pepper your statements with the words "always" and "never." Examples of aggressive behavior include blowing up at someone, verbally cutting them down, acting dismissively ("blowing them off"), complaining belligerently, or threatening someone.

A passive-aggressive style of communicating is a more covert aggressive style. Instead of overtly blaming, criticizing, or attacking, passive-aggressive people act out their aggression in small ways. They may use pseudohumor and "make jokes" that aren't funny but are directed at the object of their anger. Then, they may "take back" their criticism, saying they were "just kidding." Forgetting important appointments, breaking things, being late, and talking behind someone's back are all examples of passive-aggressive behaviors.

Aggression is the flip side of nonassertion. Typically, both nonassertion and aggression stem from feeling threatened and helpless. Aggression is often a means of trying to get control of a situation that feels out of control. It is also a means of releasing tension. Nonassertion is an attempt to escape by ducking the situation. It relieves the anxiety associated with the fear of being criticized or becoming the target of someone's anger. Both tactics put someone in the inferior position and are win/lose strategies. Aggression puts the other person one down, while nonassertive behavior makes you the "less than" person. Assertiveness aims to create a win/win for both parties. It helps people to feel good about themselves and the other person involved.

Eating Disorders and Assertiveness

The lack of assertive behavior can be either the result of not having had a good role model for assertive behavior or from not knowing how to be appropriately assertive. However, acquiring assertiveness skills may not be the problem for some people with eating disorders. Often they can be appropriately assertive in some situations but fail to be in others. For example, they may be able to assert themselves with a boss or co-workers, but not with a spouse or with parents.

Lack of assertiveness comes from assertion-inhibiting beliefs and fears. The failure to realize and accept that every person has certain rights in any interpersonal situation is one reason that some people fail to be assertive. Fears about damaging the relationship, hurting the other person's feelings, or displeasing him or her can interfere with being assertive. In this case, not being assertive results from taking responsibility for someone else's feelings. Lack of assertiveness can also stem from a fear of being rejected or fear of becoming the object of retaliation for speaking up. Some people feel guilty at the thought of asking for something they want or for denying a request from someone else. Unwillingness to give up the benefits of nonassertion—for example, being able to play the victim role—can also be part of the problem.

Personal Rights in Relationships

Rules about what constitutes "good" and "bad" behavior are taught to children by parents and other role models. Often a child is taught that it is selfish to put her needs before others', that it is shameful to make mistakes, that she should respect those in authority, that feelings aren't important or legitimate, that she should accommodate others, that she should help those in trouble or need, and so forth.

Although these rules may be appropriate to socialize a child, they do not necessarily apply to adults. Rather, there are certain legitimate rights that apply to all adults in relationships. Some of these are listed below. Failure to understand and accept these rights is the basis for much nonassertive behavior, as well as increased stress and interpersonal conflict.

Some Personal Rights in Relationships

- To be treated with respect

- To follow my own values and standards, as long as they do not interfere with the rights of others

- To make mistakes and not be perfect

- To have feelings

- To have my own opinions and convictions

- To change my mind or decide on a different course of action

- To protest any treatment that feels bad, disrespectful, or harmful to me

- To ask questions and seek clarification
- To ask for what I want or to negotiate for change
- To say "no" and to refuse requests from others
- To ignore the advice of others
- To receive recognition for my work and accomplishments
- To make my own decisions
- To be in a nonabusive environment
- To not take responsibility for someone else's thoughts, feelings, or behavior
- To not take responsibility for someone else's problems or pain
- To not have to anticipate other's needs and wishes

Fears About Being Assertive

If you tend to be nonassertive, you need to identify the fears or beliefs that keep you stuck being subservient to other people. Remember that you are responsible only for *your own* thoughts, feelings, and behavior—not for anyone else's. If someone becomes upset because you are appropriately assertive, which has at its core treating the other person with respect, and granting him or her the identical rights you claim for yourself, then it is the other person who is causing their own upset, not you.

Benefits of Nonassertiveness

Sometimes it is appropriate to choose to be nonassertive. If a masked man shoves a gun in your ribs and demands money, give it to him. If the guy behind you is tailgating you, just pull over and let him pass. When being assertive presents a danger to you, or the situation is trivial, you may choose not to be assertive. On the other hand, if you tend to act passively when assertive behavior might be more appropriate, you need to examine your motives. What are you getting out of being passive? What would you have to give up if you behaved more assertively? If you are benefiting by not being assertive, ask yourself what it costs you to remain passive or to act with aggression. It may be that binge eating is one cost of not being appropriately assertive.

Making an Assertive Request

Nonassertive people don't ask that their needs be met. Aggressive people demand that they get what they want. Assertive people use some variation on the following "DEAR" approach, suggested by Marsha Linehan, [10] to make an assertive request.

"D" reminds you to *Describe* the situation or problem objectively and without judgment. "E" means *Express* your feelings and opinions about the situation using "I" statements. (Avoid using "You should," "I need," or "I can't.") The "A" stands for *Ask for what you want* or say no clearly. Assume that others cannot read minds and will not figure out what you want unless you ask. The "R" means *Reinforce* or *Reward* the person. That is, tell him or her the positive effects of getting what you want or need. If necessary, spell out the negative consequences if you don't get what you are asking for. Help the person feel good about complying. Consider the following example in which Donna tells Eric what she wants from him.

D: "I notice that our son comes home from school and turns on the TV instead of getting started on his homework."

E: "I get frustrated that I have to ask him repeatedly to turn off the TV and get started on his homework."

A: "I need your help in this situation. I'd like you to have a talk with him and decide on a specific time that he must start his homework after school. We also need to decide on appropriate consequences if he doesn't comply."

R: "If he knows that you and I are united and determined to enforce this, I think he is more likely to do his homework and his grades will improve. If we work together on this, I think things will be more peaceful between us."

Other Assertiveness Skills

Assertiveness includes a number of other skills in addition to making requests. These include the *broken record technique*, which involves repeatedly saying "no" or otherwise setting limits with someone who is having difficulty getting your message. It involves using a short, easy-to-understand statement about what you want and does not include an excuse, explanation, or apology. For example, "No, thank you" or "Thank you but I'm not interested." You may choose to briefly acknowledge the other person's ideas, feelings, or wishes before saying no. For example, "I understand that you want me to work overtime, but I'm not able to do so tonight." Calmly and firmly repeat your statement as many times as necessary for the person to get the message and understand that you won't change your mind.

Calling a time-out can be helpful when the discussion is at an impasse or when the interaction is becoming aggressive. You may want to call a time-out when you need time to think or to get control of your feelings or behavior. Be sure when calling a time-out to specify when you will re-engage, and don't use time-outs as a way to manipulate the situation. Thus, if you and a co-worker have a dispute about something and no solution is in sight, you might say, "I think this is important and I need time to think about it. Let's talk about it again tomorrow." Or if you become overwhelmed with tears or anger, say, "I'm really upset right now. I need time to collect myself. Let's discuss this tomorrow." Be sure you do return to the problem when you say you will.

If you need more help learning assertiveness skills, find a book that discusses these matters or attend an assertiveness training class. Remember that knowing what to do and doing it are two different things. In order to be assertive, you must recognize and own that you have the right to be.

Notes

1. Klerman, G. L., M. M. Weissman, B. J. Rounsaville, and E. S. Chevron. 1984. *Interpersonal Psychotherapy of Depression*. New York: Basic Books.

2. Fairburn, C. G. 1997. Interpersonal psychotherapy for bulimia nervosa. In D. M. Garner and P. E. Garfinkle, eds., *Handbook of Treatment for Eating Disorders, 2nd ed*. New York: Guilford. 278–294; Fairburn, C. G., R. Jones, R. C. Peveler, R. A. Hope, and M. O'Connor. 1993. Psychotherapy and bulimia nervosa: The longer-term effects of interpersonal psychotherapy, behavior therapy, and cognitive behavior therapy. *Archives of General Psychiatry, 50*, 419–428.

3. Wilfley, D. E., S. W. Agras, C. F. Telch, E. M. Rossiter, J. A. Schneider, A. G. Cole, et al. 1993. Group cognitive-behavioral therapy and group interpersonal psychotherapy for the nonpurging bulimic individual: A controlled comparison. *Journal of Consulting and Clinical Psychology, 61*, 296–305.

4. Fairburn, C. G., R. Jones, R. C. Peveler, R. A. Hope, and M. O'Connor. 1993. Psychotherapy and bulimia nervosa: The longer-term effects of interpersonal psychotherapy, behavior therapy, and cognitive behavior therapy. *Archives of General Psychiatry, 50*, 419–428.

5. Christiano, B., and J. S. Mizes. 1997. Appraisal and coping deficits associated with eating disorders: Implications for treatment. *Cognitive and Behavioral Practice, 4,* 263–290.

6. Klerman, G. L., M. M. Weissman, B. J. Rounsaville, and E. S. Chevron. 1984. *Interpersonal Psychotherapy of Depression*. New York: Basic Books.

7. Gottman, J. 1994. Why marriages fail. *The Family Therapy Networker*. May/June, 41–48.

8. McKay, M., M. Davis, and P. Fanning. 1983. *Messages: The Communication Book*. Oakland, CA: New Harbinger Publications.

9. Jakubowski, P., and A. J. Lange. 1978. *The Assertive Option: Your Rights and Responsibilities*. Champaign, IL: Research Press.

10. Linehan, M. M. 1993. *Skills Training Manual for Treating Borderline Personality Disorder*. New York: Guilford. 125.

Chapter 12

Overcoming Backsliding

Mary Ann, whose story opened chapter 1, was a thirty-eight-year-old, working mother and an obese binge eater. She had made some important changes in her diet and was exercising regularly, despite her full schedule. Then she caught the flu, which kept her in bed for several days and prevented her from exercising for nearly three weeks. At first her appetite fell away, but as she began to recover, it returned. She continued to feel weak and lethargic for several weeks and unable to exercise. One night she allowed herself a few cookies as a treat and a pick-me-up, only to feel guilty immediately afterward. Disgusted with herself, she gave up and binged.

Karen's experience with bulimia was introduced in chapter 10. Although she had managed not to binge and purge for several months, she suddenly had four days in a row of doing so. At first, she didn't know why, but eventually she was able to see that several things had happened more or less simultaneously that had triggered her relapse. One factor was discovering she unexpectedly owed money to the IRS that she didn't have. She was also late with several projects at work, and she had just had a fight with her mother.

Backsliding is a relapse process involving the voluntary choice or decision to make a behavior change, the achievement of some level of success in doing so, followed by an erosion of commitment and sometimes a precipitous return to former behavior. Mary Ann had successfully maintained changes in her diet and exercise behavior for about six weeks when she relapsed. Karen had stopped bingeing and purging for several months and then she binged and purged for four successive days.

The Relapse Process

Alan Marlatt and Judith Gordon[1] have described the relapse process. When a person has made a behavior change and is able to maintain the new behavior for a period of time, he or she feels more in control and more self-confident. The longer this perception of control lasts, the greater the self-confidence. All goes well until a high-risk situation is encountered. A *high-risk situation* is any event or set of circumstances that threatens this sense of control and increases the risk of potential relapse.

Mary Ann's relapse was set up by illness, which interrupted her exercise routine and made her feel weak and lethargic. In this vulnerable state, she ate several cookies, resulting in her berating herself and then giving up in disgust. Karen's stress was already high because of her late projects at work. Her anxiety escalated when she realized she owed money she didn't have. The fight with her mother pushed her stress through the roof. Unable to cope with the anxiety, fear, and anger, she resorted to her former coping strategy, the binge/purge.

Following a period of success in coping more adaptively, a high-risk situation may be encountered that precipitates a first slip and subsequent cognitive and emotional reactions. Situations that can trigger relapse are those associated with high levels of stress. Such stress usually generates painful negative emotions. Often these emotions are created by interpersonal conflict. However, relapse can also be triggered by positive emotions, especially those associated with celebrations and happy social occasions. In some cases, negative physical states such as fatigue, hunger, and pain set the stage for relapse. When the conditions that create a high-risk situation are encountered, you must cope with the demands of the situation. If you do not have available a means of coping effectively, you will use whatever means of coping you have.

Many people with eating disorders use escape or avoidance strategies to cope with painful emotions, rather than using problem-focused coping or more adaptive emotion-focused coping strategies (see chapter 10). Even if they have adaptive coping strategies in their repertoires, they may still fall back on their old ways of coping if they become overwhelmed and lose sight of better ways to cope. In some cases, fear or anxiety inhibits the use of more adaptive coping. Or perhaps the person fails to recognize and respond to the stress involved before it is too late.

If you do cope successfully, you experience an improved sense of mastery and increased control, leading to greater self-confidence. Successful coping reduces the probability of relapse. Success in overcoming one problematic situation increases confidence that you can cope successfully with the next challenging event. With more and more successes, the perception of control increases in cumulative fashion. Success breeds success.

Failure to cope successfully results in a loss of self-confidence, frequently coupled with a sense of helplessness and a tendency to give in passively to the situation. A common reaction is to conclude, "What's the use? I can't handle this. I may as well give up." As the expectation for coping successfully begins to erode, vulnerability to slipping back into old, less adaptive coping increases. If the situation also involves a temptation to eat something good, you may lose sight of your long-term goals and abandon previous intentions to make healthy choices.

Failure to cope decreases self-confidence and promotes focusing on the rewards of eating something good-tasting. As attention narrows to the idea of eating, the thoughts turn to why it is okay to have "just one." Excuses and rationalizations such as, "I deserve a reward" or "I need something to help me cope," pave the way for the binge.

The next step in the relapse process involves the first slip—having "just one." One bite leads to another. You start to feel guilty and try and rationalize that eating is okay or inevitable. Deciding that the slip was awful and unforgivable, or that you are bad and incapable of succeeding because you broke the rules, you give up on yourself.

Now your focus is entirely on eating. At this point you may be aware that a binge is underway, although you no longer care. The binge may be pleasurable for a while, or it can take on an automatic, frantic quality in which you eat fast, shoving the food in, hardly tasting anything after the first few bites. A single lapse or slip—just one miss, one instance of giving in to temptation—has escalated quickly to a full-blown relapse, a total collapse of resolve and commitment to change. With it comes self-recrimination and guilt, and loss of confidence that you can ever overcome disordered eating.

How Backsliding Happens

The high-risk situation and the first slip it triggers, along with the attendant emotional and cognitive reactions, are the immediate determinants of relapse. Often the high-risk situation is unexpected, and the person is not prepared to cope. This was the case for Mary Ann. Not only did she unexpectedly get the flu, she was not prepared for the disruption her illness would cause to her exercise routine. Often people suddenly find themselves in a rapidly escalating situation, and they become overwhelmed by events. Karen was already under pressure when she unexpectedly discovered she owed a large amount of money.

Even though backsliding may seem to come out of nowhere, as in Karen's case, in fact it is part of a pattern that involves certain thoughts and behaviors that set the stage. The ABC model of behavior was discussed in chapter 6. Behavior never just happens, and neither does backsliding. One event—whether it be an external circumstance or a private thought or action—leads to another, culminating in a loss of focus and a return to old coping behaviors. Sometimes it appears that a high-risk situation is unpredictable, although on further inspection, it becomes clear that a number of events led up to it.

The Covertly Planned Relapse

In some cases, the high-risk situation is the last link in a chain of events preceding the first slip. With closer analysis, it is apparent that backsliding can sometimes be the result of covert planning. The antecedents of the relapse episode include a variety of thoughts, fantasies, decisions, and behaviors, any one of which may have provided the opportunity for making a different choice that could have averted the relapse.

Peter, whose story was introduced in chapter 1, provides an example of covert planning of a relapse. Forty-year-old Peter was an obese binge eater who worked two full-time jobs as a computer programmer. He had successfully implemented structured eating to overcome his "grazing" style of binge eating, and he had not overeaten in some time. As usual, Peter looked forward to the weekend, when he would not be working virtually every waking hour, and he could have some time to himself. This weekend was Mother's Day, and he planned to visit his mother who was an hour's drive away and whom he did not see very often. As he was in the car driving to his parents' home, he began ruminating about how abusive his father had been to his mother for as long as Peter could remember. The more he thought about the situation, the angrier he became. At one point on his trip, he had a choice of two routes to his parents' house, one of which took him past a fast-food restaurant. He rationalized that if he stopped there and got a soft ice cream, he would feel less angry. Arriving at the restaurant, Peter ordered the double burger with fries and a milk shake, rather than the ice cream cone he had originally planned. Later at his parents' home, he had a full dinner. By the time he left, he was upset and angry with himself for having eaten so much. Telling himself that he was no good and beyond help, he stopped at the fast-food restaurant again on the way home and ordered two double burgers with the trimmings.

Peter's experience illustrates the role of lifestyle, decision making, thinking, and feelings in the covert planning of a relapse episode. Looking back over the sequence of events, it should first be apparent that Peter's life is nearly devoid of positive experiences, which creates a major vulnerability to backsliding. He spends most of his time working and has few opportunities for pleasure.

The first major choice-point for him was deciding to visit his mother for Mother's Day. Although Peter was well aware that visiting home is always stressful for him because of his father's continuing abusive behavior, he decided to visit for his mother's sake. Apparently, Peter did not consider other, less stressful ways of honoring his mother on her day.

The next choice-point came when Peter had two routes to choose from, one of which led him directly in the path of temptation. He rationalized this choice by telling himself he would have only an ice cream cone, which would help him calm down. Once at the fast-food restaurant, however, his ability to stick to his original plan was undermined, as his focus narrowed to the gratification available from eating burgers and fries. This "first slip" set up the subsequent full-blown relapse. Upset with himself for eating more than he planned, he angrily berated himself for being weak and disgusting.

Why Do People Create Their Own Relapses?

The question arises, "Why do people set up their own relapses?" Do they consciously plan to relapse, or is inadvertent error and poor planning at work? Although the latter explanation is possible, it is also true that a relapse is the result of a series of conscious choices and decisions that can lead step by step to disaster. Consider the fact that eating provides immediate gratification, and the reward of instant gratification far outweighs potential negative effects that may occur sometime in the future. If you then deny to yourself the intent to relapse, ignore the importance of long-range negative consequences, and make excuses and rationalizations that allow you to eat, it is easy to set up your own relapse.

One of the most lethal rationalizations, in terms of causing backsliding, is that eating to feel better is justified. Peter felt justified when he stopped at the fast-food restaurant because he told himself that eating would help him to calm down. Some people justify overeating or not exercising with excuses such as, "It's been a difficult day and I deserve a reward" or "With my schedule how can I be expected to get up earlier to exercise."

Lifestyle Imbalances

Justification excuses are usually the result of having a daily lifestyle that is out of balance. That is, there is too much work and too many obligations to meet and not enough rewards, satisfaction, pleasure, or downtime. The balance is weighted toward activities perceived as "hassles" or demands (the "shoulds"), and activities that bring pleasure or self-fulfillment (the "wants") are minimal or missing. A lifestyle weighted down with a preponderance of shoulds creates feelings of deprivation and a corresponding desire to engage in some want or self-indulgence, especially at the end of the day. Eating fills the bill.

Another kind of imbalance that can play a role in relapse involves rules and regulations. Some people perceive the need to manage calories or to minimize their choice of certain foods as a threat to their personal freedom and choice. Having to do so provokes internal rebellion against restriction or the need to change. This mutinous reaction may be particularly strong in those who feel obliged to change because of the demands of significant others or the dictates of authority figures.

The desire for indulgence is an attempt to restore balance when there is imbalance in daily life, either as the result of too many "shoulds" or the feeling that there are too many rules and regulations. The prospect of obtaining the immediate gratification available from binge eating or purging can create urges and cravings, which are intensified by fantasizing about eating the desired food. When combined with certain types of thinking and decision making, a chain of events occurs that sets up the first lapse.

Rationalization is one type of thought that provides an ostensibly legitimate excuse to binge or purge. An example is the thought, "I deserve a treat." *Denial* involves the refusal to recognize important aspects of the situation or set of events. It is a means of not knowing what you know. You may deny the existence of any motive to engage in relapse, or you may deny awareness of the delayed negative consequences of disordered eating.

In addition to relapse-facilitating thinking, a person who is headed for a relapse makes a number of small decisions along the way, each of which brings her or him closer to the brink of the high-risk situation and the first lapse. Peter decided to visit his mother, even though he could have met her somewhere for brunch or sent her flowers. Likewise, he could have taken the other route to her home, rather than the one that led past the fast-food restaurant.

Overcoming Backsliding

Strategies for overcoming backsliding fall into three main categories: skills for coping with high-risk situations, alternative ways of thinking about the change process, and lifestyle changes that right imbalances.

Coping with High-Risk Situations

Both cognitive and behavioral skills are needed for coping with high-risk situations. Although some high-risk situations are unexpected, it is often possible to anticipate and plan for them.

Identify Your High-Risk Situations

The first step in coping with high-risk situations is to recognize the situations that may trigger a relapse for you, including the fantasies that may make you more prone to binge eating or purging. The earlier you become aware of the chain of events leading to the first slip, the sooner you can intervene. In chapter 6 you learned to use self-monitoring to identify the behavior patterns involved in binge eating. You also learned to identify the "chain of events" leading up to a binge. Both of these methods help you to identify the particular high-risk situations that pose a danger for you.

Plan How to Respond

Having anticipated possible high-risk situations, you should decide in advance how you will handle them. In earlier chapters of this book, you learned a number of ways to cope with stress. Some of these included using positive self-talk, problem-focused and adaptive emotion-focused coping, and various strategies for managing conflict and improving interpersonal functioning.

Learn to Recover from a First Slip

Ideally, it is best to avoid a first slip. When this fails, focus on getting back on track as soon as possible. Make a contract with yourself in advance that sets a limit on how much you will eat. Create reminder cards (see chapter 8) to tell you what to do in the case of a slip. Avoid berating yourself for slipping, and turn this event into an opportunity to learn from your mistake. Avoid a succession of having "just one," because the cumulative effect can be a slide into total relapse. When an unexpected high-risk situation occurs, do your best to cope.

Adopt Alternative Ways of Thinking About Change

All-or-nothing thinking characterizes most people with an eating disorder. Either they are perfect, or they are failures. If they take one bite of something they shouldn't, they give up on themselves completely and binge. To be human is to make errors and mistakes. Inevitably in overcoming disordered eating, there will be successes and lapses. Rather than demanding perfection of yourself, it is better to apply the 80/20 rule—80 percent of the time make the healthy choice or implement adaptive coping and 20 percent of the time expect that you are just human. Backsliding happens. The key is to be able to recover sooner than later, and with less damage. When backsliding does occur, use the experience as an opportunity to learn what went wrong and how the outcome might have been prevented.

In chapter 8 you learned about your internal Critic voice— the one who berates you when you make a mistake. The Critic is the voice that is heard when you have a slip, and it can push you into a full-blown relapse. You also learned in chapter 8 the importance of programming a positive voice, which some call the Coach or the Wise Self. Positive self-talk, embodied by the positive "voices," can reduce the incidence of self-induced emotional pain and provide support and direction in coping with the difficulties that are inevitable when you try to change behavior patterns. In order to recover from a slip and avoid a total relapse, you need to listen to your positive voice.

Likewise, in chapter 9, you learned the importance of balancing your desire for change with what is possible. Messages in the media suggest that the body is infinitely malleable, if only you find the right diet, drug, or doctor. In fact, genes and lifestyle, together with what constitutes healthy behavior, place limitations on how much body weight and shape can be changed. Dwelling on fantasies of what you wished you looked like or weighed causes unhappiness and prompts a never-ending search for an answer that doesn't exist—and is a factor in backsliding.

Correct Lifestyle Imbalances

Your lifestyle can be yet another major cause of backsliding. A balanced lifestyle is one that has a relative degree of balance between the things you must do and the things you want to do. One way to achieve this is to substitute activities that provide some form of self-gratification for eating or purging. These might include getting a massage, meditating, eliciting the relaxation response, going shopping, visiting a friend, working out with a personal trainer, and so forth. These can also serve as last-minute alternative behaviors to use in the face of temptation. Programming periods of free time during the day to pursue your own interests can help provide balance in an otherwise crowded schedule of "shoulds."

Balancing the demands of your lifestyle with opportunities for pleasure or satisfaction may require that you set priorities. Take a moment and write a list of all the daily activities in which you engage. If necessary, take several days or a week to complete your list. Once you feel that the list includes all or most of your daily activities, rate each one. Use a "W" to indicate it is something you want to do, an "H" if it is something you have to do, and an "M" if it is a mixture of a "want to" and a "have to." Next, rate each activity according to how much pleasure, satisfaction, or fulfillment each activity gives you—high, medium, or low. If the balance of "have to" and "want to" activities is weighted to one side or the other, or if your satisfaction ratings are predominantly medium or low, your lifestyle is probably out of balance. Consider how to eliminate or delegate "have to" and low satisfaction activities and include more "want to" and high satisfaction activities to create more balance.

When the imbalance involves the perception of too many rules and not enough autonomy, it can be helpful to adopt a position of moderation. Moderation represents a balance point between the extremes of absolute restraint or control (the rules) and abdication of all constraints. The person who embraces the principle of moderation maintains awareness of her choices and exercises personal responsibility for them.

Rather than oscillating between bristling at the rules and abandoning all self-discipline, those who adopt moderation make informed choices in their own long-term best interests.

Note

1. Marlatt, G. A., and J. R. Gordon. 1984. *Relapse Prevention: A Self-control Strategy for the Maintenance of Behavior Change.* New York: Guilford.

Resources

Academy for Eating Disorders (AED)
6728 Old McLean Village Drive
McLean, VA 22101
(703) 556-9222
www.acadeatdis.ord
email: aed@degnon.org

AED is an organization for professionals who conduct research with or treat eating disorders. AED promotes effective treatment, develops prevention initiatives, stimulates research, and sponsors an annual international conference.

American Anorexia/Bulimia Association, Inc. (AABA)
165 West 46th Street, #1108
New York, NY 10036
(212) 575-6200
Fax: (212) 278-0698
www.aabainc.org
email: info@aabainc.org

AABA provides information on eating disorders; information on support groups, speakers, educational programs, and professional training; a quarterly newsletter; and referrals to qualified therapists nationally.

Anorexia Nervosa and Related Eating Disorders, Inc. (ANRED)
P. O. Box 5102
Eugene, OR 97405

(541) 344-1144
www.anred.com
email: jarinor@rio.com

ANRED merged with NEDO in 1997. NEDO took over production and distribution of all printed information, as well as providing referrals to qualified therapists nationally and in some foreign countries. ANRED maintains a website providing information on eating disorders. All correspondence is forwarded to NEDO and ANRED does not respond to phone calls.

Eating Disorders Awareness and Prevention, Inc. (EDAP)
603 Stewart Street, Suite 803
Seattle, WA 98101
(206) 382-3587
Toll-free information line: (800) 931-2237
Http.//members.aol.com/edapinc

EDAP provides educational resources on eating disorders and their prevention for schools, health professionals, community organizations, and individuals. EDAP sponsors the development of educational and prevention programs. EDAP sponsors educational eating disorders programs, including Eating Disorders Awareness Week in February, and provides educational information to the general public, an annual conference, and a newsletter.

Gurze Books
P. O. Box 2238
Carlsbad, CA 92018
(800) 756-7533
(760) 434-7533
Fax: (760) 434-5476
www.gurze.com
email: gzcatl@aol.com

Gurze Books distributes an Eating Disorders Resource Catalogue that collects and makes available books on eating disorders. They also distribute a newsletter for clinicians.

International Association of Eating Disorders Professionals (IAEDP)
427 Whopping Loop, #1819
Altamone Springs, FL 32701
(800) 800-8126
www.iaedp.com

IAEDP is a professional organization for health professionals who treat eating disorders. IAEDP provides certification, education, local chapters, a newsletter, and an annual symposium.

> National Association of Anorexia Nervosa and Associated
> Disorders (ANAD)
> P. O. Box 7
> Highland Park, IL 60035
> (847) 831-3438
> www.members.aol.com/anad20/index.html
> email: anad20@aol.com

ANAD maintains a referral list of over 2,000 therapists, hospitals, and clinics who treat eating disorders in the U.S. and Canada and several other countries. ANAD distributes information about eating disorders to health professionals and the general public, and provides informative materials on eating disorders, including a national newsletter. It sponsors support groups, conferences, research, and a crisis hotline.

> National Association to Advance Fat Acceptance, Inc.
> (NAAFA)
> P. O. Box 188620
> Sacramento, CA 95818
> (916) 558-6880
> www.naafa.org
> email: naafa@naafa.org

NAAFA is an advocacy group that provides a newsletter, educational materials, an annual convention, a pen-pal program, and regional chapters to promote fat acceptance.

> National Eating Disorders Information Centre (Canada)
> (NEDIC)
> CW 1-211, 200 Elizabeth Street
> College Way
> Toronto, Ontario M5G 2C4
> (416) 340-4156
> Fax: (416) 340-4736
> www.nedic.on.ca
> email: josullivan@torhosp.toronto.on.ca

The National Eating Disorders Information Centre provides information and resources to the general public on eating disorders and weight preoccupation. NEDIC maintains a nationwide listing of treatment services and resources for Canada. It has a nondiet-ing, client-centered, feminist philosophy and will not refer to serv-ices that advocate restrictive eating patterns.

> National Eating Disorders Organization (NEDO)
> 6655 South Yale Avenue
> Tulsa, OK 74136
> (918) 481-4044
> www.laureate.com/nedo/nedointro.asp

NEDO is an educational and international treatment referral resource for individuals, families, students, health care profession-als, and the media. NEDO provides information about, and treat-ment referrals for, all forms of eating disorders and obesity.

> Overeaters Anonymous Headquarters (OA)
> 6075 Zenith Court NE
> Rio Rancho, NM 87124
> (505) 891-2664
> Fax: (505) 891-4320
> www.overeatersanonymous.org
> email: overeatr@technet.nm.org

OA provides volunteer support groups worldwide. Patterned after the Twelve-Step Alcoholics Anonymous program, the OA recovery program addresses physical, emotional, and spiritual recovery aspects of compulsive overeating.

Bibliography

Abraham, S. 1996. Characteristics of eating disorders among young ballet dancers. *Psychopathology, 29,* 223-229.

Abraham, S. 1998. Sexuality and reproduction in bulimia nervosa patients over 10 years. *Journal of Psychosomatic Research, 44,* 491-502.

Adami, G. F., P. Gandolfo, B. Bauer, and N. Scopinaro. 1995. Binge eating in massively obese patients undergoing bariatric surgery. *International Journal of Eating Disorders, 17,* 45-50.

Agras, W. S. 1997. Pharmacotherapy of bulimia nervosa and binge eating disorder: Long-term outcomes. *Psychopharmacology Bulletin, 33,* 433-436.

Ainsworth, M. D. S. 1989. Attachments beyond infancy. *American Psychologist, 44,* 709-716.

Alexander, N. 1986. Characteristics and treatment of families with anorectic offspring. *Occupational Therapy in Mental Health, 6,* 117-135.

American Psychiatric Association. 1994. *Diagnostic and statistical manual of mental disorders 4th (Ed.)* Washington, DC:

Anderson, A. E. 1995. Eating disorders in males. In K. D. Brownell and C. G. Fairburn (Eds.) *Eating Disorders and Obesity.* New York: Guilford. Pp. 177-182.

Anderson, A. E. 1997. Males with eating disorders: Challenges for treatment and research. *Psychopharmacology Bulletin, 33,* 391-397.

Aronne, L. J. 1998. Modern medical management of obesity: The role of pharmaceutical intervention. *Journal of the American Dietetic Association, 98 Supplement (2),* S23-S26.

Aronoff, N. J. 1997. Obesity-related eating patterns. In S. Dalton (Ed.), *Overweight and Weight Management: The Health Professional's Guide to Understanding and Practice.* Gaithersburg, MD: Aspen Publishers. Pp. 107-141.

Barrios, B. A., and J. W. Pennebaker. 1983. A note on the early detection of bulimia nervosa. *The Behavior Therapist, 6,* 18-19.

Beren, S. E., H. A. Hayden, D. E. Wilfley, and C. M.Grilo. 1996. The influence of sexual orientation on body dissatisfaction in adult men and women. *International Journal of Eating Disorders, 20,* 135-141.

Beresin, E. V., C. Gordon, and D. B. Herzog. 1989. The process of recovering from anorexia nervosa. *Journal of the American Academy of Psychoanalysis, 17,* 103-130.

Bion, W. R. 1959. Attacks on linking. *International Journal of Psychoanalysis, 40,* 308-315.

Bjorvell, H., S. Ronnberg, and S. Rossner. 1985. Eating patterns described by a group of treatment seeking overweight women and normal weight women. *Scandinavian Journal of Behavior Therapy, 14,* 147-156.

Bouchard, C. 1994. Genetics of obesity: Overview and research directions. In C. Bouchard, (Ed.), *The Genetics of Obesity.* Boca Raton, FL: CRC Press. Pp. 223-233.

Bouchard, C. 1995. Genetic influences on body weight and shape. In K. D. Brownell and C. G. Fairburn (Eds.), *Eating Disorders and Obesity: A Comprehensive Handbook.* New York: Guilford. Pp. 21-26.

Bouchard, C. 1997. Genetic factors and body weight regulation. In S. Dalton (Ed.), *Overweight and Weight Management.* Gaithersburg, MD: Aspen Publishers. Pp. 161-186.

Bowlby, J. 1988. *A Secure Base: Parent-Child Attachment And Healthy Human Development.* NY: Basic Books.

Bowman, M. L. 1998. Bulimia: From syncope to obsession. *Psychology of Addictive Behaviors, 12,* 83-92.

Bradshaw, J. 1988. *Bradshaw On the Family.* Pompano Beach, FL: Health Communications.

Brehm, B. J., and J. J. Steffen. 1998. Relation between obligatory exercise and eating disorders. *American Journal of Health Behavior, 22,* 108-119.

Brewerton, T. D., R. B. Lydiard, D. B. Herzog, A. W. Brotman, P. M. O'Neil, and J. C. Ballenger. 1995. Comorbidity of Axis I psychiatric disorders in bulimia nervosa. *Journal of Clinical Psychiatry, 56,* 77-80.

Briere, J., and M. Runtz. 1988. Multivariate correlates of childhood psychological and physical maltreatment among university women. *Child Abuse and Neglect, 12,* 331-341.

Briere, J., and M. Runtz. 1990. Differential adult symptomatology associated with three types of child abuse histories. *Child Abuse and Neglect, 14,* 357-364.

Brisman, J., and M. Siegel. 1985. The bulimia workshop: A unique integration of group treatment approaches. *International Journal of Group Psychotherapy, 35,* 585-601.

Brisman, J., and M. Siegel. 1986. Bulimia and alcoholism—Two sides of the same coin? *Journal of Substance Abuse and Treatment, 1,* 113-118.

Brody, M., M. J. Devlin, and B. T. Walsh. 1992, April 24-26. *Reliability and validity of binge eating disorder.* Paper presented at Fifth International Conference on Eating Disorders, New York.

Brone, R. J., and C. B. Fisher. 1988. Determinants of adolescent obesity: A comparison with anorexia nervosa. *Adolescence, 23,* 155-169.

Bruce, B., and D. Wilfley. 1996. Binge eating among the overweight population: A serious and prevalent problem. *Journal of the American Dietetic Association, 96,* 58-61.

Bruce, B., and W. S. Agras. 1992. Binge eating in females: A population-based investigation. *International Journal of Eating Disorders, 12,* 365-373.

Bruch, H. 1952. Psychological aspects of reducing. *Psychosomatic Medicine, 14,* 337-346.

Bruch, H. 1965. Anorexia nervosa. *Journal of Nervous and Mental Diseases, 141,* 555-566.

Bruch, H. 1988. Disturbed concepts of food, body, and self. In D. Czyzewski and M. A. Suhr (Eds.), *Conversations With Anorexics.* New York: Basic Books. Pp. 114-152 .

Brumberg, J. J. 1989. *Fasting Girls: The History of Anorexia Nervosa.* New York: Plume.

Bulik, C. M. 1987. Drug and alcohol abuse by bulimic women and their families. *American Journal of Psychiatry, 144,* 1604-1606.

Bulik, C. M., P. F. Sullivan, J. L. Fear, and P. R. Joyce. 1997. Eating disorders and antecedent anxiety disorders: A controlled study. *Acta Psychiatrica Scandinavica, 96*, 101-107.

Butterfield, P. S., and S. LeClair. 1988. Cognitive characteristics of bulimic and drug-abusing women. *Addictive Behaviors, 13*, 131-138.

Calam, R., and G. Waller. 1998. Are eating and psychosocial characteristics in early teenage years useful predictors of eating characteristics in early adulthood? A 7-year longitudinal study. *International Journal of Eating Disorders, 24*, 351-362.

Campfield, L. A. 1993. Simple solutions for complex problems? Occam's razor, the FDA, and the pharmacological treatment of obesity. Proceedings of Seminar on Human Obesity: Current Status of Scientific and Clinical Progress. Boston: American Association for the Advancement of Science.

Campfield, L. A. 1995. Treatment options and the maintenance of weight loss. In D. B. Allison and F. X. Pi-Sunyer (Eds.), Obesity Treatment: Establishing Goals, Improving Outcomes, and Reviewing the Research Agenda. New York: Plenum Press. Pp. 93-95.

Canals, J., G. Carbajo, J. Fernandez, C. Marti-Henneberg, and E. Domenech. 1996. Biopsychopathologic risk profile of adolescents with eating disorder symptoms. *Adolescence, 31*, 443-450.

Carlat, D. J., C. A. Camargo, and D. B. Herzog. 1997. Eating disorders in males: A report on 135 patients. *American Journal of Psychiatry, 154*, 1127-1132.

Carter, J. C., and C. G. Fairburn. 1998. Cognitive-behavioral self-help for binge eating disorder: A controlled effectiveness study. *Journal of Consulting and Clinical Psychology, 66*, 616-623.

Cash, T. F., B. A. Winstead, and L. H. Janda. 1986 (April). The great American shape-up: Body image survey report. *Psychology Today*, 30-34, 36-37.

Casper, D., and D. Zachary. 1984. The eating disorder as a maladpative conflict resolution. *Individual Psychology Journal of Adlerian Theory, Research, and Practice, 40*, 445-452.

Casper, R. C. 1983. On the emergence of bulimia nervosa as a syndrome: A Historical view. *International Journal of Eating Disorders, 2*, 3-16.

Casper, R. C., E. D. Eckert, K. A. Halmi, S. C. Goldberg, and J. M. Davis. 1980. Bulimia: Its incidence and clinical importance in patients with anorexia nervosa. *Archives of General Psychiatry, 37*, 1030-1034.

Castellanos, V. H., and B. J. Rolls. 1997. Diet composition and the regulation of food intake and body weight. In S. Dalton (Ed.), *Overweight and Weight Management*. Gaithersburg, MD: Aspen. Pp. 254-283.

Christiano, B., and J. S. Mizes. 1997. Appraisal and coping deficits associated with eating disorders: Implications for treatment. *Cognitive and Behavioral Practice, 4*, 263-290.

Clark, N. 1994. Counseling the athlete with an eating disorder: A case study. *Journal of the American Dietetic Association, 94*, 656-658.

Colditz, G. A., W. C. Willet, M. J. Stampfer, S. J. London, M. R. Segal, and F. E. Speizer. 1990. Patterns of weight change and their relation to diet in a cohort of healthy women. *American Journal of Clinical Nutrition, 51*, 1100-1105.

Cooper, P. J., and C. G. Fairburn. 1986. The depressive symptoms of bulimia nervosa. *British Journal of Psychiatry, 148*, 268-274.

Cooper, P. J., and C. G. Fairburn. 1986. The depressive symptoms of bulimia nervosa. *British Journal of Psychiatry, 148*, 268-274.

Cooper, P. J., and I. Goodyear. 1997. Prevalence and significance of weight and shape concerns in girls aged 11-16 years. *British Journal of Psychiatry, 171*, 542-544.

Coovert, D. L., B. N. Kinder, and J. K. Thompson. 1989. The psychosexual aspects of anorexia nervosa and bulimia nervosa: A review of the literature. *Clinical Psychology Review, 9,* 169-180.

Craighead, L. W. 1995. Conceptual models and clinical interventions for treatment of bulimia and binge eating. In L. VandeCreek (Ed.), *Innovations in clinical practice: A sourcebook: Vol. 14* pp. 67-87. Sarasota, FL: Professional Resource Exchange.

Crisp, A. H. 1997. Anorexia nervosa as a flight from growth: Assessment and treatment based on the model. In D. M. Garner and P. E. Garfinkel (Eds.), *Handbook of Treatment for Eating Disorders, 2ᵈ Edition.* NY: Guilford Press. Pp. 248-277.

D'Zurilla, T. J., and M. R. Goldfried. 1971. Problem solving and behavior modification. *Journal of Abnormal Psychology, 78,* 107-126.

Dansky, B. S., T. D. Brewerton, D. G. Kilpatrick, and P. M. O'Neil. 1997. The National Women's Study: Relationship of victimization and posttraumatic stress disorder to bulimia nervosa. *International Journal of Eating Disorders, 21,* 213-228.

Davis, C., D. K. Katzman, S. Kaptein, C. Kirsh, H. Brewer, K. Kalmbach, et al. 1997. The prevalence of high-level exercise in the eating disorders: Etiological implications. *Comprehensive Psychiatry, 38,* 321-326.

Davis, C., S. Kaptein, A. S. Kaplan, M. P. Olmsted, and D. B. Woodside. 1998. Obsessionality in anorexia nervosa: The moderating influence of exercise. *Psychosomatic Medicine, 60,* 192-197.

Deep, A. L., L. R. Lilenfeld, K. H. Plotnicov, C. Pollice, and W. H. Kaye. 1999. Sexual abuse in eating disorders subtypes and control women: The role of comorbid substance dependence in bulimia nervosa. *International Journal of Eating Disorders, 25,* 1-10.

Dennis, A. B., and R. A. Sansone. 1997. Treatment of patients with personality disorders. In D. M. Garner and P. E. Garfinkel (Eds.), *Handbook of Treatment for Eating Disorders, 2ᵈ Edition.* NY: Guilford Press. Pp. 437-449.

Desmond, S. M., J. H. Price, N. Gray, and J. K. O'Connell. 1986. The etiology of adolescents' perception of their weight. *Journal of Youth and Adolescence, 15,* 461-474.

Devlin, M. J., and B. T. Walsh. 1995. Medication treatment for eating disorders. *Journal of Mental Health UK, 4,* 459-468.

Dittmar, H., and B. Bates. 1987. Humanistic approaches to the understanding and treatment of anorexia nervosa. *Journal of Adolescence, 10,* 57-69.

Dreon, D. M., B. Frey-Hewitt, N. Ellsworth, P. T. Williams, R. B.Terry, and P. D. Wood. 1988. Dietary fat:carbohydrate ratio and obesity in middle-aged men. *American Journal of Clinical Nutrition, 47,* 995-1000.

Drewnowski, A., D. K. Yee, C. L. Kurth, and D. D. Krahn. 1994. Eating pathology and DSM-III-R bulimia nervosa: A continuum of behavior. *American Journal of Psychiatry, 151,* 1217-1219.

Elmore, D. K., and J. M. de Castro. 1990. Self-related moods and hunger in relation to spontaneous eating behavior in bulimics, recovered bulimics, and normals. *International Journal of Eating Disorders, 9,* 179-190.

Etringer, B. D., E. M. Altmaier, and W. Bowers. 1989. An investigation into the cognitive functioning of bulimic women. *Journal of Counseling and Development, 68,* 216-219.

Fabian, L. J., and J. K. Thompson. 1989. Body image and eating disturbance in young females. *International Journal of Eating Disorders, 8,* 63-74.

Fairburn, C. G. 1997. Interpersonal psychotherapy for bulimia nervosa. In D. M. Garner and P. E. Garfinkle, (Eds.), *Handbook of Treatment for Eating Disorders, Second Edition.* NY: Guilford. Pp. 278-294.

Fairburn, C. G., and S. J. Beglin. 1990. Studies of the epidemiology of bulimia nervosa. *American Journal of Psychiatry, 147,* 401-408

Fairburn, C. G., R. Jones, R. C. Peveler, R. A. Hope, and M. O'Connor. 1993. Psychotherapy and bulimia nervosa: The longer-term effects of interpersonal psychotherapy, behavior therapy, and cognitive behavior therapy. *Archives of General Psychiatry, 50,* 419-428.

Faith, M. S., D. B. Allison, and A. Geliebter. 1995. Emotional eating and obesity: Theoretical considerations and practical recommendations. In S. Dalton (Ed.), *Overweight and Weight Management.* Gaithersburg, MD: Aspen. Pp. 439-465.

Fallon, P., and S. A. Wonderlich. 1997. Sexual abuse and other forms of trauma. In D. M. Garner and P. E. Garfinkle, (Eds.), *Handbook of Treatment for Eating Disorders, Second Edition.* NY: Guilford. Pp. 394-414.

Federation of American Societies for Experimental Biology, Life Sciences Research Office. 1995. *Third Report on Nutrition Monitoring in the United States: Volume 1.* Prepared for the Interagency Board for Nutrition Monitoring and Related Research. Washington, DC: US GPO.

Ferguson, C. P., M. C. La Via, P. J. Crossan, and W. H. Kay. 1999. Are serotonin selective reuptake inhibitors effective in underweight anorexia nervosa? *International Journal of Eating Disorders, 25,* 11-17.

Fernstrom, J. D. 1988. Tryptophan, serotonin and carbohydrate appetite: Will the real carbohydrate craver please stand up! *Journal of Nutrition, 118,* 1417-1419.

Fowler, S. J., and C. M. Bulik. 1997. Family environment and psychiatric history in women with binge-eating disorder and obese controls. *Behaviour Change, 14,* 106-112.

Franko, D. L., and P. Orosan-Weine. 1998. The prevention of eating disorders: Empirical, methodological, and conceptual considerations. *Clinical Psychology: Science and Practice, 5,* 459-477.

Friedberg, N. L., and W. J. Lyddon. 1996. Self-other working models and eating disorders. *Journal of Cognitive Psychotherapy: An International Quarterly, 10,* 193-203.

Garfinkel, P. E., H. Moldofsky, and D. M. Garner. 1980. The heterogeneity of anorexia nervosa. *Archives of General Psychiatry, 37,* 1036-1040.

Garner, D. M., and S. C. Wooley. 1991. Confronting the failure of behavioral and dietary treatments for obesity. *Clinical Psychology Review, 11,* 729-780.

Garner, D. M., M. P. Olmstead, and P. E. Garfinkel. 1983. Does anorexia nervosa occur on a continuum? *International Journal of Eating Disorders, 2,* 11-27.

Gartner, A. F., R. N. Marcus, K. Halmi, and A. Loranger. 1989. DSM-III-R personality disorders in patients with eating disorders. *American Journal of Psychiatry, 146,* 1585-1591.

Gilbert, E. H., and R. R. Deblassie. 1984. Anorexia nervosa: Adolescent starvation by choice. *Adolescence, 19,* 839-846.

Gilbert, P. 1998. What is shame? Some core issues and controversies. In P. Gilbert and B. Andrews (Eds.), *Shame: Interpersonal Behavior, Psychopathology, and Culture.* New York: Oxford University Press.

Goldbloom, D. S., M. Olmsted, R. Davis, J. Clewes, M. Heinmaa, W. Rockert, et al. 1997. A randomized controlled trial of fluoxetine and cognitive behavioral therapy for bulimia nervosa: Short-term outcome. *Behavior Research and Therapy, 35,* 803-811.

Golden, N., and I. M. Sacker. 1984. An overview of the etiology, diagnosis, and management of anorexia nervosa. *Clinical Pediatrics, 23,* 209-214.

Goldfein, J., B. T. Walsch, M. J. Devlin, J. LaChaussee, and H. Kissileff. 1992, April 24. *Eating behavior in binge eating disorder.* Paper presented at the Fifth International Conference on Eating Disorders, New York.

Goldman, E. L. 1996. Eating disorders on the rise in preteens and adolescents. *Psychiatry News, 24,* 10.

Goodman, A. 1993. Diagnosis and treatment of sex addiction. *Journal of Sex and Marital Therapy, 19,* 225-242.

Goodrick, G. K., W. S. C Poston, K. T. Kimball, R. S. Reeves, and J. P. Foreyt. 1998. Nondieting versus dieting treatment of overweight binge-eating women. *Journal of Consulting and Clinical Psychology, 66,* 363-368.

Gottman, J. 1994, May/June. Why marriages fail. *The Family Therapy Networker.* Pp. 41-48.

Grigg, D. N., J. D Friesen, and M. I. Sheppy. 1989. Family patterns associated with anorexia nervosa. *Journal of Marital and Family Therapy, 15,* 29-42.

Grilo, C. M. 1998. The assessment and treatment of binge eating disorder. *Journal of Practical Psychiatry and Behavioral Health, 4,* 191-201.

Grissett, N. I., and M. L. Fitzgibbon. 1996. The clinical significance of binge eating in an obese population: Support for BED and questions regarding its criteria. *Addictive Behaviors, 21,* 57-66.

Gross, J., and J. C. Rosen. 1988. Bulimia in adolescents: Prevalence and psychosocial correlates. *International Journal of Eating Disorders, 7,* 51-61.

Guidano, V. F. 1987. *Complexity of the self: A developmental approach to psychopathology and therapy.* NY: Guilford Press.

Guidano, V. F., and G. Liotti. 1983. *Cognitive processes and emotional disorders: A structural approach to psychotherapy.* NY: Guilford Press.

Gustafson-Larson, A. M., and R. D. Terry. 1992. Weight-related behaviors and concerns of fourth-grade children. *Journal of the American Dietetic Association, 92,* 818-822.

Haimes, A. L., and J. L. Katz. 1988. Sexual and social maturity versus social conformity in restricting anorectic, bulimic, and borderline women. *International Journal of Eating Disorders, 7,* 331-341.

Hall, R. C. W., L. Tice, T. P. Beresford, B. Wooley, and A. K. Hall. 1989. Sexual abuse in patients with anorexia nervosa and bulimia. *Psychosomatics, 30,* 79-88.

Harding, T. P., and J. R. Lachenmeyer. 1986. Family interaction patterns and locus of control as predictors of the presence and severity of anorexia nervosa. *Journal of Clinical Psychology, 42,* 440-448.

Heatherton, T. F., and R. F. Baumeister. 1991. Binge eating as escape from self-awareness. *Psychological Bulletin, 110,* 86-108.

Herpertz-Dahlmann, B. M., C. Wewetzer, E. Schulz, and H. Remschmidt. 1996. Course and outcome in adolescent anorexia nervosa. *International Journal of Eating Disorders, 19,* 335-345.

Hill, A. J., and V. Pallin. 1998. Dieting awareness and low self-worth: Related issues in 8-year-old girls. *International Journal of Eating Disorders, 24,* 405-413.

Hoek, H. W., A. I. Bartelds, M. A. Bosveld, et al. 1995. Impact of urbanization on detection rates of eating disorders. *American Journal of Psychiatry, 152,* 1272-1278.

Hsu, L. K. G. 1996. Epidemiology of the eating disorders. *Psychiatric Clinics of North America, 19,* 681-700.

Hsu, L. K. G., A. H. Crisp, and B. Harding. 1979. Outcome in anorexia nervosa. *Lancet, I,* 61-65.

Hudson, J. I., H. G. Pope, J. Wurtman, D. Yurgelun-Todd, S. Mark, and N. E. Rosenthal. 1988. Bulimia in obese individuals: Relationship to normal-weight bulimia. *Journal of Nervous and Mental Disease, 176,* 144-152.

Humphrey, L. L. 1986. Structural analysis of parent-child relationships in eating disorders. *Journal of Abnormal Psychology, 95,* 395-402.

Humphrey, L. L. 1987. Comparison of bulimic-anorexic and nondistressed families using structural analysis of social behavior. *American Academy of Child and Adolescent Psychiatry, 26,* 248-255.

Humphrey, L. L. 1989. Observed family interactions among subtypes of eating disorders using structural analysis of social behavior. *Journal of Consulting and Clinical Psychology, 57,* 206-214.

Jakubowski, P., and A. J. Lange. 1978. *The Assertive Option: Your Rights and Responsibilities.* Champaign, IL: Research Press.

Janzen, B. L., I. W. Kelly, and D. H. Sakolfske. 1992. Bulimic symptomatology and coping in a nonclinical sample. *Perceptual and Motor Skills, 75,* 395-399.

Jarry, J. L., and F. J. Vaccarino. 1996. Eating disorder and obsessive-compulsive disorder: Neurochemical and phenomenological commonalities. *Journal of Psychiatry and Neuroscience, 21,* 36-48.

Jimerson, D. C., B. E. Wolfe, A. W. Brotman, and E. D. Metzger. 1996. Medications in the treatment of eating disorders. *The Psychiatric Clinics of North America,* Vol. 19, No. 4, pp. 739-754.

Johnson, C., and A. Flach. 1985. Family characteristics of 105 patients with bulimia. *American Journal of Psychiatry, 142,* 1321-1324.

Johnson, W. G., J. Y. Tsoh, and P. J. Varnado. 1996. Eating disorders: Efficacy of pharmacological and psychological interventions. *Clinical Psychology Review, 16,* 457-478.

Jones, D. A., N. Cheshire, and H. Moorhouse. 1985. Anorexia nervosa, bulimia and alcoholism: Association of eating disorder and alcohol. *Journal of Psychiatric Research, 19,* 377-380.

Kanakis, D., and M. H. Thelen. 1995. Parental variables associated with bulimia nervosa. *Addictive Behaviors, 20,* 491-500.

Kaplan, A. S., and D. B. Woodside. 1987. Biological aspects of anorexia nervosa and bulimia nervosa. *Journal of Consulting and Clinical Psychology, 55,* 645-653.

Karen, R. 1992, February. Shame. *The Atlantic Monthly,* 40-70.

Katz, J. L. 1990. Eating disorders: A primer for the substance abuse specialist: I. Clinical features. *Journal of Substance Abuse Treatment, 7,* 143-149.

Kaufman, G. 1989. *The Psychology of Shame.* New York: Springer.

Kaye, W. H., T. Welzin, and L. K. Hsu. 1996. Anorexia nervosa. In Hollander (Ed.), *Obsessive Compulsive Related Disorders.* Washington, DC: American Psychiatric Press.

Kearney-Cooke, A. M. 1988. Group treatment of sexual abuse among women with eating disorders. *Women and Therapy, 7,* 5-21.

Kendler, K. S., C. MacLean, M. Neale, R. Kessler, A. Heathy, and L. Eaves. 1991. The genetic epidemiology of bulimia nervosa. *American Journal of Psychiatry, 148,* 1627-1637.

Kennedy, S. H., G. McVey, and R. Katz. 1990. Personality disorders in anorexia nervosa and bulimia nervosa. *Journal of Psychiatric Research, 24,* 259-269.

Keys, A., J. Brozek, A. Henschel, O. Mickelsen, and H. L. Taylor. 1950. *The Biology of Human Starvation* 2 vols. Minneapolis: University of Minnesota Press.

Killen, J. D., C. B. Taylor, M. J. Telch, K. E. Saylor, D. J. Maron, and T. N. Robinson. 1986. Self-induced vomiting and laxative and diuretic use among teenagers: Precursors of the binge-purge syndrome? *Journal of the American Medical Association, 255,* 1447-1449.

King, A. 1963. Primary and secondary anorexia nervosa syndromes. *British Journal of Psychiatry, 109,* 470-479.

Kirschenbaum, D. S., and M. L. Fitzgibbon. 1995. Controversy about the treatment of obesity: Criticisms or challenges? *Behavior Therapy, 26,* 43-68.

Klerman, G. L., M. M. Weissman, B. J. Rounsaville, and E. S. Chevron. 1984. *Interpersonal Psychotherapy of Depression.* NY: Basic Books.

Kog, E., H. Vertommen, and W. Vandereycken. 1989. Self-report study of family interaction in eating disorder families compared to normals. In W. Vandereycken, E. Kob, and J. Vanderlinden (Eds.), *The Family Approach to Eating Disorders.* NY: PMA. Pp. 107-118.

Kratina, K. 1998, Summer. Finding a nutritionist skilled in treating eating disorders. *NEDO Newsletter,* Tulsa, OK: National Eating Disorders Organization.

Kuczmarski, R. J., K. M. Flegal, S. M. Campbell, and C. L. Johnson. 1994. Increasing prevalence of overweight among US adults. *Journal of the American Medical Association, 272,* 205-211.

Kushner, R. F. 1993. Body weight and mortality. *Nutrition Review, 51,* 127-136.

Lapiano, D. A., and C. Zotos. 1992. Modern athletics: The pressure to perform. In K. D. Brownell, J. Rodin, and J. H. Wilmore (Eds.) *Eating, Body Weight, and Performance in Athletes: Disorders of Modern Society.* Philadelphia: Lea and Febiger. Pp. 275-292.

Lazarus, R. S., and S. Folkman. 1984. *Stress, Appraisal, and Coping.* New York: Springer.

Leach, A. 1995. The psychopharmacotherapy of eating disorders. *Psychiatric Annals, 25,* 623-633.

Lehman, A. K., and J. Rodin. 1989. Styles of self-nurturance and disordered eating. *Journal of Consulting and Clinical Psychology, 57,* 117-122.

Leibowitz, S. F. 1995. Central physiological determinants of eating behavior and weight. In K. D. Brownell and C. G. Fairburn (Eds.), *Eating Disorders and Obesity: A Comprehensive Handbook.* New York: Guilford. Pp. 3-7.

Leitenberg, H., J. Gross, F. Peterson, and J. C Rosen. 1984. Analysis of an anxiety model and the process of change during exposure plus response prevention treatment of bulimia nervosa. *Behavior Therapy, 15,* 3-20.

Levine, M. P., L. Smolak, A. F. Moodey, M. D. Shuman, and L. D. Hessen. 1994. Normative developmental challenges and dieting and eating disturbances in middle school girls. *International Journal of Eating Disorders, 15,* 11-20.

Levine, M. P., L. Smolak, and H. Hayden. 1994. The relation of sociocultural factor to eating attitudes and behaviors among middle school girls. *Journal of Early Adolescence, 14,* 471-490.

Lieberman, H. R., J. J. Wurtman, and B. Chew. 1986. Changes in mood after carbohydrate consumption among obese individuals. *American Journal of Clinical Nutrition, 44,* 772-778.

Lilenfield, L. R., W. H. Kaye, C. G. Greeno, K. R. Merikangas., K. Plotnicove, C. Pollice, et al., 1998. A controlled family study of anorexia nervosa and bulimia nervosa: Psychiatric disorders in first-degree relatives and effects of proband comorbidity. *Archives of General Psychiatry, 55,* 603-610.

Linehan, M. M. 1993a. *Cognitive-Behavioral Treatment of Borderline Personality Disorder.* NY: Guilford.

Linehan, M. M. 1993b. *Skills Training Manual for Treating Borderline Personality Disorder.* New York: Guilford. P. 125.

Lissner, L., L. Sjostrom, C. Bengtsson, et al. 1994. The natural history of obesity in an obese population and associations with metabolic aberrations. *International Journal of Obesity, 18,* 441-447.

Lucas, A. R., M. Beard, W. M. O'Fallon, and L. T. Kurland. 1991. 50-year trends in the incidence of anorexia nervosa in Rochester, Minn.: A population-based study. *American Journal of Psychiatry, 148,* 917-922.

Maloney, M. J., J. B. McGuire, S. R. Daniels, and B. Specker. 1989. Dieting behaviors and eating attitudes in children. *Pediatrics, 84*, 482-489.

Marcus, M. D., R. R. Wing, and D. M. Lamparski. 1985. Binge eating and dietary restraint in obese patients. *Addictive Behaviors, 10*, 163-168.

Marcus, M. D., R. R. Wing, L. Ewing, E. Kern, W. Gooding, and M. McDerott. 1990. Psychiatric disorders among obese binge eaters. *International Journal of Eating Disorders, 9*, 69-77.

Marlatt, G. A., and J. R. Gordon. 1984. *Relapse Prevention: A Self-control Strategy for the Maintenance of Behavior Change*. NY: Guilford Press.

McCann, U. D., E. M. Rossiter, R. J. King, and W. S. Agras. 1991. Nonpurging bulimia: A distinct subtype of bulimia nervosa. *International Journal of Eating Disorders, 10*, 679-687.

McKay, M., M. Davis, and P. Fanning. 1983. *Messages: The Communication Book*. Oakland, CA: New Harbinger.

McNulty, P. A. F. 1997. Prevalence and contributing factors of eating disorder behaviors in active duty Navy men. *Military Medicine, 162*, 753-758.

Miller, W. C., A. K. Lindeman, J. P. Wallace, and M. G. Niederpruem, M. G. 1990. Diet composition, energy intake, and exercise in relation to body fat in men and women. *American Journal of Clinical Nutrition, 52*, 426-430.

Miller, W. C., M. G. Niederpruem, J. P. Wallace, and A. K. Lindeman. 1994. Dietary fat, sugar, and fiber predict body fat content. *Journal of the American Dietetic Association, 94*, 612-615.

Mitchell, J. E., C. Pomeroy, and D. E. Adson. 1997. Managing medical complications. In D. M. Garner and P. E. Garfinkel (Eds.), *Handbook of Treatment for Eating Disorders, 2nd Edition*. NY: Guilford Press. Pp. 383-393.

Mitchell, J. E., D. Hatsukami, E. D. Eckert, and R. L. Pyle. 1985. Characteristics of 275 patients with bulimia. *American Journal of Psychiatry, 142*, 482-485.

Mitchell, J. E., R. Pyle, E. D. Eckert, D. Hatsukami, and E. Soll, E. 1990. The influence of prior alcohol and drug abuse problems on bulimia nervosa treatment outcome. *Addictive Behaviors, 15*, 169-173.

Mitchell, J. E., S. Specker, and K. Edmonson. 1997. Management of substance abuse and dependence. In D. M. Garner and P. E. Garfinkel (Eds.), *Handbook of Treatment for Eating Disorders, 2nd Edition*. NY: Guilford Press. Pp. 415-423.

Mizes, J. S. 1988. Personality characteristics of bulimic and non-eating-disordered female controls: A cognitive-behavioral perspective. *International Journal of Eating Disorders, 7*, 541-550.

Mizes, J. S. 1989. Assertion deficits in bulimia nervosa: Assessment via behavioral, self-report, and cognitive measures. *Behavior Therapy, 20*, 603-608.

Mizes, J. S., and E. L. Fleece. 1986. On the use of progressive relaxation in the treatment of bulimia: A single-subject design study. *International Journal of Eating Disorders, 5*, 169-176.

Mizes, J. S., and J. M. Lohr. 1983. The treatment of bulimia binge-eating and self-induced vomiting : A quasi-experimental investigation of the effects of stimulus narrowing self-reinforcement, and self-control relaxation. *International Journal of Eating Disorders, 2*, 58-65.

Nash, J. D. 1995. *What Your Doctor Can't Tell You About Cosmetic Surgery*. Oakland, CA: New Harbinger Publications.

National Institutes of Health. 1998. http//www.nhlbi.nih.gov/nhlbi/nhlbi.htm.

Neckowitz, P., and T. L. Morrison. 1991. Interactional coping strategies of normal-weight bulimic women in intimate and non-intimate situations. *Psychological Reports, 69*, 1167-1175.

Newman, M. M., and M. S. Gold. 1992. Preliminary findings of patterns of substance abuse in eating disorder patients. *American Journal of Drug and Alcohol Abuse, 18,* 207-211.

Norman, D., M. Blais, and D. Herzog. 1993. Personality characteristics of eating disordered patients as identified by the Millon Clinical Multiaxial Inventory. *Journal of Personality Disorders, 7,* 1-9.

Oliver, K. K., and M. H. Thelen. 1996. Children's perceptions of peer influence on eating concerns. *Behavior Therapy, 27,* 25-39.

Olson, M. S., H. N. Williford, L. A. Richards, J. A. Brown, and S. Pugh. 1996. Self-reports on the Eating Disorder Inventory by female aerobic instructors. *Perceptual Motor Skills, 82,* 1051-1058.

Oppenheimer, R., K. Howells, L. Palmer, and D. Chaloner. 1985. Adverse sexual experiences in childhood and clinical eating disorders: A preliminary description. *Journal of Psychiatric Research, 19,* 157-161.

Patton, G. C., E. Johnson-Sabine, K. Wood, A. H. Mann, and A. Wakeling. 1990. Abnormal eating attitudes in London schoolgirls—A prospective epidemiological study: Outcome at twelve month follow-up. *Psychological Medicine, 20,* 383-394.

Patton, G. C., J. B. Carlin, Q. Shao, M. E. Hibbert, et al. 1997. Adolescent dieting: Healthy weight control or borderline eating disorder? *Journal of Child Psychology and Psychiatry and Allied Disciplines, 38,* 299-306.

Perusse, L., A. Tremblay, C. Leblanc, et al. 1988. Familial resemblance in energy intake: Contribution of genetic and environmental factors. *American Journal of Clinical Nutrition, 47,* 629-635.

Phelps, L., and E. Bajorek. 1991. Eating disorders of the adolescent: Current issues in etiology, assessment, and treatment. *School Psychology Review, 20,* 9-22.

Pike, K. M., and J. Rodin. 1991. Mothers, daughters, and disordered eating. *Journal of Abnormal Psychology, 100,* 198-204.

Piran, N., P. Lerner, P. E. Garfinkel, S. H. Kennedy, and C. Brouillette. 1988. Personality disorders in anorexic patients. *International Journal of Eating Disorders, 7,* 589-599.

Pope, H. G., and J. I. Hudson. 1992. Is childhood sexual abuse a risk factor for bulimia nervosa? *American Journal of Psychiatry, 149,* 455-463.

Porzelius, L. K., C. Houston, M. Smith, C. Arfken, and E. Fisher. 1995. Comparison of a standard behavioral weight loss treatment and a binge eating weight loss treatment. *Behavior Therapy, 26,* 119-134.

Pratt, E. M., S. H. Niego, and W. S. Agras. 1998. Does the size of a binge matter? *International Journal of Eating Disorders, 24,* 307-312.

Romieu, I., W. C. Willett, M. J. Stampfer, et al. 1988. Energy intake and other determinants of relative weight. *American Journal of Clinical Nutrition, 47,* 406-412.

Root, M. P., and P. Fallon. 1988. The incidence of victimization experiences in a bulimic sample. *Journal of Interpersonal Violence, 3,* 161-173.

Rorty, M., and J. Yager. 1998. Speculations on the role of childhood abuse in the development of eating disorders among women. In M. F. Schwartz and L. Cohn Eds. , *Sexual Abuse and Eating Disorders.* NY: Brunner/Mazel. Pp. 23-35.

Rosen, J. C., and H. Leitenberg. 1990. Bulimia nervosa: Treatment with exposure and response prevention. *Behavior Therapy, 13,* 117-124.

Rosen, J. C., P. Orosan, and J. Reiter. 1995. Cognitive behavior therapy for negative body image in obese women. *Behavior Therapy, 26,* 25-42.

Sansone, R. A., and M. A. Fine. 1992. Borderline personality as a predictor of outcome in women with eating disorders. *Journal of Personality Disorders, 6,* 176-186.

Schteingart, D. C. 1995. Phenylpropanolamine in the management of moderate obesity. In: T. B. Van Itallie, and A. P. Simopoulos, (Eds.), *Obesity: New Directions in Assessment and Management*. Philadelphia: The Charles Press. Pp. 220-226.

Schwalberg, M. D., D. H. Barlow, S. A. Alger, and L. J. Howard. 1992. A comparison of bulimics, obese binge eaters, social phobics, and individuals with panic disorders or comorbidity across DSM-III-R anxiety disorders. *Journal of Abnormal Psychology, 101*, 675-681.

Shapiro, S., M. Newcomb, and T. B. Loeb. 1997. Fear of fat, disregulated-restrained eating, and body esteem: Prevalence and gender differences among eight-to ten-year-old children. *Journal of Clinical Child Psychology, 26*, 358-365.

Siever, M. D. 1994. Sexual orientation and gender as factors in socioculturally acquired vulnerability to body dissatisfaction and eating disorders. *Journal of Consulting and Clinical Psychology, 62*, 252-260.

Smalley, K. J., A. N. Kneer, Z. V. Kendrick, J. A. Colliver, and O. E. Owen. 1990. Reassessment of body mass indices. *American Journal of Clinical Nutrition, 52*, 405-408.

Smith, D. E., M. D. Marcus, C. Lewis, M. Fitzgibbon, and P. Schreiner. 1998. Prevalence of binge eating disorder, obesity, and depression in a biracial cohort of young adults. *Annals of Behavioral Medicine, 20*, 227-232.

Sobal, J., and A. J Stunkard,. 1989. Socioeconomic status and obesity: A review of the literature. *Psychological Bulletin, 105*, 260-275.

Soukup, V. M., M. E. Beiler, and F. Terrell. 1990. Stress, coping style, and problem-solving ability among eating disordered patients. *Journal of Clinical Psychology, 46*, 592-599.

Specker, S., M. de Zwaan, R. Pyle, N. Raymond, and J. Mitchell. 1992, April 24. *Psychiatric disorders among obese patients with binge eating disorder BED*. Paper presented at Fifth International Conference on Eating Disorders, New York.

Spitzer, R. L., M. Devlin, B. T. Walsch, D. Hasin, R. Wing, M. Marcus, et al. 1992a. Binge eating disorder: A multisite field trial of the diagnostic criteria. *International Journal of Eating Disorders, 11*, 191-203.

Spitzer, R. L., M. J. Devlin, B. T. Walsh, D. Hasin, R. Wing, M. Marcus, et al. 1992b. Binge eating disorder: Its further validation in a multisite study. *International Journal of Eating Disorders, 13*, 137-153.

Spitzer, R. L., S. Z. Yanovski, T. Wadden, et al. 1993. Binge eating disorder: Its further validation in a multisite study. *International Journal of Eating Disorders, 13*, 137-153.

Steiger, H., K. Liquornik, J. Chapman, and N. Hussain. 1991. Personality and family disturbances in eating disorder patients: Comparison of "restricters" and "bingers" to normal controls. *International Journal of Eating Disorders, 10*, 501-512.

Steiner, H., P. Rahimzadeh, and N. B. Lewiston. 1990. Psychopathology in cystic fibrosis and anorexia nervosa: A controlled comparison. *International Journal of Eating Disorders, 9*, 675-683.

Stice, E., and W. S. Agras. 1998. Predicting onset and cessation of bulimic behaviors during adolescence: A longitudinal grouping analysis. *Behavior Therapy, 29*, 257-276.

Stice, E., C. Ziemba, J. Margolis, and P. Flick. 1996. The dual pathway model differentiates bulimics, subclinical bulimics, and controls: Testing the continuity hypothesis. *Behavior Therapy, 27*, 531-549.

Stice, E., E. Schupak-Neuber, H. E. Shaw, and R. I. Stein. 1994. The relationship of media exposure to eating disorder symptomatology: An examination of mediating mechanisms. *Journal of Abnormal Psychology, 103*, 836-840.

Stierlin, H., and G. Weber. 1989. Anorexia nervosa: Lessons from a follow-up study. *Family Systems Medicine, 7,* 120-157.

Striegel-Moore, R. H., L. R. Silberstein, and J. Rodin. 1986. Toward an understanding of risk factors for bulimia. *American Psychologist, 41,* 246-263.

Strober, M., and L. L. Humphrey. 1987. Familial contributions to the etiology and course of anorexia nervosa and bulimia. *Journal of Consulting and Clinical Psychology, 55,* 654-659.

Stunkard, A. J., W. J. Grace, and H. G. Wolff. 1955. The night-eating syndrome: A pattern of food intake among certain obese patients. *American Journal of Medicine, 19,* 78-86.

Telch, C. F., and E. Stice. 1998. Psychiatric comorbidity in women with binge eating disorder: Prevalence rates from a non-treatment-seeking sample. *Journal of Consulting and Clinical Psychology, 66,* 768-776.

Telch, C. F., E. M. Pratt, and S. H. Niego. 1998. Obese women with binge eating disorder define the term binge. *International Journal of Eating Disorders, 24,* 313-317.

Telch, C. F., W. S. Agras, and E. M. Rossiter. 1988. Binge eating increases with increasing adiposity. *International Journal of Eating Disorders, 7,* 115-119.

Telch, C. F., W. S. Agras, E. M. Rossiter, D. Wilfley, and J. Kenardy. 1990. Group cognitive behavioral treatment for the nonpurging bulimic: An initial evaluation. *Journal of Consulting and Clinical Psychology, 58,* 629-635.

Teusch, R. 1988. Level of ego development and bulimics' conceptualization of their disorder. *International Journal of Eating Disorders, 7,* 607-615

Thelan, M. H., J. Farmer, L. McLaughlin, and J. Pruitt. 1990. Bulimia and interpersonal relationships: A longitudinal study. *Journal of Counseling Psychology, 37,* 85-90.

Thelen, M. H., A. L. Powell, C. Lawrence, and M. E. Kuhnert. 1992. Eating and body image concerns among children. *Journal of Clinical Child Psychology, 21,* 41-46.

Thelen, M. H., C. M. Lawrence, and A. L. Powell. 1992. Body image, weight control, and eating disorders among children. In J. H. Crowther, S. E. Hobfoll, M. A. P. Stephens, and D. L. Tennenbaum (Eds.), *Etiology of Bulimia: The Individual and Family Context.* Washington, DC: Hemisphere Publishers. Pp. 81-98.

Thiel, A., A. Broocks, M. Ohlmeier, G. E. Jacoby, and G. Schufler. 1995. Obsessive-compulsive disorder among patient with anorexia nervosa and bulimia nervosa. *American Journal of Psychiatry, 152,* 72-75.

Thiel, A., M. Zuger, G. Jacoby, and G. Schussler. 1998. Thirty-month outcome in patients with anorexia or bulimia nervosa and concomitant obsessive-compulsive disorder. *American Journal of Psychiatry, 155,* 244-249.

Thompson, J. K. 1991. Body shape preferences: Effects of instructional protocol and level of eating disturbance. *International Journal of Eating Disorders, 10,* 193-198.

Thompson, J. K., and K. Psaltis. 1988. Multiple aspects and correlates of body figure ratings: A replication and extension of Fallon and Rozin, 1985. *International Journal of Eating Disorders, 7,* 813-818.

Troop, N. S., A. Holbrey, and J. S. Treasure. 1998. Stress, coping, and crisis support in eating disorders. *International Journal of Eating Disorders, 24,* 157-166.

Troop, N. S., A. Holbrey, R. Trowler, and J. S. Treasure. 1994. Ways of coping in women with eating disorders. *Journal of Nervous and Mental Disease, 182,* 535-540.

Tucker, L. A., and M. J. Kano. 1992. Dietary fat and body fat: A multivariate study of 205 adult females. *American Journal of Clinical Nutrition, 56,* 616-622.

Vandereycken, W. 1990. The relevance of body-image disturbance for the treatment of bulimia. In M. M. Fichter (Ed.), *Bulimia Nervosa: Basic Research, Diagnosis, and Treatment.* New York: Wiley. Pp. 320-330.

Vandereycken, W. 1995. The families of patients with an eating disorders. In K. D. Brownell and C. G. Fairburn (Eds.), *Eating Disorders and Obesity: A Comprehensive Handbook.* New York: Guilford. Pp. 219-223.

Vanderlinden, J., and W. Vandereycken. 1996. Is sexual abuse a risk factor for developing an eating disorder? In M. F. Schwartz and L. Cohn (Eds.), *Sexual Abuse and Eating Disorders.* NY: Brunner/Mazel. Pp. 17-22.

Vaz, F. J. 1998. Outcome of bulimia nervosa: Prognostic indicators. *Journal of Psychosomatic Research, 45,* 391-400.

Wade, T., N. G. Martin, and M. Tiggemann. 1998. Genetic and environmental risk factors for weight and shape concerns characteristic of bulimia nervosa. *Psychological Medicine, 28,* 761-771.

Wall, D. 1998. Obsessive compulsive disorder and eating disorders. 1998, Summer. *AABA Newsletter.* NY: American Anorexia Bulimia Association. Pp. 4-5.

Walsh, T. B., and M. J. Devlin. 1995. Pharmacotherapy of bulimic nervosa and binge eating disorders. *Addictive Behaviors, 20,* 757-764.

Walsh, T. B., and M. J. Devlin. 1998, May. Eating disorders: Progress and problems. *Science, 280,* 1387-1390.

Weingarten, H. P., and D. Elston. 1990. The phenomenology of food cravings. *Appetite, 15,* 231-246.

Weinsier, R. L., G. R. Hunter, A. F. Heini, M. I. Goran, and S. M. Sell. 1998. The etiology of obesity: Relative contribution of metabolic factors, diet, and physical activity. *American Journal of Medicine, 105,* 145-150.

Weintraub, M. and G. A. Bray. 1989. Drug treatment of obesity. *Medial Clinics of North America, 73,* 237-250.

White, F. 1998 Summer. Treating overeating disorders: A 3 stage nutrition therapy approach. *NEDO Newsletter.* Tulsa, OK: National Eating Disorders Organization. Pp. 1-4.

Wilfley, D. E., and L. R. Cohen. 1997. Psychological treatment of bulimia nervosa and binge eating disorder. *Psychopharmacology Bulletin, 33,* 437-454.

Wilfley, D. E., S. W. Agras, C. F. Telch, E. M. Rossiter, J. A. Schneider, A. G. Cole, et al. 1993. Group cognitive-behavioral therapy and group interpersonal psychotherapy for the nonpurging bulimic individual: A controlled comparison. *Journal of Consulting and Clinical Psychology, 61,* 296-305.

Wilson, G. T. 1991. The addiction model of eating disorders: A critical analysis. *Advances in Behavior Research and Therapy, 13,* 27-72.

Wilson, G. T. 1995. Eating disorders and addictive disorders. In K. D. Brownell and C. G. Fairburn (Eds.), *Eating Disorders and Obesity: A Comprehensive Handbook.* New York: Guilford. Pp. 165-170.

Wilson, G. T., C. A. Nonas, and G. D. Rosenblum. 1993. Assessment of binge-eating in obese persons. *Internatioal Journal of Eating Disorders, 13,* 23-33.

Wilson, G. T. 1996. Acceptance and change in the treatment of eating disorders and obesity. *Behavior Therapy, 27,* 417-439.

Wing, R. R., and C. G. Greeno. 1994. Behavioural and psychosocial aspects of obesity and its treatment. *Baillieres Clinical Endocrinology and Metabolism, 8,* 689-703.

Wiseman, C. V., J. J. Gray, J. E. Mosimann, and A. H. Ahrens. 1992. Cultural expectations of thinness: An update. *International Journal of Eating Disorders, 11,* 85-89.

Wonderlich, S. A., and W. J. Swift. 1990. Perceptions of parental relationships in eating disorder subtypes. *Journal of Abnormal Psychology, 99,* 353-360.

Wonderlich, S. A., M. H. Klein, and J. R. Council. 1996. Relationship of social perceptions and self-concept in bulimia nervosa. *Journal of Consulting and Clinical Psychology, 6,* 1231-1237.

Wonderlich, S. A., W. J. Swift, H. B. Slotnick, and S. Goodman. 1990. DSM-III-R personality disorders in eating-disorder subtypes. *International Journal of Eating Disorders, 9,* 607-616.

Woodside, D. B., L. L. Field, P. E. Garfinkel, and M. Heinmaa. 1998. Specificity of eating disorders diagnoses in families of probands with anorexia nervosa and bulimia nervosa. *Comprehensive Psychiatry, 39,* 261-264.

Wurtman, J. J. 1983. The Carbohydrate Craver's Diet. Boston: Houghton Mifflin.

Wurtman, J. J. 1993. Depression and weight gain: The serotonin connection. *Journal of Affective Disorders, 29,* 183-192.

Wurtman, R. J., and J. J. Wurtman. 1986. Carbohydrate craving, obesity, and brain serotonin. *Appetite, 7,* 99-103.

Yanovski, S. Z., J. E. Nelson, B. K. Dubbert, and R. L. Spitzer. 1993. Association of binge eating disorder and psychiatric comorbidity in obese subjects. *American Journal of Psychiatry, 150,* 1472-1479.

Index

A

ABC model of behavior, 109-110
Academy for Eating Disorders
    (AED), 261
active listening, 239-240
activity anorexia, 6
adaptive coping, 198-199, 252-253
addiction model of binge eating,
    85-87
addictive personality, 86
adolescents: body image develop-
    ment in, 174-175, 178; develop-
    ment of eating disorders in, 30-31,
    66-72; dysfunctional families and,
    72-74; parental influences on,
    70-72; peer influences on, 77-78;
    school influences on, 77. See also
    children
adults: body image development in,
    179; development of eating disor-
    ders in, 8, 10, 31, 34
affective signs of shame, 214
aggressive behavior, 243-244
agreements: broken, 228-229; negoti-
    ating, 228-229
alcohol abuse. See substance abuse
all-or-nothing thinking, 152-153
alternative activities, 142
amenorrhea, 56
American Anorexia/Bulimia Associa-
    tion, Inc. (AABA), 261
American Psychiatric Association
    (APA), 6
analyzing your eating behavior, 116,
    119-123
anemia, 56
anger, 231-235; avoidance of, 231-232;
    expression of, 232-233; getting

control of, 233; productive and
    appropriate use of, 234-235;
    vengeful binges and, 99-100, 232.
    See also emotions
anorexia nervosa, 5-6, 11-14; charac-
    teristics of, 11; co-occurring prob-
    lems with, 13-14; description of
    binges in, 12; exercise anorexia
    and, 6, 11-12; families of people
    with, 66-67; hunger binges and,
    96; medical complications caused
    by, 53-57; medications for, 23;
    obsessive-compulsive disorder
    and, 14, 23, 37, 38; origins of, 13;
    personality disorders and, 41-42,
    44, 45; psychological complica-
    tions of, 14, 57-58; resources on,
    261-264; substance abuse and, 35
Anorexia Nervosa and Related Eat-
    ing Disorders, Inc. (ANRED),
    261-262
antecedents, 109
antidepressant medications, 21-22
anxiety, coping with, 188
anxiety disorders: eating disorders
    and, 37-38; obsessive-compulsive
    disorder, 37-38
appraisal process: cognitive appraisal,
    151; deficits in, 199-200; stages in,
    194-195
assertiveness, 243-248; eating disor-
    ders and, 244-245; making asser-
    tive requests, 247; personal fears
    about, 246; skills in, 247-248
assessing your eating behavior,
    109-127; ABC model of behavior,
    109-110; analyzing your eating

behavior records, 116, 119-123;
identifying behavior patterns,
124-126; self-monitoring process,
111, 114-116, 117-118;
understanding behavior chains,
110-111, 112-113; weighing
yourself, 126-127
athletes: development of eating
disorders in, 33-34. *See also*
exercise
attractiveness: benefits of, 172-173;
body image and, 174-175;
self-perception of, 172
avoidance behaviors: anger and,
231-232; coping through, 80,
197-198; negative body image and,
180, 187-188; overcoming, 188;
shame and, 215
avoidant personality organization,
41-43

B

backsliding, 251-260; covertly
planned, 254-255; justification
excuses and, 256; lifestyle
imbalances and, 256-257;
overcoming, 257-260; relapse
process and, 252-253
behavior: ABC model of, 109-110;
aggressive, 243-244; analyzing,
119-123; avoidance, 80, 180,
187-188; chain of events leading
to, 110-111, 112-113; identifying
patterns of, 124-126; inappropriate,
230-231; recording, 114-116,
117-118; shaping, 145-146
Best Friend (inner voice), 164
binge eating: ABC model of, 109-110;
addiction model of, 85-87;
analyzing behaviors related to,
116, 119-123; behavior chains
analogy and, 110-111, 112-113;
characteristics of, 6-7; deprivation
binges, 96-97; four stages in,
102-103; grazing binges, 7; habit
binges, 101-102; hunger binges,
95-96; identifying behavior
patterns related to, 124-126;
intervening in, 103-105; nutritional
deficits and, 85, 86; opportunity
binges, 98-99; pleasure binges,
100-101; reinforcers of, 105;
self-monitoring, 111, 114-116,
117-118; stress binges, 97-98; tips
for preventing, 143-144; triggers
for, 103-104; vengeful binges,
99-100, 232
binge eating disorder (BED), 3-4, 7-9;
characteristics of, 7; co-occurring

problems with, 9; description of
binges in, 8; families of people
with, 66; medical complications
caused by, 53-57; medications for,
21-23; obesity and, 4, 7, 9; origins
of, 8; personality disorders and,
40; psychological complications of,
9, 59; resources on, 261-264;
simple overeating compared to,
7-8
binge/purge syndrome, 9
biological factors in eating disorders,
80-87; chemical dependency and
addiction, 85-87; genes and
heredity, 82-83; hunger and
starvation, 83-85; physiological
determinants, 81-82
black-and-white thinking, 152-153
blaming, 236-237
body image, 174-192; avoidance
behavior and, 187-188; changes in,
175; development of, 174-175;
distressing situations related to,
187-189; domino thinking and,
182-183, 185, 186; making friends
with your body, 184-185; negative
body talk and, 180-181; personal
history of, 176-180; positive body
talk and, 184; self-esteem and, 189,
192
Body Image History form, 176-180
body mass index (BMI), 15-16; table
for determining, 18-19
body talk. *See* self-talk
body weight and shape: acceptance
of, 171-174; importance of,
170-171; perceived attractiveness
and, 172-173; self-image related to,
174-192
bone problems, 55-56
borderline personality organization
(BPO), 39-40, 86
boredom, 125
boys. *See* males
brainstorming, 201-202
breathing deeply, 204
broken record technique, 247-248
bulimia nervosa, 4-5, 9-10;
characteristics of, 9-10;
co-occurring problems with, 10;
description of binges in, 10;
families of people with, 66;
medical complications caused by,
53-57; medications for, 21;
opportunity binges and, 98-99;
origins of, 10; peer influences on,
78; personality disorders and, 40,
41; psychological complications of,

10, 58-59; resources on, 261-264; substance abuse and, 10, 35

C

caffeine, 23
calorie restrictions, 130
carbohydrate craving, 81-82
cardiovascular problems, 55
Caretaker (inner voice), 97, 158
catastrophizing, 153, 206
character assassination, 238
chemical dependency, 85-87
children: body image development in, 176-177; development of eating disorders in, 30-31, 66-72; dysfunctional families and, 72-74; parental influences on, 70-72; peer influences on, 77-78; school influences on, 77; self- concept emergence in, 74-76; sexual abuse of, 67. *See also* adolescents
clarification, 240
clouding, 241-242
Coach (inner voice), 164
cognitive appraisal, 151
cognitive errors, 152-154; disputing, 154-155; identifying, 125; types of, 152-154
cognitive signs of shame, 214
cognitive-behavioral therapy (CBT), 221-222
communication, 235-243; blocks to effective, 236-239; coping with criticism in, 240-242; gender differences in, 235-236; issuing criticism to others, 242-243; listening skills and, 239-240; managing conflict, 240
comparison processes, 79
conflict, 225-231; blocks to resolving, 236-239; broken promises and, 228-229; intolerance of shortcomings and, 229; managing, 240; misunderstandings and, 230-231; productive vs. unproductive, 226; threats to self-worth and, 230; unmet expectations and, 226-228
conflict-avoidant families, 74
consequences, 109
contagion, 78
contemptuous treatment, 238-239
coping: adaptive, 198-199, 252-253; avoidance strategies for, 80, 187-188, 197-198, 215; with criticism, 240-242; definition of, 194; emotion- focused, 197-198, 202-213; with food cravings, 139-143; with high-risk situations,

257-258; with painful feelings, 207-212; problem-focused, 195-197, 200-202; relapse process and failure of, 253; with shame, 216-217; strategies used for, 195-198, 199; with stressful situations, 188-189; styles of, 199
coping skills, 200-213; brainstorming alternatives, 201-202; changing dysfunctional thinking, 206-207; distress tolerance skills, 209-210; eliciting the relaxation response, 203-206; emotion regulation skills, 210-212; expanding your emotional palette, 212-213; implementing solutions to problems, 202; mindfulness skills, 207-209; problem definition, 201; seeking social support, 206
covertly planned relapses, 254-255
cravings: coping with, 139-143; Five D's of dealing with, 143; indulging with moderation, 142
Critic (inner voice), 97, 156-157, 258
criticism: acknowledging, 241; as block to conflict resolution, 236-237; coping with, 240-242; and development of eating disorders, 68-70; issuing to others, 242-243; self-criticism, 142
cross-complaining, 237
cultural influences on eating disorders, 64-65

D

Daily Eating Behavior Record: analyzing, 119-123; blank copy of form, 118; completed sample of, 117; identifying behavior patterns from, 124-126; instructions for using, 114-116
deep breathing, 204
defensiveness, 237-238
denial, 257
dental problems, 56
dependency, chemical, 85-87
dependent personality organization, 43-44
depression: eating disorders and, 36-37; medications for treating, 21-22; symptoms of, 36-37
deprivation: behavior patterns associated with, 124; binge eating induced by, 96-97, 124
developmental factors in eating disorders, 78
diabetes, 9
dichotomous thinking, 152-153
diet pills, 131-132

dieting: alternatives to, 131-133; development of eating disorders from, 30, 31, 84-85, 86, 95, 129-131; nutritional problems caused by, 85, 86, 130
disengagement, 73
disordered eating syndromes, 14-15. *See also* eating disorders
dissociation, 97
distress tolerance skills, 209-210, 212
diuretics, 9, 131
domino thinking, 182-183; fighting back against, 183, 185, 186; worry and, 157-158
drug abuse. *See* substance abuse
dysfunctional families, 72-74

E

eating behavior, 129-146; coping with food cravings, 139-143; dieting, 129-131; normalizing, 134, 136-137; self-reward methods and, 144-146; shaping, 145-146; structured eating, 138-139; tips for preventing binges, 143-144
eating disorders: addiction model of, 85-87; appraisal process and, 199-200; assertive behavior and, 244-245; biological factors and, 80-87; body weight/shape and, 170-171; complicating factors with, 35-45; conflict in relationships and, 225-231; cultural factors and, 64-65; developmental factors and, 78; dieting and development of, 30, 31, 84-85, 86, 95, 129-131; environmental influences on, 76-78; family influences on, 70-74; grief and, 222-223; hurts to others caused by, 59-62; inner voice of, 160; interpersonal deficits and, 224-225; interpersonal relationships and, 65-72; medical complications caused by, 53-57; obesity and, 15-16; parental influences on, 70-72; peer influences on, 77-78; people at risk for, 29-35; personality disorders and, 38-45; predisposing psychological factors and, 79-80; psychological complications caused by, 57-59; resources on, 261-264; role transitions and, 223-224; self-concept and, 74-76; shame and, 10, 67-68, 217-218; subclinical, 14-16; treatments for, 16-25. *See also* anorexia nervosa; binge eating disorder; bulimia nervosa

Eating Disorders Awareness and Prevention, Inc. (EDAP), 262
edema, 55
electrolyte balance, 55
emotion regulation skills, 210-212
emotional discharge strategies, 197
emotional thinking, 153
emotion-focused coping, 197-198, 202-213; changing dysfunctional thinking, 206-207; distress tolerance skills for, 209-210; eliciting the relaxation response, 203-206; emotion regulation skills for, 210-212; expanding your emotional palette, 212-213; mindfulness skills for, 207-209; seeking social support, 206; shame and, 216-217. *See also* problem-focused coping
emotions: anger, 99-100, 231-235; associated with eating disorders, 79-80; behavior influenced by, 151-152; cognitive appraisal and, 151; cognitive errors and, 152-154; desire to escape from, 80; eating binges triggered by, 7, 8, 80, 97-98, 99-100; identifying and labeling, 210, 212-213; intuitive knowing through, 150; mood swings and, 84;obstacles to changing, 210-211; painful, coping with, 207-212; shame, 213-218; stress binges and, 97-98; thinking as influence on, 150; vengeful binges and, 99-100
enemas, 9
Enforcer (inner voice), 98, 159
enmeshment/disengagement dimension, 72-73
errors, cognitive, 152-154
estrogen, 55
Excuse-Maker (inner voice), 157
exercise: excessive, 6, 9, 11-12, 132; health benefits of, 25; obligatory, 12. *See also* athletes
exercise anorexia, 6, 11-12
expectations, examining, 227-228

F

families, 72-74; development of eating disorders in, 65-74; dysfunctional, 72-74; enmeshment/disengagement dimension in, 72-73; functional, 72; hostile/conflict-avoidant dimension in, 73-74; hurts caused by eating disorders in, 59-62; parental influences in, 70-72; self-concept emergence in, 74-76. *See also* interpersonal relationships

family counseling, 20
fasting, 9, 95, 130
father/daughter relationship, 71-72
feared foods, 133
feelings. *See* emotions
females: anorexia nervosa among, 5, 6; binge eating disorder among, 4; bulimia nervosa among, 4; development of eating disorders in, 29, 30-31. *See also* gender differences
fluid retention, 55
Folkman, Susan, 194
Food Pyramid, 133, 134
foods: coping with cravings for, 139-143; forbidden, 96-97, 124, 132-133, 140; hunger-induced preoccupation with, 84; making better choices of, 133, 135-136; nutritional value of, 125-126; sweet, addiction to, 86
forbidden foods: deprivation binges and, 96-97, 124; dietary fads and, 130-131; food cravings and, 140; "legalizing," 97, 132-133
forgiveness, 217
functional families, 72

G
gastrointestinal disturbances, 54
gay men, 33
gender differences: communication styles and, 235-236; eating disorders and, 4, 5, 29-33. *See also* females; males
generalized anxiety disorder, 37
genetic factors in eating disorders, 82-83
girls. *See* females
Gordon, Judith, 252
governing scenes of shame, 218
gratification seeking, 125
grazing binges, 7
grief, 222-223
groups, self-help, 19, 263, 264
guilt, 142
gunnysacking, 238
Gurze Books, 262

H
habit binges, 101-102, 125
hair problems, 56
health problems. *See* medical problems
heredity and eating disorders, 82-83
heterosexual males, 33
high achievers, 76
high profile occupations, 34-35
high-risk situations, 252; coping with, 257-258

histrionic personality organization, 40-41
homosexual males, 33
hostile/conflict-avoidant dimension, 73-74
hunger: behavior patterns associated with, 124; binge eating induced by, 95-96, 124; food cravings and, 140; learning to identify, 134; preoccupation with food caused by, 84
hypoglycemia, 55

I
imagery, 204-206
imbalanced lifestyles, 256-257, 259-260
inner voices, 156-160
insulin, 9
International Association of Eating Disorders Professionals (IAEDP), 262-263
interpersonal deficits, 224-225
Interpersonal Psychotherapy (IPT), 221-222
interpersonal relationships: anger in, 231-235; assertiveness in, 243-248; communicating effectively in, 235-243; conflicts in, 225-231, 236-239; coping with criticism in, 240-242; gender differences in, 235-236; hurts caused by eating disorders in, 59-62; increasing effectiveness in, 221-222; issuing criticism to others in, 242-243; listening skills in, 239-240; managing conflict in, 240; personal rights in, 245-246; role disputes in, 225-231; signs of shame in, 214-215; unsatisfying, and eating disorders, 198. *See also* families
interrupting conversations, 237-238
interventions, 103-105
intolerance, 229
intuition, 150
ipecac syrup, 9, 55
irritable bowel syndrome (IBS), 54

J
joint problems, 56
journal writing, 218
justification excuses, 256

K
Kaufman, Gershen, 213
Keys, Ansel, 83
kitchen sinking, 238
Klerman, Gerald, 221

L
laxatives, 9, 131
Lazarus, Richard, 194

licensed therapists, 20
lifestyle imbalances: correcting, 259-260; relapses caused by, 256-257
Linehan, Marsha, 207, 247
listening skills, 239-240

M

macronutrients, 130, 131
males: binge eating disorder among, 4; development of eating disorders in, 29, 31-33; exercise anorexia among, 6; homosexual, 33. *See also* gender differences
Marlatt, Alan, 252
medical problems, 53-57; bone problems, 55-56; cardiovascular problems, 55; dental problems, 56; electrolyte abnormalities, 55; gastrointestinal disturbances, 54; menstrual/reproductive complications, 56-57; metabolism problems, 55-56; obesity and, 16; skin and hair problems, 56
medications, 21-24; for anorexia nervosa, 23; for binge eating disorder, 21-23; for bulimia nervosa, 21; ineffective, 23, 131-132; over-the- counter, 23, 131-132
men. *See* males
menstrual complications, 5, 56-57
mental health professionals, 19-20
Meridia (obesity drug), 22
metabolism problems, 55-56
micronutrients, 130
military personnel, 34
mind reading, 153
mindfulness skills, 207-209, 211-212
minerals, 130
misunderstandings, interpersonal, 230-231
monitoring your eating behavior. *See* self-monitoring process
moods: eating binges triggered by, 7, 84; extreme swings in, 84. *See also* emotions
mother/daughter relationship, 70-71

N

National Association of Anorexia Nervosa and Associated Disorders (ANAD), 263
National Association to Advance Fat Acceptance, Inc. (NAAFA), 263
National Eating Disorders Information Centre (NEDIC), 263-264
National Eating Disorders Organization (NEDO), 264

negative self-talk, 125, 160-161; body image and, 180-181; characteristics of, 164-165; reducing, 167; voice of, 159-160
Negativity voice, 159-160
negotiating agreements, 228-229
new beginning stage, 103
night-eating syndrome (NES), 14-15
nocturnal sleep-related eating disorder, 15
nonassertiveness, 243; benefits of, 246
nonreciprocal role expectations, 225
nonverbal behavior, 239-240
normalizing eating patterns, 134, 136-137
nutrition: binge eating and lack of, 85, 86; macronutrient requirements and, 130, 131; relationship of body weight to, 126
nutritional counseling, 20-21

O

obesity: binge eating disorder and, 4, 7, 9; definition of, 15; and development of eating disorders, 31; fat consumption and, 126; health problems caused by, 16; psychological problems associated with, 16; treatments for, 24-25. *See also* weight issues
obligatory exercise, 12
obsessive-compulsive disorder (OCD), 37-38; anorexia nervosa and, 14, 23, 37, 38
obsessive-compulsive personality organization (OCPO), 44-45
opportunity binges, 98-99
osteoporosis, 55
overanxious disorder, 37
Overeaters Anonymous (OA), 19, 264
overgeneralization, 153
over-the-counter diet pills, 131-132
overweight people: development of eating disorders among, 31, 32; fat consumption by, 126. *See also* obesity; weight issues

P

painful feelings: shame, 213-218; skills for coping with, 207-212
paraphrasing, 240
parental influences on eating disorders, 70-72; father/daughter relationship, 71-72; mother/daughter relationship, 70-71. *See also* families
passive-aggressive communication style, 244
peer influences, 77-78
people pleasers, 75-76

perfectionism, 10, 13, 14, 45;
dichotomous thinking and,
152-153, 258-259; domino thinking
and, 183
personality disorders, 38-46; avoidant
personality organization, 41-43;
borderline personality
organization, 39-40; dependent
personality organization, 43-44;
histrionic personality organization,
40-41; obsessive-compulsive
personality organization, 44-45
personality traits, 38
physical abuse, 67
physiological determinants of eating
disorders, 81-82
pleasure binges, 100-101, 125
positive self-talk, 161, 258-259; body
image and, 184; characteristics of,
164, 165; programming, 164-166;
reminder cards for, 165-166; stress
inoculation and, 188-189, 190-191
post-traumatic stress disorder (PTSD),
37
pregnancy complications, 56-57
primary appraisal process, 194-195;
deficits in, 199-200
problem solving, 202
problem thinking, 125; cognitive
errors and, 152-154; disputing,
154-155
problem-focused coping, 195-197,
200-202; brainstorming
alternatives, 201-202; defining the
problem, 201; implementing a
solution, 202. *See also* emotion-
focused coping
productive conflict, 226
progressive deep muscle relaxation,
203-204
promises, broken, 228-229
Prozac, 21, 22, 23
psychiatrists, 20
psychological abuse, 67
psychological problems: anorexia
nervosa and, 14, 57-58; anxiety
disorders, 37-38; binge eating
disorder and, 9, 59; bulimia
nervosa and, 10, 58-59; depression,
36-37; obesity and, 16, 36;
obsessive-compulsive disorder,
37-38; personality disorders, 38-45
psychologists, 19-20
psychotherapy, 19-21
purging behaviors, 9

R
rationalizations, 256, 257
Rebel Eater, 97, 100

record-keeping process, 114-116;
analyzing records, 119-123;
instructions for engaging, 115-116;
sample form used in, 117-118
recovery stage, 103
refocusing attention, 216-217
reinforcers of binge eating, 105
relapse process, 252-257; covertly
planned relapses, 254-255; lifestyle
imbalances and, 256-257. *See also*
backsliding
relationships. *See* interpersonal
relationships
relaxation response, 203-206
reminder cards, 165-166, 258
reproductive complications, 56-57
restrictive dieting. *See* dieting
rewarding good behavior, 144-146;
examples of, 144-145;
perfectionism trap and, 146;
principles for, 146; shaping
behavior through, 145-146
risk. *See* high-risk situations
role expectations, 225
role transitions, 223-224

S
school environment, 77
secondary appraisal process, 195;
deficits in, 200
secrecy, and shame, 215-216
selective serotonin reuptake inhibitors
(SSRIs), 21
self-acceptance, 182; obstacles to,
173-174
self-concept, 74-76
self-esteem: body image and, 189,
192; eating disorders and, 9, 10;
family influences on, 74-76; threats
to, 230
self-forgiveness, 217
self-fulfilling prophecy, 153-154
self-help methods, 17, 19
self-monitoring process, 111, 114-116;
analyzing your eating behavior,
116, 119-123; concerns about
record keeping, 114; identifying
behavior patterns from, 124-126;
problem definition and, 201;
recording your eating behavior,
114-116; sample form used for,
117-118; weighing yourself,
126-127. *See also* Daily Eating
Behavior Record
self-reward methods, 144-146;
examples of, 144-145;
perfectionism trap and, 146;
principles for using, 146; shaping
behavior through, 145-146

self-talk, 149, 155-167; body-image and, 180-181; developing awareness of, 161-163; domino thinking and, 157-158, 182-184, 185, 186; explanation of, 155-156; identifying your inner voices, 156-160; negative, 125, 159-161, 164-165; positive, 164, 165-166, 184, 188-189, 258-259; reminder cards for, 165-166; taking control of, 160-166. *See also* thinking
sensory longing, 141
Serenity Prayer, 169
serotonin, 81
sexual abuse, 10, 67
sexuality: anorexia nervosa and, 13; binge eating disorder and, 7; bulimia nervosa and, 10, 56-57
shame, 213-218; avoidance behaviors and, 215; eating disorders and, 10, 67-68, 217-218; governing scenes of, 218; repair of, 217-218; signs of, 214-215; tolerating, 216-217. *See also* emotions
shame spirals, 216-217
shaping behavior, 145-146
shyness, 224-225
skin problems, 56
sleep apnea, 9, 15
sleep disturbances, 15
social phobia, 37
social support, 206
starvation: binge eating induced by, 84-85, 95-96, 130; preoccupation with food caused by, 84; self-imposed, 5, 13, 95
stonewalling, 239
stress: appraising, 194-195; behavior patterns associated with, 124-125; binge eating induced by, 97-98, 102, 125; definition of, 194; eating disorders triggered by, 79-80, 194; managing, 188-189, 203-206; reducing vulnerability to, 211; relaxation response and, 203-206; tension buildup caused by, 102
stress eating, 97-98
stress inoculation, 188-189; planning worksheet for, 190-191
structured eating: benefits of, 139; worries about, 138-139
subclinical eating disorders, 14-16
substance abuse, 10, 35-36
sugar addiction, 86
suicidal ideation, 37
support groups, 19, 263, 264
"surfing an urge," 142
sweet foods, 86

T
teasing, 68-70, 77-78
teenagers. *See* adolescents
temptation, avoiding, 141
tension building stage, 102; intervening in, 103-104
tension release stage, 102
therapists, licensed, 20
therapy, 19-20
thinking: behavior influenced by, 151-152; cognitive errors in, 152-154; dichotomous, 152-153; domino, 157-158, 182-184, 185, 186; dysfunctional, 206-207; emotional influences on, 150, 153; human change process and, 258-259; as influence on emotions, 150; internal voices and, 155-160; intuition and, 150; problem, 125, 152-154; reducing negative thoughts, 167; relapse-facilitating, 257; taking control of, 160-166. *See also* self-talk
thought stopping, 99, 141
thyroid medication, 9
time-outs, 248
tolerance: distress, 209-210; increasing, 230
trauma, 37, 67-68
treatments for eating disorders, 16-25; exercise and, 25; medications, 21-24; nutritional counseling, 20-21; psychotherapy, 19-20; self-help methods, 17, 19; weight reduction efforts and, 24-25
triggers for binge eating, 103-104

V
vengeful binges, 99-100, 232
Victim (inner voice), 158-159
visualization, 204-206
vitamins, 130
voices, internal, 156-160
vomiting, self-induced, 9, 54

W
weight issues: body shape and, 170-174; exercise and, 25; frequency of weighing yourself, 126-127; genetic factors and, 82-83; good nutrition and, 126; weight cycling, 31. *See also* obesity
Wise Mind concept, 207
Wise Self (inner voice), 164
women. *See* females
Worrier (inner voice), 97, 157-158
worthless self-concept, 75

X
Xenical (diet drug), 22

Joyce D. Nash is a clinical psychologist specializing in the treatment of eating disorders. Dr. Nash is in private practice in San Francisco and Menlo Park, CA. She holds two Ph.D.s—one in clinical psychology from the Pacific Graduate School of Psychology, and one in communication from Stanford University, where she went on to do postdoctoral work at the School of Medicine. Dr. Nash is the author of several books on various behavioral medicine subjects. For more information about Dr. Nash, visit her web site at www.joycenashphd.com.

Other Books by the Author

The New Maximize Your Body Potential

What Your Doctor Can't Tell You About Cosmetic Surgery

Now That You've Lost It

Maximize Your Body Potential

Taking Charge of Your Smoking

Taking Charge of Your Weight and Well-Being
(with Linda Ormiston)

More New Harbinger Titles

THE BODY IMAGE WORKBOOK

Shows you how to evaluate a negative body image, change self-defeating "private body talk" and appearance-preoccupied rituals, and create a more pleasurable, affirming relationship with your appearance   *Item IMAG $17.95*

THE DEADLY DIET

Provides essential techniques for confronting the inner voice that's responsible for the shame, guilt, and low self-worth that fuels eating disorders.   *Item DD2 $14.95*

FACING 30

A diverse group of women who are either teetering on the brink of thirty or have made it past the big day talk about careers, relationships, the inevitable kid question, and dashed dreams. *Item F30 $12.95*

HIGH ON STRESS

A variety of enlightening exercises help women rethink the role of stress in their lives, rework their physical and mental responses to it, and find ways to boost the potentially positive impact that stress can have on their well-being.   *Item HOS $13.95*

SEX SMART

"Sex Smart is *the* book on everything you probably didn't know about why you turned out the way you did sexually and what to do about it." Arnold Lazarus, Ph.D.   *Item SESM $14.95*

Call toll-free 1-800-748-6273 to order. Have your Visa or Master-card number ready. Or send a check for the titles you want to New Harbinger Publications, 5674 Shattuck Avenue, Oakland, CA 94609. Include $3.80 for the first book and 754 for each additional book to cover shipping and handling. (California residents please include appropriate sales tax.) Allow four to six weeks for delivery.

Prices subject to change without notice.

Some Other New Harbinger Self-Help Titles

The Self-Esteem Companion, $10.95
The Gay and Lesbian Self-Esteem Book, $13.95
Making the Big Move, $13.95
How to Survive and Thrive in an Empty Nest, $13.95
Living Well with a Hidden Disability, $15.95
Overcoming Repetitive Motion Injuries the Rossiter Way, $15.95
What to Tell the Kids About Your Divorce, $13.95
The Divorce Book, Second Edition, $15.95
Claiming Your Creative Self: True Stories from the Everyday Lives of Women, $15.95
Six Keys to Creating the Life You Desire, $19.95
Taking Control of TMJ, $13.95
What You Need to Know About Alzheimer's, $15.95
Winning Against Relapse: A Workbook of Action Plans for Recurring Health and Emotional Problems, $14.95
Facing 30: Women Talk About Constructing a Real Life and Other Scary Rites of Passage, $12.95
The Worry Control Workbook, $15.95
Wanting What You Have: A Self-Discovery Workbook, $18.95
When Perfect Isn't Good Enough: Strategies for Coping with Perfectionism, $13.95
Earning Your Own Respect: A Handbook of Personal Responsibility, $12.95
High on Stress: A Woman's Guide to Optimizing the Stress in Her Life, $13.95
Infidelity: A Survival Guide, $13.95
Stop Walking on Eggshells, $14.95
Consumer's Guide to Psychiatric Drugs, $16.95
The Fibromyalgia Advocate: Getting the Support You Need to Cope with Fibromyalgia and Myofascial Pain, $18.95
Healing Fear: New Approaches to Overcoming Anxiety, $16.95
Working Anger: Preventing and Resolving Conflict on the Job, $12.95
Sex Smart: How Your Childhood Shaped Your Sexual Life and What to Do About It, $14.95
You Can Free Yourself From Alcohol & Drugs, $13.95
Amongst Ourselves: A Self-Help Guide to Living with Dissociative Identity Disorder, $14.95
Healthy Living with Diabetes, $13.95
Dr. Carl Robinson's Basic Baby Care, $10.95
Better Boundries: Owning and Treasuring Your Life, $13.95
Goodbye Good Girl, $12.95
Fibromyalgia & Chronic Myofascial Pain Syndrome, $19.95
The Depression Workbook: Living With Depression and Manic Depression, $17.95
Self-Esteem, Second Edition, $13.95
Angry All the Time: An Emergency Guide to Anger Control, $12.95
When Anger Hurts, $13.95
Perimenopause, $16.95
The Relaxation & Stress Reduction Workbook, Fourth Edition, $17.95
The Anxiety & Phobia Workbook, Second Edition, $18.95
I Can't Get Over It, A Handbook for Trauma Survivors, Second Edition, $16.95
Messages: The Communication Skills Workbook, Second Edition, $15.95
Thoughts & Feelings, Second Edition, $18.95
Depression: How It Happens, How It's Healed, $14.95
The Deadly Diet, Second Edition, $14.95
The Power of Two, $15.95
Living Without Depression & Manic Depression: A Workbook for Maintaining Mood Stability, $18.95
Couple Skills: Making Your Relationship Work, $14.95
Hypnosis for Change: A Manual of Proven Techniques, Third Edition, $15.95
Letting Go of Anger: The 10 Most Common Anger Styles and What to Do About Them, $12.95
Infidelity: A Survival Guide, $13.95
When Anger Hurts Your Kids, $12.95
Don't Take It Personally, $12.95
The Addiction Workbook, $17.95
It's Not OK Anymore, $13.95
Beyond Grief: A Guide for Recovering from the Death of a Loved One, $14.95
The Chemotherapy & Radiation Survival Guide, Second Edition, $14.95
An End to Panic: Breakthrough Techniques for Overcoming Panic Disorder, Second Edition, $18.95
Dying of Embarrassment: Help for Social Anxiety and Social Phobia, $13.95
The Endometriosis Survival Guide, $13.95
Grief's Courageous Journey, $12.95
Flying Without Fear, $13.95
Stepfamily Realities, $14.95
Coping With Schizophrenia: A Guide For Families, $15.95
Conquering Carpal Tunnel Syndrome and Other Repetitive Strain Injuries, $17.95
The Three Minute Meditator, Third Edition, $13.95
The Chronic Pain Control Workbook, Second Edition, $17.95
The Power of Focusing, $12.95
Living Without Procrastination, $12.95
Kid Cooperation: How to Stop Yelling, Nagging & Pleading and Get Kids to Cooperate, $13.95

Call **toll free, 1-800-748-6273**, or log on to our online bookstore at **www.newharbinger.com** to order. Have your Visa or Mastercard number ready. Or send a check for the titles you want to New Harbinger Publications, Inc., 5674 Shattuck Ave., Oakland, CA 94609. Include $3.80 for the first book and 75¢ for each additional book, to cover shipping and handling. (California residents please include appropriate sales tax.) Allow two to five weeks for delivery.

Prices subject to change without notice.